The Menu Cookbook Company
P.O. Box 204015
Austin, TX 78727-4015
(512) 258-5617

Library of Congress Cataloging-in-Publication Data

Heerensperger, Leonard, 1941 -

Features all food groups with a different full-course meal every day of the year. Accompanied by weekly grocery lists, calendar guides, cooking methods, it can be used as a day-to-day guide to food preparation or as a general cookbook with indices.

ISBN 0-966-1614-0-8
Includes index

1. Menu. 2. Recipes 3. Cookbooks

Published by The Menu Cookbook Company

Printed in the United States of America

First Edition
1 2 3 4 5 6 7 8 9 10

Volume 2

More Than Recipes Organization

June

The Best Month Overall!

Only halfway through this set of books and you're about to get the best.

June has the best variety. The pace of the menus, the balance of heavy meals to lighter fares and the different cooking methods impress us as the best. This was more by chance than choice; over the years it worked out this way. The menu on the flip side should show you what we mean.

June begins with the best of the Monday at Ease menus: The *Steak Ragoutant* is a an easy-to-fix ground meat and pasta hash that everyone raves about. The *Street Vendor Hot Dog* is a chili-less hot dog that will taste more like a sandwich than a hot dog. The *Herbed Chicken Breasts*, a healthy, fresh chicken sandwich that is a snap to fix and will satisfy any hunger.

June also has one of the best assortments of shrimp menus, from the familiar *Cocktail Shrimp and Potatoes* to a most unusual and tasty *Shrimp and Pesto Salad* that is loaded with healthy tomatoes and red peppers, broccoli and sugar peas -- a very sensual meal when topped with the pesto dressing that you will make from scratch (it takes about 1 minute!).

June will also be remembered for some of the best pasta you've had. The *Heavenly Roma* is just that: heavenly. It is angel hair pasta with ripe olives, canned tuna or chicken, and capers, the fine Italian spices.

The June pork menus are to die for. We offer an *Italian Pork Chops* plus the very best method of cooking them: braising.

The meat eaters in the family will love the *Hawaiian Steak* grilled out of doors and the *Sliced Beef Tenderloin* with a great mushroom sauce and mashed potatoes, a meal unsurpassed in quality and taste.

It is like the opening song of a great musical: we open the second act with a powerhouse. That is June: the best month overall. Not by design but by chance.

June Menus

Chicken

Grilled Barbecued Chicken with Cole Slaw and Baked Beans

Wild Rice Chicken Breasts with Corn and Caesar Salad

Chicken in Beer Marinade with Mashed Potatoes and Onion Rings

Chicken w/ Lemon Caper Sauce with Wild Rice and Chopped Vegetables

Swiss Chicken Rolls with Rice and Vegetable Caesar Salad

Quick & Easy

Steak Ragoutant with French Bread and Italian Salad

Stir Fry Beef with Rice and Egg Rolls

Herbed Chicken Sandwich with Caesar Salad

Street Vendor Hot Dogs with Red Beans

Barbecued Meat Loaf with Corn and Spinach

Shrimp

Shrimp With Chilies with Rice

Cocktail Shrimp with Baked Potatoes and Green Wedge Salad

Shrimp Curry with Rice and Fruit Cocktail

Shrimp and Pesto Salad

New Orleans Shrimp with Rice and Green Wedge Salad

Pork

Brown Rice Pork Chops with Herbed Tomatoes

Elegant Italian Pork Chops with Rice and Green Beans

Italian Pork Chops with Pasta, Italian Salad and Fresh Bread

Braised Pork Chops with Prunes and Macaroni & Cheese

Pasta / Soup

Pasta Salad w/ Spinach & Feta with Fresh Bread, Cheese Spread

Minestrone Soup with Broiled Chicken and Cheese Assortment

Pasta Cochon with Garlic Bread

Heavenly Roma with French Bread & Tossed Salad

Tangy Pasta Salad with Fresh Bread

Fish

Lemon-Garlic Salmon with Broccoli Spears and New Potatoes

Tuna Casserole with Baked Bell Peppers and Fresh Bread

Mushroom Onion Baked Fish with Rice and Vegetable Platter

Cod Fillets with Pesto Sauce with Corn and Herbed Cucumbers

Simple Salmon Spinach Pasta Salad

Citrus Cooked Halibut with Baked Potato & Cucumber Slices

Red Meats

Steak Kabob with Baked Potatoes and Fruit Salad

Sliced Beef Tenderloin with Mashed Potatoes and Carrots

Pan-Broiled Sirloin with Cubed Potatoes and Green Peas

Veal Stir-fry with Dutch Potatoes and Green Beans

Grilled Hawaiian Steak with New Potatoes and Green Peas

JUNE

Sunday	Monday	Tuesday	Wednesday	Thursday	Friday	Saturday
Wild Rice Chicken Breasts Corn, Caesar Salad	**Steak Ragoutant** French Bread Italian Salad	**Shrimp with Chilies** Rice	**Brown Rice Pork Chops** Herbed Tomatoes	**Pasta Salad w/ Spinach & Feta** Fresh Bread Cheese Spread	**Lemon-Garlic Salmon** Broccoli Spears, New Potatoes 3-C Salad	*Plan Ahead* **Steak Kabob** Baked Potato, Fruit Salad
Swiss Chicken Rolls Rice Vegetable Caesar Salad	**Stir-Fried Beef** Rice, Egg Rolls	**Cocktail Shrimp** Baked Potato, Green Wedge Salad	**Elegant Italian Pork Chops** Rice, Green Beans	*Plan Ahead* **Mine-strone Soup** Chicken, Cheese Assortment	**Mushroom Onion Baked Fish** Rice, Vegetable Platter	**Sliced Beef Tenderloin** Mashed Potatoes, Carrots
Chicken w/ Lemon Caper Sauce Wild Rice, Chopped Vegetables	**Barbecued Meat Loaf** Corn, Spinach	**New Orleans Shrimp** Rice, Green Wedge Salad	**Pasta Cochon** Garlic Bread	**Heavenly Roma** French Bread, Tossed Salad	**Cod Fillet w/ Pesto Sauce** Corn, Herbed Cucumbers	*Plan Ahead* **Grilled Hawaiian Steak** New Potatoes, Green Peas
Plan Ahead **Chicken in Beer Marinade** Mashed Potatoes, Onion Rings	**Street Vendor Hot-Dogs** Red Beans	**Shrimp & Pesto Salad**	**Italian Pork Chops** Pasta, Italian Salad, Fresh Bread	**Tangy Pasta Salad** Fresh Bread	*Plan Ahead* **Citrus Cooked Halibut** Baked Potato, Cucumber Slices	**Pan-broiled Sirloin** Cubed Potatoes, Green Peas
Plan Ahead **Grilled Barbecued Chicken** Cole Slaw, Baked Beans	**Herbed Chicken Sandwich** Caesar Salad	**Shrimp Curry** Fruit Cocktail, Rice	**Braised Pork Chops** Prunes, Macaroni Cheese	**Tuna Casserole** Baked Bell Peppers, Fresh Bread	**Simple Salmon** Spinach, Pasta Salad	**Veal Stir-Fry** Dutch Potatoes, Green Beans

First week JUNE

Sunday	*Monday*	*Tuesday*	*Wednesday*	*Thursday*	*Friday*	*Saturday*
Wild Rice Chicken Breasts Corn, Caesar Salad	**Steak Ragoûtant** French Bread Italian Salad	**Shrimp with Chilies** Rice	**Brown Rice Pork Chops** Herbed Tomatoes	**Pasta Salad Spinach & Feta** Fresh Bread Cheese Spread	**Lemon-Garlic Salmon** Broccoli Spears, New Potatoes, 3-C Salad	*Plan Ahead* **Steak Kabob** Baked Potato, Fruit Salad

Fresh Vegetables \ Fruits		*Herbs \ Spices*	*Basics*
broccoli bunches -2 corn ears - 4 romaine lettuce iceberg lettuce - 1 lemons - 6 white onions - 2 red onion - 1 celery bundle tomatoes - 7 salad tomatoes - 6 carrot bundle	garlic pod - 1 fresh thyme - 2 tsp. fresh spinach -1 bag zucchini - 1 cucumber - 1 new potatoes - 3 potatoes - 4 green pepper - 1 yellow pepper - 1 summer squash - 1 jalapeño - 1 Serrano chili - 1	lemon pepper red pepper flakes dry mustard chili powder ginger thyme	olive oil extra-virgin olive oil peanut oil sea salt flour red wine vinegar Worcestershire sauce soy sauce kosher salt honey Converted rice

Entrée Food	*Dairy*	*Miscellaneous*	*Cans \ Jars*
skinless, boneless chicken breasts -2 ground sirloin 1 lb. medium or large shrimp 10-20 pork chops 2-4 salmon filets - 2 beef kabob - 1 lb. **Frozen** chopped broccoli - pkg	eggs - 2 milk - 1 cup butter - 1 stick buttermilk - ½ cup Cheddar cheese- 6 oz. Feta cheese - pkg cheese variety - 3 **Wine** red wine - bottle dry white wine ½ C	long grain and wild rice - pkg. converted brown rice - pkg croutons pkg. fresh French bread 2 pine nuts - 4 oz rotelle pasta - 1 lb. spaghetti pasta 1 lb. fruit-flavored gelatin 1 pkg.	whole tomatoes - 1 tomato paste - 1 ripe olives - 4 oz chicken broth - 1 salad pepper vlasic® Pepperoncini 4 oz. canned fruit - 4 oz.

WILD RICE CHICKEN BREASTS

with Corn, Caesar Salad

2 skinless, boneless chicken breasts
1 (6 oz.) pkg. serving of Long Grain & Wild Rice
2 cups chopped broccoli
½ cup dry white wine

4 ears fresh corn

2 hard-cooked eggs
¼ cup olive oil
1 tsp. Worcestershire sauce
½ teaspoon salt
1 clove garlic
Ground black pepper
¼ tsp. dry mustard
1 bunch romaine lettuce
2 lemons

Preheat oven to 325° F .

Pound **chicken breasts** to obtain an even thickness. Spoon a layer of **wild rice** onto chicken, fold one end over and secure with toothpicks. (The leftover rice will be prepared separately.) Arrange chicken pieces in a lightly- greased baking dish. We spray the dish with a fat-free vegetable spray. Add white wine. Bake, covered, at 325° F for 45 minutes; uncover and bake another 10-15 minutes to brown.

While the chicken cooks, prepare the **hard-cooked eggs.** Use the 10-10 method: 10 minutes boiling water, ten minutes in hot. Remove the eggs from water, run under cold water to stop the cooking process and refrigerate until needed.

Cook remaining wild rice according to package directions.

Prepare the **Caesar salad.** Mix the olive oil, Worcestershire sauce, salt, garlic, pepper and mustard in a bowl; toss with the romaine lettuce until all leaves are coated. Squeeze the lemons over the salad and toss.

Before serving, slice the cooked eggs and place atop the salad.

At time of uncovering chicken, prepare the **corn.** We normally boil our corn in water for approximately ten minutes.

STEAK RAGOÛTANT

with French Bread and Italian Salad

3 Tbsps. cooking oil (peanut)
1 small onion, chopped
1 cup chopped celery
1 lb. ground sirloin
1 (14 oz.) can whole tomatoes
1 (6 oz.) can tomato paste
1 teaspoon chili powder
1 teaspoon salt
½ teaspoon pepper
1 cup uncooked spaghetti

Italian Salad Ingredients:
lettuce
tomato, in wedges
carrot, shredded
ripe olives
salad pepper (Pepperoncini)
Croutons (optional)

Fresh French bread
Red wine (optional)

Ragoûtant: a French word that means to restore the appetite.

If you're having fresh **French bread**, bake it now, following package directions.

Prepare the **Steak Ragoûtant**. In a large skillet, cook onions and celery in oil until yellow. Add meat and cook until meat is light brown. Add tomatoes with liquid, tomato paste, chili powder, salt and pepper and simmer for 45 minutes. Add water as needed. Before the meat is done, prepare spaghetti according to package directions.

While the meat cooks, prepare the **Italian salad.** Tear lettuce into bite-size pieces. Cut tomato into wedges in desired thickness. Shred the carrot on top. Add a few ripe olives. Toss well. Add a salad pepper to top and spread croutons around.

Serve with **French bread** and a **red wine**.

SHRIMP WITH CHILIES

with Rice

1 jalapeño, sliced in rounds*
1 Serrano chili, julienned*

10-20 medium or large shrimp
2 Tbsps. kosher salt

2 Tbsps. peanut oil
1 clove garlic, minced
¾ teaspoon ground ginger
½ teaspoon lemon juice

Converted Rice

* *Any Mexican chili will do. Try Anaheim or Chiptole, fresh or in can.*

Prepare the **rice** before proceeding, following package directions.

To prepare the **chilies**: clean them; cut Serrano chilies in half, lengthwise. Remove white ribs and seeds; with paring knife remove ribs and seed from jalapeño. If you are using the canned version of peppers, wash them under water. The chilies may be roasted to sweeten them up a bit. Set on broiler plate a few inches from heat source. Allow them to blister. Remove from heat, cool and separate skin. Cut into rounds or julienne strips.

Meanwhile, salt-leach the **shrimp**; peel the shrimp and wash clean. Sprinkle with kosher salt, coating evenly. Let sit for one minute. Rinse and drain. Repeat salting again, let sit for another minute, rinse and drain well; set aside.

When rice is about done, begin the stir-fry. Heat a frying pan or wok to a high temperature. Pour in peanut oil, garlic, ginger and lemon juice. Immediately, add the peppers and the salt-leached shrimp. Chow (cook) for a minute or two; remove and serve with the rice.

BROWN RICE PORK CHOPS

with Herbed Tomatoes

1 pkg. frozen chopped broccoli
1 small onion, chopped
2 Tbsps. peanut oil
3 Tbsps. butter
3 Tbsps. flour
¾ cup chicken broth
½ cup milk
½ teaspoon sea salt
1 clove garlic, minced
Freshly ground pepper, to taste

½ cup buttermilk
1 cup uncooked Converted brown rice
3 oz. Cheddar cheese

2 - 4 pork chops, braised
Herbed Tomatoes:
2 tomatoes
1 clove minced garlic
red wine vinegar

For the **Herbed Tomatoes**, slice the tomatoes into ¼ inch slices. Sprinkle minced garlic on top as well as fresh ground black pepper. Pour some red wine vinegar over the slices. Place tomatoes in refrigerator until ready to serve.

Preheat oven to 350°F.

Using a colander, thaw the **frozen broccoli** by running water over it and separating it with your fingers. Set broccoli aside.

Add peanut oil to skillet over low heat. Sauté onion pieces until they become clear. Remove onions and set aside. To skillet add margarine to melt, then add flour and stir for one minute, do NOT brown. Add chicken broth and milk and stir over medium heat until mixture comes to a boil. Add salt, garlic and pepper. Cook 1 minute more. To this mixture, add the onions from above, broccoli, buttermilk and the cup of uncooked brown rice. Mix well; pour into a covered baking dish. Top with Cheddar cheese.

Bake about 40 minutes.

While the brown rice cooks, prepare **pork chops** by braising. Season the chops with salt and pepper. Brown on both sides in pan of hot peanut oil. Add small amount of water to pan, cover tightly and simmer over medium-low heat for about 40 minutes, turning once.

PASTA SALAD SPINACH AND FETA

with Fresh Bread and Cheese Spread

½ cup pine nuts
1 bag fresh spinach
4 ripe tomatoes
2 teaspoons fresh thyme, chopped
5 Tbsps. extra-virgin olive oil
½ teaspoon freshly ground black pepper

½ lb. fresh rotelle pasta
1 zucchini, julienned
Feta cheese

Fresh bread
Cheeses (variety)

If you are having **fresh bread**, preheat the oven to 400° F for making the **bread**. Bake it now according to package directions.

When bread is cooked, remove and reduce oven heat to 350° F. Toast the pine nuts for about 5 minutes.

Combine **spinach**, cut tomatoes, thyme and 5 tablespoons of extra-virgin olive oil in a large mixing/serving bowl. Season the ingredients with pepper. Prepare the pasta following the package directions. Cook until *al dente* and add the zucchini for a maximum of one minute. Drain pasta and zucchini, rinse with cold water and drain again. Toss pasta with spinach mixture above. Add pine nuts and crumble some of the **feta cheese** for a topping.

Cut **cheeses** into various shapes and sizes.

LEMON GARLIC SALMON

with Broccoli Spears, New Potatoes and 3-C Salad

2 salmon fillets
1 teaspoon lemon pepper seasoning
2 Tbsps. butter
1 clove garlic, minced
2 lemons
1 bunch broccoli
Cheddar cheese

3-C Salad Ingredients:
carrot
celery
cucumber
red wine vinegar
3 new potatoes
1 Tbsp. sea salt

To prepare the **new potatoes**, wash the skins but do not peel. Add new potatoes to pot of boiling water. Add sea salt depending on the number of potatoes: 1 tablespoon for three potatoes can be tried. Let the potatoes boil 15-20 minutes. Test for softness. Drain and set aside.

Before you begin the fish, prepare the **broccoli spears**. Remove any large leaves from the broccoli bunch. Cut the stalks lengthwise from end to broccoli head to make spears. Cook by steaming over boiling water for about five minutes. When serving, sprinkle with shredded Cheddar cheese.

Prepare the **3-C salad** by slicing the carrot, celery and cucumber and placing in a serving dish. A red-wine vinegar will do the trick for the topping. Let this salad marinate for about ten minutes before serving.

Next, rinse **fish** and pat dry. Season with lemon pepper on both sides. Melt butter in large skillet over medium-high heat. Sauté garlic for a moment. Place fillets in pan and cook in butter, turning once, until the fish flakes in the center when tested with a fork. You may need to add additional butter during the cooking process. Sprinkle with lemon juice before serving and cut lemon into wedges as garnish.

3 hours - Plan ahead

STEAK KABOB

with Baked Potato and Fruit Salad

2 Tbsps. soy sauce
2 Tbsps. honey
1 clove garlic, crushed
1 teaspoon lemon peel
1 teaspoon ground ginger
½ teaspoon red pepper flakes
1 lb. beef kabob meat*

4 potatoes

Vegetables:
6 salad tomatoes
green & yellow bell peppers
red onion
summer squash
1 (3 oz.) pkg. fruit-flavored gelatin
2 cups well-drained, canned fruit
1 lemon

* *If kabob meat is unavailable, purchase sirloin steak and cut into cubes.*

In a bowl large enough to hold all of the **beef cubes**, mix together the soy sauce, honey, crushed garlic, lemon peel, ground ginger and red pepper flakes. Stir well.

Into this dish, lay the beef cubes and toss to coat well. Cover the dish and marinate the beef in the refrigerator for a *couple of hours (or overnight).*

Take the time now to make the **fruit salad**, prepare gelatin according to package directions. Chill. When partially set, add fruit and juice from one lemon. Pour into individual molds. Chill until firm. When serving, unmold on plate and garnish with lettuce.

When ready for the meal prepare **baked potatoes**. Wash the potatoes and pierce with fork. Place potatoes in the microwave and cook on HIGH for 4 minutes per potato per side, turning once. (3 or 4 potatoes will cook in 24 minutes.)

Preheat the oven broiler.

Cut the **vegetables** into bite-size squares. Remove beef from marinade and slide onto metal (flat) skewers alternating the beef with cubes of vegetables.

Place the completed skewers on the top of a baking dish and broil 2-3 inches from heat. Turn after a few minutes. The meat should cook to medium-rare and this should take approximately 10 minutes total broiling time.

Second week JUNE

Sunday	*Monday*	*Tuesday*	*Wednesday*	*Thursday*	*Friday*	*Saturday*
Swiss Chicken Rolls Rice, Vegetable Caesar Salad	**Stir-Fried Beef** Rice, Egg Roll	**Cocktail Shrimp** Baked Potato, Green Wedge Salad	**Elegant Italian Pork Chops** Rice, Green Beans	*Plan Ahead* **Mine-strone Soup** Chicken, Cheese Assortment	**Mushroom Onion Baked Fish** Rice, Vegetable Platter	**Sliced Beef Tenderloin** Mashed Potatoes, Carrots

Fresh Vegetables \ Fruits		*Herbs \ Spices*	*Basics*
parsley bunch green beans - 2 lb. white onions - 3 green onions - 6 potatoes - 7 iceberg lettuce- 1 cucumber - 1	garlic pod - 1 red bell peppers - 1 mushrooms- 2 carrot bundle radish bunch celery bundle zucchini - 1 lemons - 2	dried oregano paprika garlic salt dry mustard ginger fennel seeds marjoram	flour vegetable oil white vinegar olive oil soy sauce peanut oil cornstarch sea salt Worcestershire sauce Converted Rice

Entrée Food	*Dairy*	*Miscellaneous*	*Cans \ Jars*
skinless, boneless chicken breasts - 3 flank beef strips - ½ lb. cooked cocktail shrimp 20-24 butterfly pork chops - 2 orange roughy fillets - 2 beef tenderloin 1 lb. ham cubes - ¼ lb.	Swiss cheese - 4 slices butter - 5 T margarine - 2 sticks Parmesan cheese 5 T bacon - 2 slices milk - ¼ cup cheese assortment - 3 **Wine** sherry wine- 4 oz. dry white wine- ½ cup Chianti wine - bot.	bread crumbs - 3 T pine nuts - ¼ cup spaghetti pasta ½ lb bean assortment - black, pinto, navy 1 cup each brown sugar 2 T barley - ¼ cup **Frozen** frozen egg rolls pkg.	chicken broth - 1 whole tomatoes - 1 pickles - 2 oz. seafood cocktail sauce - 4 oz. mushrooms (4 oz.)

SWISS CHICKEN ROLLS

with Rice and Vegetable Caesar Salad

2 whole chicken breasts, boneless, skinless

2 slices Swiss cheese
½ teaspoon black pepper
2 Tbsps. flour
1 Tbsp. butter
½ cup chicken broth
¼ cup dry white wine
¼ teaspoon dried oregano
¼ cup fresh parsley

Converted Rice

¾ lb. fresh green beans
1 slice bacon, uncooked
Vegetable Caesar Salad:
1 Tbsp. vegetable oil
½ Tbsp. minced onions
½ Tbsp. vinegar
Clove garlic, crushed
Dash salt and pepper
1 Tbsp. dried bread crumbs
1 Tbsp. Parmesan cheese
½ Tbsp. butter
Paprika

Prepare the cooked **green beans** first. To a pot of water, add a slice of bacon and the green beans with ends removed then cut in half. Let beans cook for 12 minutes then drain.

To make the **Vegetable Caesar salad**: combine the cooked beans and the oil, minced onions, vinegar, garlic, salt and pepper. Mix well. Place in an ungreased 1-quart casserole dish. Mix bread crumbs, Parmesan cheese and sprinkle over the green beans. Drizzle butter and sprinkle the paprika over the mixture and set aside for oven cooking later.

Preheat the oven to 350° F.

While the oven heats, prepare the **rice** by following package directions. Begin the **Swiss Chicken.** Pound the chicken breasts to achieve an even thickness. Place a Swiss cheese slice on each half-breast. Roll the breast into a tube. Using string or skewers secure the tubes. On wax paper, mix the pepper and flour. Coat the chicken with this mixture. In a heavy skillet melt the butter; when hot, brown the breasts on all sides. Add chicken broth, wine and oregano to skillet and bring to a boil. Cover and simmer until the chicken is cooked though, about 10 minutes.

While the chicken cooks, put the green beans into the oven to heat through. Leave the beans in until the chicken is ready, then serve immediately. Garnish with parsley.

STIR - FRIED BEEF

with Rice and Egg Roll

2 Tbsps. olive oil
½ lb. flank beef strips,
or beef stroganoff
¼ cup pine nuts
Garlic salt to taste
¼ lb. green beans
1 onion, cut in wedges

Frozen egg rolls (chicken or beef)

2 Tbsps. vinegar
½ cup sherry wine
2 Tbsps. brown sugar
4 Tbsps. soy sauce
2 Tbsps. cornstarch
½ teaspoon ground ginger
½ teaspoon dry mustard

Converted Rice

If having **egg rolls**, prepare the oven according to package directions.

Cook **rice** NOW! following package directions.

If using **flank steak**, cut across grain into small strips. Heat oil in a large skillet or wok. Add beef and pine nuts and sprinkle with garlic salt.

Cook and stir over high heat for 1 minute.

Add beans and onion. Cover and cook over medium heat for about 5 minutes, shaking or stirring often.

Combine vinegar, sherry, sugar, soy sauce and cornstarch; add to skillet. At the same time, add the seasonings: ginger and dry mustard. Cook, stirring, about 1 minute, until sauce is thick.

Serve the beef over rice. Don't forget the egg rolls! A mistake that we sometimes make, but only once a year!

COCKTAIL SHRIMP

with Baked Potato and Green Wedge Salad

20-24 cooked cocktail shrimp
4 potatoes, for baking

Seafood cocktail sauce
Pickles

Green Wedge Salad Ingredients:
½ head iceberg lettuce
½ cucumber, in thick slices
2 radishes, in thin slices
2 celery stalks, julienned

For this menu, make sure the **cooked shrimp** are icy cold.

Bake **potatoes** according to your favorite method. We typically use the microwave to completely bake or to at least partially bake the potatoes. Wash the potatoes and pierce with fork. Place potatoes in the microwave and cook on HIGH for 4 minutes per potato per side, turning once. (3 or 4 potatoes will cook in 24 minutes.)

While the potatoes cook, prepare the **green wedge salad.** Cut the iceberg lettuce in half, then into large wedges. Cut the cucumber and place in the curve portion of lettuce wedge. Slice the radishes and place on cucumbers. Julienne the celery and place on top of and around the wedge.

Serve cooked shrimp on plate with a **pickle** as relish. Don't forget the cocktail sauce!

ELEGANT ITALIAN PORK CHOPS

with Rice and Green Beans

2 butterfly pork chops
Salt and pepper, to taste
1 teaspoon fennel seeds
1 Tbsp. peanut oil
1 clove garlic, minced
Chianti red wine

1 lb. green beans
1 slice bacon, uncooked

Converted Rice

This is simply an elegant meal. A candlelight evening. One guaranteed to please!

Sprinkle both sides of **pork chops** with salt and pepper. Lay chops flat and cut a slit into the side of the chop. Place a few, say 10, fennel seeds into the opening.

Sauté minced garlic in small amount of peanut oil then brown chops on both sides in same peanut oil. Use low heat to avoid overcooking.

When barely brown, add a half-cup of Chianti or red table wine. Cover and simmer for 40 minutes.

While pork chops cook, prepare the **rice** according to package directions.

When the pork chops are simmering, cook **green beans** by the boiling method. Cut off ends of beans. Cut in half or leave long. Barely cover them with water and add one slice of bacon; add beans and sprinkle with salt. Cook until they are tender: 20 minutes for *al dente.*

Overnight - Plan ahead

MINESTRONE SOUP

with Broiled Chicken and Cheese Assortment

1 cup soup mix (see below)
1 onion, chopped
1 (9 oz.) can tomatoes
¼ cup barley
¼ lb. ham, cut in cubes
Garlic, to taste
Sea salt and pepper, to taste
4 stalks chopped celery
Chopped zucchini

Assortment of cheeses
1 whole boneless, skinless chicken breast
1 Tbsp. butter, melted

½ lb. spaghetti pasta

4 Tbsps. Parmesan cheese, grated

Soak 1 cup of dried beans ***overnight*** in cold water: Drain, rinse and cover with 6 cups cold water in a large pot. See note below.

Prepare an **assortment of sharp cheeses**.

If you want to add the **chicken** to the soup do this: pound the chicken to achieve an even thickness. Rub chicken with garlic, brush on softened butter and place under oven broiler turning once.

For the **soup,** add chopped onion, tomatoes, ¼ cup barley and ham. Bring to a slow boil, then simmer until all beans are tender. Add seasonings: garlic, sea salt, or pepper as desired. Add celery and zucchini. Continue to cook.

Fifteen minutes before serving, add spaghetti, broken into small pieces. Sprinkle with Parmesan cheese. Add chicken from above, cut into small pieces.

Soup Mix Preparation

Buy 7 or 8 different kinds of beans: lentils or split peas, black beans, red beans, pinto beans, white navy beans, green and yellow spilt peas, etc. Divide these into as many pint jars as you have. Layer them evenly according to colors so that they end up making a pretty jar of soup mix. If there is space at the top of the jar, fill with barley.

MUSHROOM-ONION BAKED FISH

with Rice and Vegetable Platter

1 Tbsp. margarine
6 green onions, chopped
1 (4 oz.) jar mushrooms, drained
1 or 2 fish fillets of orange roughy
¼ cup dry white wine
Juice from 1 lemon
½ teaspoon dried marjoram
Black pepper
2 slices Swiss cheese, in strips
2 Tbsps. dry bread crumbs
Converted Rice
Vegetable platter:
1 red bell pepper
1 Tbsp. olive oil

Note: Cod or sole fillets are good substitutes

Preheat oven to 400° F.

Prepare the **rice** according to package directions.

For the **fish,** lightly grease a baking dish with margarine. Chop the green onions and mix with the jar of mushrooms; scatter evenly on bottom of baking dish. Place the fish fillets in a single layer (folding under thin ends). Mix the wine and lemon juice together and pour over fish. Sprinkle with marjoram and black pepper. Distribute the cheese slices evenly over the fillets. Add ¼ cup water. Cover baking dish and bake at 400° F for about 7 minutes.

Remove cover and spread the bread crumbs on top. Bake for another 7 minutes or until fish is done.

Cut the **red bell pepper** in large pieces. Coat with virgin olive oil. Place the bell pepper and the cooked fish under broiler and broil for 1 minute until brown.

SLICED BEEF TENDERLOIN

with Mashed Potatoes and Carrots

2 Tbsps. butter
1 lb. beef tenderloin
2 mushrooms, sliced
2 Tbsps. finely chopped onions
1 lemon, juiced
1 teaspoon Worcestershire sauce
Sea salt, to taste
1 clove garlic, crushed
¼ cup margarine
2 Tbsps. parsley

3 potatoes
½ stick margarine
¼ cup milk

2-3 carrots

Prepare **mashed potatoes.** Wash and peel potatoes and cut into halves then quarter into smaller pieces. Heat a pot of water and add in the potato pieces. Salt the water to your taste. Cook for approximately 20 minutes; drain. Into hot potatoes, place ½ stick of butter or margarine, ¼ cup of milk and whip to desired smoothness.

Meanwhile, cut the **carrots** in half and steam them until they are *al dente.*

Melt 2 tablespoons butter in heavy skillet. Cook **beef** over medium-high heat, turning once, until desired doneness. We allow about 5 minutes per side. Cut into beef to test.

While the beef cooks, prepare the **mushroom sauce**. Cook and stir mushrooms, onion, lemon juice, Worcestershire sauce, salt and garlic in ¼ cup margarine until mushrooms are tender. Stir in parsley and keep warm.

Serve beef with mushroom sauce.

Third week JUNE

Sunday	*Monday*	*Tuesday*	*Wednesday*	*Thursday*	*Friday*	*Saturday*
Chicken w/ Lemon Caper Sauce Wild Rice, Chopped Vegetables	**Barbecued Meat Loaf** Corn Spinach	**New Orleans Shrimp** Rice, Green Wedge Salad	**Pasta Cochon** Garlic Bread	**Heavenly Roma** French Bread, Tossed Salad	**Cod Fillet w/ Pesto Sauce** Corn, Herbed Cucumbers	*Plan Ahead* **Grilled Hawaiian Steak** New Potatoes, Green peas

Fresh Vegetables \ Fruits		*Herbs \ Spices*	*Basics*
lemons - 3 romaine lettuce - 1 cauliflower - 1 cup broccoli - ½ lb. white onions - 2 corn - 8 ears spinach bunch - 1 parsley bunch - 1	garlic pod - 1 fresh basil iceberg lettuce - 1 greenleaf lettuce 1 cucumbers - 2 radish bunch tomatoes - 2 new potatoes - 4 celery bundle green bell pepper - 1 lemon - 1	cayenne pepper dried thyme dried marjoram paprika red pepper flakes bay leaf dried parsley	Dijon mustard extra-virgin olive oil olive oil red wine vinegar white wine vinegar Converted Rice soy sauce

Entrée Food	*Dairy*	*Miscellaneous*	*Cans \ Jars*
skinless, boneless chicken breasts - 2 ground sirloin steak -1 lb. cooked shrimp 20-24 cod, snapper, or flounder fish fillets - 2 sirloin steaks - 2 **Frozen** green peas pkg.	eggs - 2 milk - ½ cup butter - 5 T margarine - 1 stick fresh Parmesan cheese - 1 cup orange juice - pint bacon - 6 slices American cheese ¾ C **Wine** Chianti wine - bottle	long grain & wild rice - pkg Quaker® oats ½ C French or Italian bread loaves - 4 Fresh bread - 1 angel hair pasta ½ lb. fusilli pasta - ½ lb. croutons - pkg.	tomato paste - 1 whole tomatoes - 1 tuna or chicken - 1 can ripe olives - 4 oz. crushed pineapple 1 capers - 4 oz. B-B-Q sauce - 8 oz.

CHICKEN WITH LEMON - CAPER SAUCE

with Wild Rice and Chopped Vegetables

1 (5.2 oz.) pkg. Long Grain & Wild Rice
1 ⅔ cups water
3 Tbsps. butter or margarine
2 skinless, boneless chicken breast
1 clove garlic, minced
Salt and pepper, to taste

1 cup romaine lettuce, torn

1 lemon, juiced
1 Tbsp. capers, drained

1 cup cauliflower, chopped
1 cup broccoli, chopped
¾ cup American cheese
1 tomato, in wedges

Prepare **wild rice** following package directions. Combine water and 1 tablespoon of butter in saucepan. Stir in contents of rice and seasoning packets; bring to a boil. Cover tightly, reduce heat and simmer until all water is absorbed, about 25 minutes.

While rice cooks, pound **chicken breasts** to achieve an even thickness. Rub garlic onto chicken and sprinkle with salt and pepper. Heat remaining butter in large skillet over medium heat. Add chicken and cook until lightly browned and cooked through, 3 to 4 minutes per side. Remove cooked chicken and keep warm. Use the skillet in the next step.

Make the **lemon-caper sauce**. Add lemon juice and capers to drippings in skillet; cook and stir 1 minute. Pour over chicken.

When rice is done, stir in the minced lettuce.

Chop the **cauliflower** and **broccoli**. Steam them for a moment. Top with grated cheese.

Place rice and chopped vegetables beside the chicken. Garnish with twisted slice of lemon. Cut tomato into wedges to add color to the meal.

BARBECUED MEAT LOAF

with Corn and Spinach

1 lb. ground sirloin steak
½ cup Quaker® oats
½ cup finely chopped onion
1 egg, beaten
½ cup barbecue sauce

4 ears of fresh corn
or 1 package frozen
1 bunch fresh spinach
or 1 package frozen

If using a conventional oven, preheat the oven to 375° F.

Prepare the **barbecue meat loaf**. Mix together the ground steak, oats, chopped onion and egg. Add about ¼ cup of barbecue sauce to give the meat some moisture. Shape into a loaf and place in a baking dish. Next, add about ¼ cup of barbecue sauce to the dish to aid the cooking process.

For conventional oven bake for about 1 hour at 375° F.

To microwave meat loaf, cook on HIGH/full power for 7 minutes, then let rest 2 minutes before turning the container and cooking again on HIGH for another 7 to 8 minutes.

For the **corn and spinach**, follow package directions, or, if using fresh vegetables, steam both vegetables in a steamer while the meat loaf rests.

NEW ORLEANS SHRIMP

with Rice and Green Wedge Salad

2 Tbsps. butter
½ cup minced onions
1 teaspoon salt
1 teaspoon minced parsley
1 bay leaf
¼ cup celery, diced
Dash cayenne pepper
½ cup chopped green pepper
1 (6 oz.) can tomato paste
2 ½ cups water

20 -24 cooked shrimp, cleaned

Converted Rice

Green Wedge Salad:
½ head iceberg lettuce
½ cucumber, in thick slices
2 radishes, in thin slices
2 celery stalks, julienned

To prepare the **green wedge salad**, cut the iceberg lettuce in half and then into wide wedges. Remove center portion and chop, spreading on salad plate. Cut the cucumber and place in the remaining curved portion of lettuce wedge. Slice the radishes and place on cucumbers. Julienne the celery and place on top of and around the wedge. Refrigerate salad until serving.

Have all ingredients prepared and measured before you proceed.

For the **New Orleans sauce**, melt butter in saucepan and sauté the onions. Blend in the remaining ingredients, except for the cooked shrimp. Cook slowly for about 30 minutes, stirring occasionally.

While the New Orleans sauce cooks, prepare the **rice** according to package directions. When rice is about done, stir the **shrimp** into the sauce and heat thoroughly, about 1 minute.

Serve the New Orleans shrimp over a mound of rice.

PASTA COCHON

with Garlic Bread

6 slices bacon
½ stick butter or margarine
½ cup milk
1 Tbsp. red wine vinegar
½ lb. fusilli pasta
1 egg, whipped
¼ cup Parmesan or Romano cheese, freshly-grated
Salt and pepper, to taste
Chianti wine

Garlic Bread Ingredients:
1 clove garlic, minced
1 tsp. extra-virgin olive oil
1 teaspoon dried thyme
½ teaspoon dried marjoram
1 Tbsp. fresh parsley
Dash paprika
1 Tbsp. Parmesan cheese
Small loaves of French or Italian bread

Prepare the **garlic bread** first. Preheat the oven to 350° F.

In a small bowl, combine the chopped garlic and the olive oil and mix well. In another bowl combine the herbs: thyme and marjoram, parsley and paprika. Add the Parmesan cheese and mix well.

Cut each of the small bread loaves in half, coat with the garlic oil and sprinkle the herbs about the loaves. Place loaves on baking sheet. Bake for about 15 minutes and serve while still hot.

For the **Pasta Cochon,** cut the raw bacon into small pieces. Use either the microwave or a small saucepan. Cook in the butter until clear. Heat the milk in the microwave for about 15 seconds then add the milk with the bacon and butter to the original saucepan. When this mixture is heated, slowly add the wine vinegar. Simmer for about 15 minutes, or until the sauce cooks smooth. The vinegar will turn the milk into cheese.

Start the water heating immediately. Boil the **fusilli pasta** until *al dente.* Consult package directions. Drain pasta and return to the pan. Whip the egg and scatter it atop the hot pasta. This will cook the egg. At the same time add the bacon sauce from above, and the Parmesan or Romano cheese. Add salt and pepper, toss and serve when Pasta Cochon is done.

Serve with **Chianti wine**.

HEAVENLY ROMA

with French Bread and Tossed Salad

½ lb. angel hair pasta
¼ cup olive oil
1 clove garlic, minced
2 Tbsps. capers
1 (15 oz.) can whole tomatoes, crushed
Dash red peppers flakes
1 cup black olives, sliced
1 (6 ½ oz.) can tuna or chicken
Salt and pepper, to taste

French bread
Chianti red wine (optional)
Tossed Salad Ingredients:
- **iceberg lettuce**
- **greenleaf lettuce**
- **cucumber**
- **radishes**
- **tomato**
- **ripe olives**
- **croutons**

This is equally good with canned tuna or canned chicken.

If you're having fresh **French bread**, bake it now, according to package directions.

Prepare the **tossed salad.** Wash and dry all vegetables. Tear the lettuces into bite-size pieces. Slice the cucumber and radishes. Cut the fresh tomato into wedges. Toss all together, then add the ripe olives and the croutons.

Cook **pasta** according to package directions.

Prepare the **Italian sauce.** Heat olive oil in large skillet and sauté garlic and capers for 1 minute. Add canned tomatoes and heat to a simmer. Add red pepper flakes, olives and tuna.

When pasta is *al dente*, drain well and add to skillet. Add salt and pepper to taste. Heat thoroughly.

Serve with **tossed salad** and French bread spread with garlic. A **red wine** such as a Chianti will compliment this meal.

COD FILLETS WITH PESTO SAUCE

with Corn and Herbed Cucumbers

2 fish fillets
(cod, snapper, flounder)
4 ears fresh corn

1 cucumber
Red wine vinegar
Pepper, to taste

Pesto Sauce Ingredients:
1 clove garlic, peeled
1 cup fresh basil leaves or
2 Tbsps. dried parsley
¼ cup Parmesan cheese
¼ cup olive oil
Juice from 1 lemon

Preheat oven to 450°F.

Prepare fresh **pesto sauce**. Mince garlic. Mince basil leaves if using fresh. Place the minced basil and garlic in a small mixing bowl. Stir in Parmesan cheese. Add olive oil and lemon juice and beat into a smooth blend.

Rinse **fish** and pat dry. Lay fish in a lightly oiled baking dish. Spread the pesto mix over the fish. Save one-half of the pesto sauce for the *Shrimp and Pesto Sauce* menu next week. This sauce will keep in the refrigerator for that length of time.

Bake fish uncovered in the 450° F oven for about 8 to 10 minutes.

While fish bakes, cook **corn,** by micro-waving 1 minute per side per corn. Or, if you prefer, boil the corn in water for 10 minutes.

While corn cooks, cut **cucumber** into slices. Sprinkle slices with balsamic or red wine vinegar and sprinkle with pepper.

4 hours - Plan ahead

GRILLED HAWAIIAN STEAK

with New Potatoes and Green Peas

2 sirloin steaks

4 new potatoes
2 Tbsps. olive oil

Green peas, frozen

Pineapple Marinade Ingredients:
1 (8 oz.) can crushed pineapple
1 cup orange juice
1 Tbsp. soy sauce
1 teaspoon Dijon mustard
2 Tbsps. white wine vinegar

This is a grill menu !!

Prepare the **Pineapple Marinade** by combing all ingredients in right column into a large baking dish large enough to hold the steaks.

Remove excess fat from **steaks**; place steaks in marinade. Cover and marinate in the refrigerator for ***4 hours***, turning at least once.

When you are ready to cook, prepare the grill with coals then light. The coals should be white before you put on the steaks.

While the grill heats, prepare the **red potatoes**. Slice new potatoes into halves, brush top with olive oil and sprinkle with pepper. Place the potatoes in a microwave-proof bowl and cook on HIGH until they are close to being done. To give the potatoes a nice browning, place them on the grill around the steak.

For a vegetable, try frozen **green peas**. Cook, following package directions.

Fourth week JUNE

Sunday	*Monday*	*Tuesday*	*Wednesday*	*Thursday*	*Friday*	*Saturday*
Plan ahead **Chicken in Beer Marinade**	**Street Vendor Hot-Dogs**	**Shrimp & Pesto Salad**	**Italian Pork Chops**	**Tangy Pasta Salad**	*Plan ahead* **Citrus Cooked Halibut**	**Pan-Broiled Sirloin**
Mashed Potatoes, Onion Rings	Red Beans		Pasta Italian Salad, Fresh Bread	Fresh Bread	Baked Potato Cucumber Slices	Cubed Potatoes Green peas

Fresh Vegetables \ Fruits		*Herbs \ Spices*	*Basics*
white onions - 3 potatoes - 10 yellow onion - 1 green bell pepper - 1 cucumber - 2 iceberg lettuce - 2 green leaf lettuce - 1 red bell pepper - 1 small red onion - 1 butter lettuce- bunch red cabbage bunch	garlic pod fresh basil parsley bunch tomatoes - 11 carrot bundle lemons - 4 limes 4-6 oranges 1-2 grapefruit - 1 broccoli - ½ lb.	red pepper flakes paprika garlic salt dried basil red pepper sauce	peanut oil Dijon mustard olive oil ketchup Worcestershire sauce

Entrée Food	*Dairy*	*Miscellaneous*	*Cans \ Jars*
chicken breasts with skin - 4 beef frankfurters - 8 cooked shrimp 20-24 pork chops - 4 halibut fillets, skinless steaks 1-3 sirloin steaks - 2 **Frozen** green peas - 2 pkg.	Parmesan cheese- ½ C Romano cheese- 6 T sour cream - 1 cup bacon - 1 slice margarine 1 stick milk - ¼ C **Wine** beer - 1 can	brown sugar - 3 T Hot Dog buns - 8 potato chips sm pkg. red beans - 1 cup bow-tie pasta ½ lb. fresh bread pkg - 2 croutons pkg sea shell pasta ½ lb. pine nuts pkg	sweet pickle relish 2 oz sugar peas - 1 can ripe olives- 4 oz. dill pickles - 4 salad peppers - 4 oz. vlasic® Pepperoncini capers - 4 oz. chili sauce - 6 oz. stuffed olives - 4 oz. chicken broth - 1

1 hour - Plan ahead

CHICKEN IN BEER MARINADE

with Mashed Potatoes and Onion Rings

Beer Marinade Ingredients:

3 Tbsps. peanut oil
3 Tbsps. brown packed sugar
1 Tbsp. Worcestershire sauce
1 teaspoon red pepper sauce
Salt and pepper to taste
1 (16 oz.) can beer
3 Tbsps. Dijon mustard

1 large onion, cut into rings
4 chicken breasts, with skin
3 potatoes
½ stick margarine
¼ cup milk

Frozen green peas

An outdoor grill recipe!

Prepare the **beer marinade** by combining all ingredients on left side into a baking dish large enough to hold marinade and chicken. Place in the onion rings.

Pound the **chicken breasts** to a achieve an even thickness. Place chicken in marinade and cover completely with the juice. Cover the dish and refrigerate for a minimum of 30 minutes. Longer will do better. Remember to turn the chicken every 30 minutes or so.

Prepare the outdoor grill with coals.

When the coals are about ready, prepare the **mashed potatoes**. Wash and peel potatoes and cut into halves then quarter into smaller pieces. Heat a pot of water and add in the potato pieces. Salt the water to your taste. Cook for approximately 20 minutes; drain. Into hot potatoes, place ½ stick of margarine, ¼ cup of milk and whip to the desired smoothness.

Drain the chicken from the marinade and place on grill. Use the marinade for basting during cooking process. Grill the **onion rings** on the side of the chicken.

We have **green peas** with this chicken and it makes a nice statement. You should steam the peas for a few minutes or follow the package directions.

1 hour - Plan ahead

STREET - VENDOR HOT DOGS

with Red Beans

1 cup red beans
1 slice bacon

The **Basics**:
All beef frankfurters
Hot dog buns
Chips
Dijon mustard

The Condiments:
Sweet-pickle relish
Yellow onion, diced
Dill-pickle chips
Green bell pepper, diced
Cucumber, chopped
Iceberg lettuce, shredded
Ketchup
Garlic salt

This menu can be found on any big city street corner. The kids will love this chili-less hot dog for a change.

We like to have **red beans** with this meal, although any bean type will substitute. Make the beans by boiling them for 2 minutes. Remove from heat and let stand for an hour. Return to heat, add bacon, salt to taste, and bring back to a boil. Let cook for about an hour.

Cook **frankfurters** according to your favorite method, or place in pot of boiling water for 10 minutes. Remove pot and let frankfurters sit in hot water for another 10 minutes.

When frankfurters are done, heat buns. Allow guest to load on the condiments that suit them.

SHRIMP AND PESTO SALAD

2 Roma tomatoes, chopped
½ red bell pepper, thinly sliced
1 small red onion, sliced into thin rings, separated
½ cup sugar peas (canned)
½ lb. fresh broccoli
20-24 cooked shrimp and washed
¼ cup Parmesan cheese
Butter lettuce, leaves separated

Get the shrimp and other ingredients ready beforehand. Chop the tomatoes, the bell pepper, slice the small onion. Add sugar peas. If you have pesto sauce left over from last week, use it. Otherwise, prepare the **Pesto dressing** below**.**

Bring 1 quart of water to boiling; add **broccoli**, cover and remove from heat. Let stand 3 minutes. Add peas to the broccoli and let stand another minute. Drain peas and broccoli, rinse in cold water until cool; drain well.

Put broccoli, peas, tomatoes, shrimp, bell pepper, onion and cheese in a bowl and stir to mix.

Serve salad on a bed of lettuce and drizzle with **Pesto dressing**.

PESTO DRESSING

1 cup fresh basil
¼ cup olive oil
1 clove garlic
2 sprigs parsley
Salt and pepper to taste
2 Tbsps. pine nuts
4 Tbsps. Romano cheese

Place the basil in a blender. Add oil, garlic, parsley, salt, pepper, pine nuts; blend until all are chopped very fine. Remove from blender and add the Romano cheese.

ITALIAN PORK CHOPS

with Pasta, Italian Salad and Fresh Bread

Romano Gravy Ingredients:
- **¼ cup olive oil**
- **½ cup chopped onions**
- **1 ½ lbs. tomatoes, chopped**
- **¼ cup fresh basil leaves**
- **2 cloves garlic, minced**
- **Dash red pepper sauce**
- **½ teaspoon red pepper flakes**
- **Salt & pepper, to taste**

4 pork chops, fat trimmed
1 Tbsp. peanut oil
¼ cup chicken broth

Italian Salad Ingredients:
- **iceberg lettuce**
- **green leaf lettuce**
- **tomato in wedges**
- **red cabbage, in slivers**
- **ripe olives**
- **carrot, shredded**
- **salad pepper**
- **croutons (opt.)**

Bow-tie pasta (½ lb.)
Fresh bread

If you are having **fresh bread**, bake it now according to package directions.

For the **Romano gravy,** heat olive oil in a medium-size skillet. Add onions; cook, covered, over low-heat for 10 to 15 minutes, until soft. Add tomatoes, basil, garlic, red pepper sauce and red pepper flakes. Simmer, uncovered, for 30 to 40 minutes or until thick. Season with salt and pepper to taste.

While the Romano sauce cooks, prepare the **Italian salad**. Tear lettuces into bite-size pieces. Cut tomato into wedges in desired thickness. Cut red cabbage into julienne strips. Add a few ripe olives. Shred the carrot on top. Toss well. Add a salad pepper to top and spread croutons around.

For the **Italian pork chops,** brown them lightly in peanut oil. Add ¼ cup of chicken broth. Add the Romano sauce, cover and simmer for about 40 minutes.

When you are ready to eat, prepare **bow-tie pasta** according to package directions. *Note: Any pasta will substitute.*

TANGY PASTA SALAD

with Fresh Bread

½ lb. sea shell pasta *
1 clove garlic, minced
1 tomato, chopped
Black pepper
4 lemons
1 Tbsp. capers
1 ½ Tbsps. parsley, chopped
¼ cup olive oil
Fresh bread

Pesto Sauce Ingredients:
1 cup fresh basil
¼ cup olive oil
1 clove garlic
2 sprigs parsley
Salt and pepper, to taste
2 Tbsps. pine nuts
2 Tbsps. Parmesan or Romano cheese

* *Use the smaller version of the sea shells.*

If there was no pesto dressing left over from last Tuesday, make the **Pesto sauce** beforehand. Place the basil in a blender. Add oil, garlic, parsley, salt, pepper, pine nuts; blend until all are chopped very fine. Remove from blender and add the Parmesan or Romano cheese.

Cook **sea shell pasta** according to package directions. Drain, rinse with cold water and drain well again.

In a large bowl, combine the pasta, minced garlic and chopped tomato. Sprinkle black pepper to your taste. Squeeze the juice from 4 lemons through a strainer and add to the bowl. Add 1 tablespoon of capers to the bowl. Note: *Some may not like the taste of capers so wait until the plates are served to add these.* Add the chopped parsley and pour olive oil over all.

Add the pesto sauce to the bowl and mix well.
Place in refrigerator to chill for about 30 minutes before serving.

If you are having **fresh bread**, make it now, following the package directions.

Overnight - Plan ahead

CITRUS COOKED HALIBUT

with Baked Potato and Cucumber Slices

4-6 limes
1-2 oranges
1 grapefruit
¼ cup chili sauce
½ red bell pepper, diced
½ green bell pepper, diced
¼ cup diced onion
¼ cup fresh parsley

1-3 halibut fillets, skinless

4 potatoes, for baking

¼ lettuce head, torn
1 tomato, quartered
Cucumber slices

This is a heatless way of "cooking" fish. The acid in the marinade reacts with the protein. Give it a try. Don't tell the kids! A cod or snapper can substitute.

Make the marinade first. In a 2 to 3 quart glass bowl, stir together the lime juice, orange juice, grapefruit sections and chili sauce. Add the bell peppers, the diced onion and the fresh parsley.

Rinse fish and pat dry. If using steaks, trim the white membrane and cut off the skin. Cut along both sides of bone to separate flesh; discard skin and bones. Cut the **halibut** into small (½ inch) cubes or pieces.

Add halibut pieces to the bowl and gently stir the mixture until the fish is completely coated with marinade. Cover and chill until halibut turns a solid white color throughout, in about 10 hours. You can cut into several pieces to test. We let ours marinate *overnight.*

When ready to eat, bake **potatoes** according to your favorite method. We typically use the microwave to completely bake or to at least partially bake the potatoes. Wash the potatoes and pierce with fork. Place potatoes in the microwave and cook on HIGH for 4 minutes per potato per side, turning once. (3 or 4 potatoes will cook in 24 minutes.)

Serve halibut pieces on torn lettuce leaves. Garnish with **tomato wedges** and slices of **cucumber**.

PAN BROILED SIRLOIN

with Cubed Potatoes and Green Peas

2 sirloin steaks or eye of round
Peanut oil

Green peas, frozen

Parsley
Paprika

Cubed Potatoes Ingredients:
- **3 medium potatoes**
- **1 cup dairy sour cream**
- **½ onion, finely chopped**
- **1 Tbsp. stuffed olives**
- **¼ teaspoon salt**
- **Pepper, to taste**

Prepare the **potatoes.** Boil the whole potatoes in water. Leave skins on the potatoes, cook in salted water for about 30 minutes.

Drain cooked potatoes and cut into ½ inch cubes, set aside for the moment.

Prepare the steaks now. For the **pan-broiled steaks**, coat the steaks on both sides with peanut oil. Heat a heavy frying pan slowly until it becomes medium hot. Add the steaks and brown them on both sides. Reduce the heat and slowly cook the steaks in their own juices until they are done to your liking, between 6 and 10 minutes.

While the steaks cook, prepare the **green peas** according to the package directions.

To complete the **potatoes,** mix the sour cream, chopped onion, pimento-stuffed olives in a skillet. Add the cubed potatoes. Season with salt and pepper. Cook on medium heat, stirring occasionally until heated thoroughly. Garnish with parsley and paprika.

The Grilling Hint Sheet

Some prerequisites:

The grill should be clean. Not just the cooking surface but the cavity of the grill itself should be as clean as you can make it. Remove any old ashes, scrub the sides with an abrasive cleaner. Wash thoroughly.

Use fresh coals. You should set the coals aflame about forty minutes before you are ready to cook.

Flavoring woods: Purchase mesquite or any flavored hardwood chips and soak a few pieces in water for about an hour before you grill. A minute or two before you are ready to toss on the food, drain the soaked wood pieces and place along the edges of the coals so that the smoke will rise and envelope the food.

Testing the Heat

This is a good tip, courtesy of the beef industry. To check the temperature of coals on a grill, cautiously hold the palm of your hand a few (4-6) inches above the coals. The length of time you can hold your hand in that position until the heat forces you to pull back will tell you the heat of the coals.

2 seconds = hot (high)
3 seconds = medium-high
4 seconds = medium
5 seconds = low

Fifth week JUNE

Sunday	Monday	Tuesday	Wednesday	Thursday	Friday	Saturday
Plan Ahead **Grilled Barbecued Chicken** Cole Slaw Baked Beans	**Herbed Chicken Sandwich** Caesar Salad	**Shrimp Curry** Rice Fruit Cocktail	**Braised Pork Chops** Prunes Macaroni Cheese	**Tuna Casserole** Baked Bell Peppers, Fresh Bread	**Simple Salmon** Spinach Pasta	**Veal Stir-Fry** Dutch Potatoes, Green Beans

Fresh Vegetables \ Fruits		*Herbs \ Spices*	*Basics*
white onions - 4 green bell pepper - 3 cabbage head - 1 carrot - 1 stick red bell pepper - 2 yellow bell pepper - 1	garlic pod - 1 fresh basil romaine lettuce -1 snow peas - 8-10 green onions - 6 potatoes - 2 parsley bunch green beans - 1 lb. lemons - 6	white pepper dried thyme hot pepper flakes curry powder cinnamon dry sage celery salt celery seeds Italian seasoning ground ginger cloves dry mustard	ketchup brown sugar sugar olive oil extra-virgin olive oil flour peanut oil mayonnaise white vinegar Worcestershire sauce Converted Rice Dijon mustard

Entrée Food	*Dairy*	*Miscellaneous*	*Cans \ Jars*
skinless, boneless chicken breasts - 6 cooked shrimp ½ lb. pork chops - 4 salmon - 6 oz. veal cutlets - 4 **Frozen** chopped spinach pkg	eggs - 2 butter - 2 sticks milk - 2 cups American cheese ¼ lb. extra-sharp Cheddar cheese -1 cup plain yogurt - pint bacon - 3 slice **Wine** red wine - ¼ cup	apple cider vinegar - 3 T horseradish sauce 1T dried navy beans - 1 cup molasses - 2 Tbsps. liquid smoke - dash whole wheat rolls 4 extra-wide noodles - pkg macaroni - 2 cups fresh bread pkg. spinach pasta - 6 oz. prunes - ¼ lb.	chopped pimiento 2 oz chicken broth - 1 fruit cocktail - 1 can tuna - 1 can (6 oz.) cream of mushroom soup - 1 can sliced mushrooms - 1 can sliced olives - 2 oz. ripe olives - 2 oz. capers - 2 oz.

2 hours - Plan ahead

GRILLED BARBECUED CHICKEN

with Cole Slaw and Baked Beans

4 skinless, boneless chicken breasts
¼ teaspoon black pepper
¼ cup ketchup
3 Tbsps. apple cider vinegar
1 Tbsp. horseradish sauce
2 teaspoons brown sugar

Dash or two dried thyme
1 clove garlic, minced

Cole Slaw Ingredients
(Facing Page ==>)
Baked Beans
(Facing Page ==>)

Prepare the **Baked Beans** beforehand. See Facing Page ===>.

This barbecued **chicken** can be prepared indoors or out of doors.

Prepare the grill.

While the grill heats, prepare the **Cole Slaw** dressing following directions. See facing page.

Prepare the sauce, or use bottled barbecue sauce if time is a factor. Mix together the ketchup, apple cider vinegar, horseradish, brown sugar, garlic and thyme. Pour into skillet and bring to a boil. Cook stirring frequently until mixture thickens, about 3-5 minutes.

Brush chicken breasts with sauce and season with pepper. Grill on or under medium hot coals for about 6 minutes each side or until done.

BAKED BEANS

2 cups water
1 cup dried navy beans
½ medium onion, sliced
2 slices bacon
2 Tbsps. packed brown sugar (optional)
½ teaspoon salt
1 ½ Tbsps. molasses
Dash dry mustard
Dash pepper
1 Tbsp. Liquid Smoke

Heat beans placed in hot water to boiling in Dutch oven; boil about 2 minutes. Remove from heat, add liquid smoke and let stand for an hour.

Add additional water to barely cover the beans. Add remaining ingredients. Cover and simmer until tender, about 1- 1 ½ hours.

COLE SLAW with OLIVE OIL

1 teaspoon salt
¼ teaspoon pepper
½ teaspoon dry mustard
Scant teaspoon celery seeds
1 Tbsp. sugar
¼ cup chopped green bell pepper
1 Tbsp. chopped pimentos
1 teaspoon grated onion
3 Tbsps. olive oil
¼ cup white vinegar
3 cups finely chopped cabbage
½ carrot, julienned
¼ cup sliced olives

Into a bowl measure salt, pepper and dry mustard, and celery seeds. Add 1 tablespoon sugar. Chop ¼ cup of green bell pepper and add to bowl. Do the same for 1 tablespoon of pimento. Grate a 1 teaspoon of onion and add to bowl. While mixing the cole slaw, pour 3 tablespoons of olive oil, then the white vinegar. Stir well.

If you are making this the day before, cover and chill through.

A half hour before serving add the chopped cabbage and carrot and stir to coat and refrigerate for about thirty minutes. Garnish with sliced stuffed olives just before serving.

HERBED CHICKEN SANDWICH

with Caesar Salad

2 chicken breasts, boneless, skinless
Garlic cloves
1 Tbsp. butter, melted
Pepper and salt to taste
2 Tbsps. extra-virgin olive oil
Dash hot pepper flakes
½ onion, sliced
½ red bell pepper
½ yellow bell pepper
2 Tbsps. ripe olives, sliced
1 Tbsp. capers
Whole wheat rolls
2 hard-cooked eggs
Basil leaves

Caesar Salad Ingredients:
1 clove garlic, minced
¼ cup olive oil
1 tsp. Worcestershire sauce
½ teaspoon salt
ground pepper
¼ teaspoon dry mustard
1 bunch romaine lettuce
2 lemons

Prepare **hard cooked eggs** for garnish. Use the 10-10 method: 10 minutes in boiling water then 10 in hot water. Remove eggs from water, run under cold water to stop the cooking process and refrigerate until needed

Prepare the **Caesar salad** next. Mix the garlic, olive oil, Worcestershire sauce, salt, pepper and mustard in a bowl; toss with the romaine lettuce until all leaves are coated. Squeeze the lemons over the salad and toss.

Prepare **chicken** next. First, pound the chicken lightly to achieve an even thickness. Rub the chicken pieces with garlic and spread with melted butter. Preheat the oven broiler and place chicken pieces about four inches from heat source. Cook for about 6 minutes on each side, turning once, until done.

While chicken cooks, in a medium saucepan over medium heat, sauté in olive oil the red pepper flakes and the sliced onion. Sauté for about 3 minutes. Cut the bell peppers in large strips and add to the sauce pan. Cook until the bell peppers are soft. Add the ripe olives and the capers, season with salt and pepper and cook until contents are heated thoroughly.

Brown the **wheat rolls** in the oven. Place ½ of chicken breast on each sandwich. (This menu calls for four small sandwiches.) Add the pepper mixture. Top with basil leaves and cover the top slice of wheat roll.

SHRIMP CURRY

with Fruit Cocktail and Rice

3 Tbsps. butter
¼ cup minced onion
1 ½ teaspoons curry powder
3 Tbsps. flour
¾ teaspoon salt
¾ teaspoon sugar
Dash ground ginger
½ cup chicken broth

½ cup milk
½ lb. cooked shrimp
1 lemon, juiced

Converted Rice

1 (8 ¼ oz.) can fruit cocktail

This is a light meal. As a first course you can add a salad of choice. We usually go light, then have a late night snack. *See snack hint sheet on page 450.*

Prepare the **rice** before proceeding.

When rice is about done, prepare the **shrimp curry.** In a heavy skillet, over low heat, melt the butter. Sauté the onion and curry powder; blend in the flour, salt, sugar and ginger. Cook over low heat until the mixture becomes smooth. Add the chicken broth and the milk. Heat to boiling, stirring constantly. Add the cooked shrimp and the lemon juice and let the mixture heat thoroughly, about 1 minute maximum.

Dish out some of the **fruit cocktail** as a garnish to this dish.

BRAISED PORK CHOPS

with Prunes, Macaroni and Cheese

4 pork chops
¼ cup ketchup
2 lemons, juiced
½ teaspoon dry mustard
1 teaspoon Worcestershire sauce
Peanut oil
1 small onion, sliced
¼ cup water

2 cups uncooked Macaroni
2 Tbsps. butter, melted
¼ lb. American cheese
¼ cup milk
Spiced Prunes:
- **¼ lb. prunes**
- **1 Tbsp. white vinegar**
- **¼ teaspoon cinnamon**
- **2 whole cloves**
- **1 Tbsp. brown sugar**

Preheat the oven to 350° F.

For the **pork chops** combine ketchup, lemon juice, mustard and Worcestershire sauce. Coat all sides of the chops. Brown in a small amount of peanut oil. Top with onion and add water. Cover and bake in oven for 1 hour.

While the pork cooks, prepare the **macaroni and cheese**. In a large pot of boiling water cook the pasta. Add salt and some olive oil. Drain the pasta.

Melt 2 tablespoons of butter; have ready. Cut thin slices of cheese to spread over macaroni. In a deep baking dish, layer cooked macaroni, cheese slices, portions of the milk, ½ of the butter. Make at least two layers. Sprinkle with salt and pepper. Place macaroni cheese in oven during the last 15 minutes of cooking the pork chops.

For the **spiced prunes**: cook the *un-pitted* prunes in 1 cup water until tender, about 20 minutes. Add vinegar, cinnamon, whole cloves and brown sugar. Cook slowly for 10 minutes.

TUNA CASSEROLE

with Baked Bell Peppers and Fresh Bread

½ pkg. extra-wide egg noodles
1 pkg. frozen chopped spinach
1 (6 ½ oz.) can tuna, drained
1 (2 oz.) jar diced pimentos, drained
1 (10 ½ oz.) can cream of mushroom soup
½ teaspoon minced onion
1 cup extra-sharp Cheddar cheese, grated

½ red bell pepper, julienned
½ yellow bell pepper, julienned
½ green bell pepper, julienned
Extra-virgin olive oil
Black pepper, to taste

Fresh bread (pkg.)

Pre-heat the oven to 400° F.

If making **fresh bread**, bake it now, before proceeding.

While the bread bakes, prepare the **tuna casserole.** Cook the extra-wide noodles according to package directions. Cook only until they are *al dente;* drain. Combine the noodles, spinach, tuna, pimientos, soup, minced onions and Cheddar cheese and pour into baking dish. Spread some extra cheese on top. Set aside.

In a separate pan, cut the **bell peppers** and coat them with the olive oil. Add black pepper if desired.

When bread is removed from oven, reset temperature to 350° F.

Place peppers and tuna casserole into oven and heat until the cheese bubbles.

Serve with a fresh cooked bread.

SIMPLE SALMON

with Spinach Pasta

3 green onions, julienned
½ red pepper, julienned
1 Tbsp. olive oil
6 ounces dry spinach pasta (linguine or fettuccine)
6 ounces salmon *
2 oz. snow peas, sliced lengthwise in half
3 green onions, chopped, garnish
Salt and pepper

Mustard Dressing:
1 clove garlic, minced
1 teaspoon dry sage
1 teaspoon Dijon mustard
Dash ground white pepper
1 lemon, juiced
2 Tbsps. plain yogurt
¼ cup mayonnaise
¼ cup milk

* *If you can find fresh smoked salmon you're in for a treat. Otherwise, use canned smoked salmon.* Either way *this menu is worthy of a restaurant!*

Prepare **mustard dressing** using ingredients on right side. In a bowl mix garlic, sage, mustard, pepper, and lemon juice. Layer in the yogurt, mayonnaise, and stir until smooth; slowly stir in milk. Makes about ½ cup.

If you prefer your **vegetables** cooked, do it now. Sauté the onions, red pepper in a tablespoon of olive oil.

Cook **pasta** in boiling salted water until *al dente*. Rinse pasta in cold water until chilled; drain, but not completely, leave a bit of water.

In a large bowl, toss pasta with dressing; add **smoked salmon pieces,** snow peas, green onions and red pepper and toss until mixed well. Season with salt and pepper.

Serve the pasta and sprinkle lightly with chopped green onions.

VEAL STIR-FRY

with Dutch Potatoes and Green Beans

¼ cup peanut oil
4 veal cutlets, sliced into thin strips
1 (4 oz.) can sliced mushrooms, drained
¼ cup chopped onion
1 green bell pepper, sliced in thin strips
½ teaspoon celery salt
Black pepper, to taste
¼ teaspoon Italian seasoning
¼ cup red wine

Dutch Potatoes Ingredients:
1 onion, chopped
1 Tbsp. peanut oil
2 baking potatoes, cubed
2 Tbsps. chopped parsley
Salt and pepper to taste

1 lb. green beans
1 slice bacon

First, prepare the **Dutch potatoes**. In a large covered skillet, slightly brown the chopped onions in peanut oil. Add the cubed potatoes. Carefully add water to skillet so that the water barely covers the potatoes. Boil covered until the potatoes are about done, say 20 minutes. Add parsley, salt and pepper and cook for another five minutes. Drain before serving.

For the **Veal**: heat slowly a frying pan to high temperature. Add the peanut oil; place the veal strips in the pan. Sauté the meat for a moment then toss in the vegetables and the seasoning. Reduce heat to low and cook until tender, about 5-10 minutes.

Add **wine** to veal and simmer another 3-4 minutes.

If using fresh **green beans,** they should be boiled in salted water with a slice of bacon for approximately 30 minutes or until done to your likeness. If using frozen green beans, follow package directions.

The Perfect Picnic Basket

What is the perfect picnic? It is one that exceeds your expectations. How to ensure that this will be a perfect picnic? Have absolutely no expectations! And no plans! We gave up having any planned events, we wanted only to get there and then to let the atmosphere of time and place dictate the best things to do. Below are the ingredients to take along with an open mind.

The necessary ingredients: first and foremost is a Swiss army knife for it has all the tools needed:

a bottle opener
a can opener
a wine cork puller, or corkscrew

The food stock:

4 six-packs of water (tap water, spring water) or water cooler. Glasses.
ribbon sandwiches (page **2**-410) Make more than you think you will eat.
fresh fruits such as oranges, peaches, grapes
a variety of cheeses
a bottle of red or white wine

The game equipment:

badminton equipment
crochet set
board games
playing cards
books to read or glance through. Any book by John McPhee will do along with books appropriate to the guests' ages.

The ground table setting:

a large, white sheet or covering
plastic knives and forks
napkins

A radio or CD player with music you like.

The Pan Poaching Month

Besides the fireworks of the Fourth of July, this month has a lot that simmers.

Pan poaching is probably as old as fire and we explore several ways to poach fish, chicken and shrimp.

The Fourth of July is left open for you to decide what to prepare, although we do offer some suggestions -- see page 325. For our family the fourth has always been one to join the crowd: at a baseball game or picnics in the park; riding the river or making long hiking trails with groups. And we usually end the evening with the sounds of *America* sung by Ray Charles or *Born to Be an American* by Lee Greenwood, or the symphony playing Tchaikovsky's *1812 Overture* while overhead the fireworks ignite in colorful display.

July is the month for meat lovers. We have the best meat loaf this side of heaven, moist and tasty with tomato slices across the top. We'll tell you how to keep meat loaf from drying out during baking. In July you'll enjoy a *Garlic Stuffed Sirloin* that will grill perfectly. Last month you enjoyed Beef Tenderloin with a mushroom sauce; compare it to this month's *Beef Tenderloin with Wine Sauce* that speaks for itself.

We'll also have *Grilled Salmon* outside and serve it with new potatoes and snow peas for the healthiest meal of the month.

The month will end on a customary sour note: two menus with sour cream. The *Fish in Sour Cream*, a fish with wine and lemon is one of our favorites, and the *Beef Cubes in Sour Cream* that replaces the usual wine with sour cream to create a tart beef taste.

Give us some feedback: how does your family celebrate Independence Day?

July Menus

Chicken

Poached Chicken w/ Mashed Potatoes, Green Vegetables and Dinner Rolls

Julienned Chicken in Cabernet with Rice and Green Beans

Chicken in Egg Noodles and Tomato Salad

Chardonnay Chicken with Snow Peas and Baked Potatoes

Chicken Enchiladas with Rice, Avocado Salad and Black Beans

Italian Chicken with Italian Salad

Quick & Easy

Old-Fashioned Meat Loaf with Corn, Rice and Green Wedge Salad

Jalisco Salad North American Style with Buttered Tortillas

Slicer's Sandwiches with Potato Wedges

Pasta Marinara with Angel Hair Pasta, Italian Salad, Hot Garlic Bread

Bell Pepper Spaghetti with French Bread and Tossed Salad

Shrimp

Spanish Rice Shrimp with Avocado Salad

Sweet Curry Shrimp Salad w/ Lemon with Avocado Wedges and Rolls

Shrimp and Avocado Salad and Rice

Indian Style Shrimp with Curried Rice and Green Salad

Pork

Savory Pork Chops with Macaroni & Cheese and Spinach

Fettucine Pork Chops with Tomato and Green Salad

Barbecued Pork Chops with Potato Salad

Pasta / Soup

Real Manicotti with Fresh Bread and Broccoli Salad

Rice and Avocado Salad with Tomato Wedges

Italian Tetrazzini with Green Wedge Salad, Tomato and Fresh Bread

Nutty Noodle Casserole with Easy Tomato Slices and Fresh Bread

Fettuccine Delight with Tossed Salad and Fresh Bread

Fish

Poached Caper Fish with Green Beans and 3-C Salad

Poached Trout in Wine with Corkscrew Noodles and Greek Salad

Baked Salmon w/ Sauce, Herbed Rice and Mustard Greens

Grilled Salmon with Snow Peas and New Potatoes

Fish in Sour Cream with Baked Potato and Green Wedge Salad

Salmon in Ribbon Pasta with Italian Bread and Sautéed Celery Salad

Citrus Charbroiled Swordfish with Saffron Rice and Baby Carrots

Red Meats

Fourth of July Cookout

Beef Tenderloin w/ Wine Sauce with Mashed Potatoes, Green Beans

Garlic Stuffed Sirloin with Baked Potatoes and Green Peas

Marinated Beef w/ Tomato Chutney and Baked Potatoes

Beef Cubes in Sour Cream with Mashed Potatoes, Broccoli, Green Beans

JULY

Sunday	Monday	Tuesday	Wednesday	Thursday	Friday	Saturday
Poached Chicken Mashed Potatoes, Green Vegetables, Dinner Rolls	**Old-Fashioned Meat Loaf** Rice, Corn, Green Wedge Salad	**Spanish Rice Shrimp** Avocado Salad	**Savory Pork Chops** Macaroni & Cheese, Spinach	**Chicken In Egg Noodles** Tomato Salad	**Poached Caper Fish** Green Beans, 3-C Salad	**Fourth of July Cookout**
Plan ahead **Julienned Chicken in Cabernet** Rice Green Beans	**Bell Pepper Spaghetti** French Bread Tossed Salad	**Indian Style Shrimp** Curried Rice Green Salad	*Plan ahead* **Rice & Avocado Salad** Tomato Wedges	**Nutty Noodle Casserole** Easy Tomato Slices, Fresh Bread	**Poached Trout in Wine** Corkscrew Noodles, Greek Salad	**Beef Tender-loin w/ Wine Sauce** Mashed Potatoes Green Beans
Char-donnay Chicken Snow Peas, Baked Potatoes	**Jalisco Salad** Buttered Tortillas	*Plan ahead* **Sweet Curry Shrimp Salad** Avocado Salad, Rice	**Fettucine Pork Chops** Tomato. Green Salad	**Real Manicotti** Fresh Bread Broccoli Salad	**Baked Salmon w/ Sauce** Herbed Rice, Mustard Greens	**Garlic Stuffed Sirloin** Baked Potatoes Green Peas
Chicken Enchiladas Rice Avocado Salad Black Beans	**Slicer's Sand-wiches** Potato Wedges, Beer	**Shrimp & Avocado Salad** Rice	**Barbecued Pork Chops** Potato Salad	**Italian Tetrazzini** Green Wedge Salad, Tomato, Fresh Bread	**Grilled Salmon** Snow Peas, New Potatoes	*Plan ahead* **Marinated Beef** w/ Tomato Chutney, Baked Potatoes
Italian Chicken One-dish Italian Salad	*Plan ahead* **Pasta Marinara** Italian Salad, Hot Garlic Bread	**Fish in Sour Cream** Baked Potato Green Wedge Salad	**Fettuccine Delight** Tossed Salad, Fresh Bread	**Salmon in Ribbon Pasta** Italian Bread, Celery Salad, Wine	*Plan ahead* **Citrus Char-broiled Swordfish** Saffron Rice Baby Carrots	**Beef Cubes in Sour Cream** Mashed Potatoes, Broccoli

First week JULY

Sunday	*Monday*	*Tuesday*	*Wednesday*	*Thursday*	*Friday*	*Saturday*
Poached Chicken Mashed Potatoes, Green Vegetables, Dinner Rolls	**Old-Fashioned Meat Loaf** Rice, Corn, Green Wedge Salad	**Spanish Rice Shrimp** Avocado Salad	**Savory Pork Chops** Macaroni & Cheese, Spinach	**Chicken In Egg Noodles** Tomato Salad	**Poached Caper Fish** Green Beans, 3-C Salad	**Fourth of July Cookout** Ingredients not listed

Fresh Vegetables \ Fruits		*Herbs \ Spices*	*Basics*
white onion - 4 celery bundle pearl onions - 6 carrots - bundle potatoes - 3 tomatoes - 2 iceberg lettuce- 1 green leaf lettuce - 1 corn - 4	lemons - 4 parsley bunch avocado - 1 green bell peppers 2 spinach bunch green beans - 1 lb. cucumbers - 2 radish bunch	garlic pod bay leaves nutmeg peppercorns dry mustard red pepper flakes	olive oil salad dressing sugar flour Tabasco® sauce Dijon mustard Converted Rice sea salt red wine vinegar Worcestershire sauce cornstarch

Entrée Food	*Dairy*	*Miscellaneous*	*Cans \ Jars*
1 hen (roaster chicken) ground chuck or sirloin - 1 lb. 20-24 large shrimp butterfly pork chops - 2 cod or roughy fish fillets - 2 whole broiler chicken **Frozen**	margarine - 1 stick egg - 3 milk - 3 cups American cheese - ¼ lb. sour cream - ½ cup bacon - 7 slices	bread crumbs 1 C macaroni 2 C wide egg noodles ½ lb. dinner rolls - dozen **Wine** white wine - 1 C	chicken broth 3 cans beef bouillon cubes 1 ripe olives - 4 oz tomatoes - 2 cans salad pepper - 4 oz. vlasic® Pepperoncini chicken gravy - 1 capers - 2 oz.

POACHED CHICKEN

with Mashed Potatoes, Green Vegetables and Dinner Rolls

1 hen (roaster chicken)
1 clove garlic
½ medium-size onion
6 peppercorns
2 celery stalks
Sea salt and ground pepper, to taste
4 cups chicken broth
1 cup white wine
Water

1 bay leaf
6 pearl onions, peeled (small white onions)
6 carrots, cut into 1 ½ inch sticks
1 pkg. dinner rolls
3 potatoes
½ stick margarine
¼ cup milk

We like to purchase the fresh roaster that comes with a built-in temperature control, a red button that pops up when the roaster is done. We have found this to be fail-proof.

Wash **roaster** thoroughly. Rub garlic on outside. Place in cavity of the roaster one-half onion, the peppercorns, 2 stalks of celery. *Do not season with salt.*

Secure the cavity with laces and tie the legs together. Season *outside* with sea salt and pepper and place in a large Dutch oven. Pour in chicken broth, wine and enough water to reach halfway up sides of the roaster. Add bay leaf.

Place pot with chicken over medium heat; bring liquid to a simmer. Reduce heat to medium-low. Cover and simmer, *do not boil,* allowing 16-18 minutes per pound for a roaster. The secret to poaching is to let the liquid simmer not boil.

Add the **pearl onions** and the sliced **carrots** to the liquid when there is about thirty minutes left to the cooking.

While roaster cooks, prepare the **dinner rolls** according to package directions. Also prepare **mashed potatoes** according to your favorite method. Wash and peel potatoes and cut into halves then quarter into smaller pieces. Heat a pot of water and add in the potato pieces. Salt the water to your taste. Cook for approximately 20 minutes; drain. Into hot potatoes, place ½ stick of margarine, ¼ cup of milk and whip to desired smoothness.

When chicken is done, remove from pot and spoon out vegetables.

OLD-FASHIONED MEAT LOAF

with Rice, Corn and Green Wedge Salad

1 lb. ground chuck or sirloin
1 glove of garlic, crushed
1 egg, beaten
¾ cup milk
1 Tbsp. Worcestershire sauce
1 ½ teaspoons salt
¼ teaspoon pepper
½ teaspoon dry mustard
1 cup bread crumbs
1 small onion, finely chopped

¼ cup water
1 beef bouillon cube
1 small tomato, sliced

4 ears of fresh corn
Converted Rice
Green Wedge Salad:
lettuce, cucumber, radish, ripe olives, carrot, salad pepper

Preheat the oven to 350° F.

For the **meat loaf**, mix all ingredients on left side. Shape into loaf. Place in ungreased loaf pan, or casserole dish. Make ¼ cup of beef bouillon by combining water and 1 beef bouillon cube. Pour into loaf pan. Spread slices of tomatoes across top of loaf. Sprinkle with pepper. Bake uncovered for 1 hour.

While meat loaf cooks, prepare the **green wedge salad** prior to serving main course. Tear lettuce leaves into bite-size pieces, slice cucumber, radish, black olives, shredded carrot and top with a salad pepper.

Thirty minutes before the meat loaf is done, prepare the **fresh corn**. You can cook the corn in the microwave by cooking on HIGH for 3 minutes then turning for another three minutes, or cook the corn in a pot of boiling water for 10 minutes.

Prepare the **rice** according to package directions.

SPANISH RICE SHRIMP

with Avocado Salad

20 - 24 large shrimp
2 Tbsps. olive oil
2 cloves garlic, crushed
1 dried chili pepper, minced
Black pepper to taste
1 teaspoon lemon juice
1 teaspoon parsley, chopped

Spanish rice (Below)
Avocado Salad Ingredients:
- **1 avocado, skinned, cut in wedges**
- **iceberg lettuce**
- **1 tomato, cut in wedges**
- **2 radishes, sliced**
- **½ cup dressing**

Prepare the **Spanish rice** before proceeding, following package directions. Most grocery stores have the Spanish version of rice. If they don't, prepare it using the instructions below.

While rice cooks, prepare the **avocado salad**. Tear the lettuce leaves into bite-size pieces, or simply chop the lettuce if time is pressing. Cut tomato and avocado in wedges. Slice radishes, add dressing to the salad and mix well.

For the **Shrimp,** wash and dry the shrimp. In a skillet, heat olive oil and add in the garlic. Cook the garlic for about 2 minutes and insert the chili pepper. Immediately, add the shrimp. Add pepper to desired amount. Cook until the shrimp turn pink then remove. Add the lemon juice to the sauce and mix well. Pour this sauce over the shrimp when serving. Add parsley as garnish.

Spanish Rice

6 slices bacon
¼ cup finely-chopped onion
¼ cup chopped green pepper

2 cups canned tomatoes
1 cup uncooked rice
1 teaspoon salt
Pepper to taste

If making **Spanish rice** from scratch, preheat the oven to 350° F. Prepare converted rice following package directions. Meanwhile, fry strips of bacon until crisp; allow to cool, then crumble them into mixing bowl.

In the same pan used for the bacon, add onion and green pepper. Cook on low heat until the onions become slightly yellow. Add remaining ingredients and the crushed bacon. Place all ingredients in a baking dish; bake for about 30 minutes.

SAVORY PORK CHOPS

with Macaroni and Cheese, Spinach

2 pork chops,
butterfly or 4 loins
¼ teaspoon pepper
1 Tbsp. olive oil
1 (10 ½ oz.) can chicken broth
2 lemons, juiced
1 Tbsp. sugar
1 teaspoon Dijon-style mustard

Macaroni and Cheese Ingredients:
2 cups uncooked macaroni
2 Tbsps. butter, melted
¼ lb. American cheese
¼ cup milk
4 teaspoons cornstarch
2 Tbsps. water
Spinach

Trim fat from **pork chops**. Sprinkle pork chops with pepper. Heat olive oil in skillet over medium heat. Brown pork chops on both sides.

Stir in broth, the juice from 2 lemons, sugar and mustard. Heat to boiling. Reduce heat to low. Cook, covered, simmering about 35 minutes.

While pork cooks, preheat oven to 350° F .

Prepare the **Macaroni and Cheese.** In a large pot, boil the pasta. You can add salt and some olive oil if you like. Drain the pasta. Melt 2 tablespoons of butter; have ready. Cut thin slices of cheese to spread over macaroni. In a deep baking dish, layer cooked macaroni, cheese slices, portions of the milk, ½ of the melted butter. Make at least two layers. Sprinkle with salt and pepper. Bake, covered, until the cheese is melted, about 10-15 minutes.

When pork chops are done, transfer chops to platter. In cup, stir together cornstarch and water until well blended; gradually stir into skillet. Cook over high heat until mixture boils and thickens, stirring often.

Just before macaroni and cheese is finished, steam the **spinach**.

CHICKEN IN EGG NOODLES

with Tomato Salad

3 Tbsps. olive oil
2 lb. broiler-fryer, cut up
½ cup chopped onion
1 can chicken gravy
¼ teaspoon crushed red pepper
1 green or red pepper,
cut into 1-inch strips
½ cup sour cream
½ pkg. wide egg noodles

Tomato Salad Ingredients:
iceberg lettuce
green leaf lettuce
tomato

The preliminaries: prepare pot of water for cooking noodles. Measure the noodles and save in cup.

Prepare the **tomato salad** by tearing washed lettuce and green leaves into bite-size pieces. Cut the tomatoes into round slices, toss together the ingredients and place in refrigerator until ready to serve. Top the salad with the dressing of your choice.

Cut the **chicken** into bite-size pieces. In skillet over medium heat, heat oil then add chicken. Cook chicken 10 minutes. Add onions; cook 10 minutes more or until chicken is well browned on all sides. Spoon off fat. Add gravy and crushed red pepper. Reduce heat to low and simmer, covered, for 20 minutes.

While the chicken cooks, prepare the **noodles** according to package directions.

Meanwhile, to the skillet chicken add red or green bell pepper strips. Cook, uncovered for 10 minutes or until pepper strips are tender.

Remove chicken and pepper to serving plate and stir sour cream into skillet. Heat thoroughly, stirring constantly. Spoon gravy over chicken and noodles.

POACHED CAPER FISH

with Green Beans and 3-C Salad

Caper Sauce:
- **2 Tbsps. olive oil**
- **1 Tbsp. flour**
- **1 cup milk**
- **2 egg yolks, beaten**
- **6 capers**
- **½ teaspoon salt**
- **¼ teaspoon Tabasco® sauce**
- **¼ teaspoon nutmeg**
- **Dash pepper**

*** cod, roughy**

- **2 fish fillets ***
- **½ teaspoon salt**
- **2 peppercorns**
- **3 lemon slices**
- **3 parsley sprigs**
- **1 bay leaf**

3-C Salad Ingredients:
- **carrots**
- **celery**
- **cucumbers**
- **red wine vinegar**

- **1 lb. green beans**
- **1 slice bacon, uncooked**

Prepare the **3-C salad** by slicing the carrots, celery and cucumbers; place in a serving dish. A red-wine vinegar will do the trick for the topping. Let this salad marinate for about ten minutes before serving.

Prepare **green beans** by the boiling method. Cut off ends of beans and if needed cut in half or leave long. Barely cover them with water and add one slice of bacon; sprinkle with salt. Cook until they are tender, 20 minutes for *al dente.*

Meanwhile prepare the **caper sauce.** Blend oil and flour in saucepan until smooth. Stir in milk and bring to a boil over low heat, stirring constantly. Boil for 1 minute then remove from heat. Stir about ½ of mixture into the egg yolks then blend this back into the liquid in pot. Blend in remaining sauce ingredients.

For the **boiled fish,** prepare the poaching liquid. To a pot of boiling water add the salt, peppercorns, lemon slices, parsley and bay leaf. Place fish fillets in the water and when it begins to boil again, reduce heat. Simmer for about 5-7 minutes until the fish flakes easily with a fork.

Remove fish. Place in serving dish and top with the caper sauce and the green beans.

FOURTH OF JULY COOKOUT

with Traditional Food and Side Dishes

So many people have their own traditions with regards to the Fourth of July that we decided to honor it by leaving the meal choices to you and your family.

Some suggestions for this day:

Hamburger and hot dog cookout with potato salad and beans.

A chicken feast meal such as the *Poached Chicken* of last Sunday.

A fried-chicken and potato salad picnic type affair.

A day at the ball park with hot dogs and chili.

Barbecue, baked beans and potato salad.

Browse the index for a menu that suits your tradition for this day!

Second week JULY

Sunday	Monday	Tuesday	Wednesday	Thursday	Friday	Saturday
Plan ahead **Julienned Chicken in Cabernet** Rice Green Beans	**Bell Pepper Spaghetti** French Bread Tossed Salad	**Indian Style Shrimp** Curried Rice Green Salad	**Rice & Avocado Salad** Tomato Wedges	**Nutty Noodle Casserole** Easy Tomato Slices, Fresh Bread	**Poached Trout in Wine** Corkscrew Noodles, Greek Salad	**Beef Tender-loin w/ Wine Sauce** Mashed Potatoes Green Beans

Fresh Vegetables \ Fruits		*Herbs \ Spices*	*Basics*
white onions - 2	green onions - 6	garlic pod	olive oil
green beans - 2 lb.	parsley bunch	thyme leaves	sugar
red bell pepper - 1	avocado - 1	red pepper flakes	wine vinegar
celery bundle	green bell pepper - 1	red pepper sauce	ketchup
iceberg lettuce - 1	carrot bundle	curry powder	vegetable oil
green leaf lettuce - 1	mushrooms - 2	dried thyme	red wine vinegar
cucumber - 2	potatoes - 3	bay leaf	flour
tomatoes - 5	cherry tomatoes 10-12	ginger	sea salt
fresh ginger - 1 oz.	radish bunch	peppercorns	kosher salt
	lemon - 1	white pepper	soy sauce
		whole clove	cornstarch
		dried parsley	Converted Rice

Entrée Food	*Dairy*	*Miscellaneous*	*Cans \ Jars*
skinless, boneless chicken breasts - 3	butter - 2 sticks	spaghetti - ½ lb.	ripe olives - 4 oz.
ground meat - 1 lb.	Parmesan cheese 2 oz.	French bread - 2 pkg	beef broth - 1 can
shrimp - ½ lb.	half and half cream 1 C	croutons 1 pkg.	Cheddar cheese soup - 1
trout fillets - 2	feta cheese - 4 oz.	egg noodles - 1 pkg.	beef broth - 1
beef tenderloin - 2 lbs.	bacon - 2	crackers - 1 column	
	milk - ¼ C	corkscrew noodles - ½ lb.	
	Wines	pecans - 4 oz.	
	Cabernet Sauvignon wine bottle		
	dry sherry - 1 T		
	white wine - 1 cup		

2 hours - Plan ahead

JULIENNED CHICKEN IN CABERNET

with Rice and Green Beans

2 whole skinless, boneless chicken breasts
1 cup Cabernet Sauvignon wine, divided
1 lb. green beans
1 slice bacon
Sea salt, to taste

Wine sauce:
1 white onion, chopped
¼ cup olive oil
1 Tbsp. sugar
1 teaspoon wine vinegar

Converted Rice

Cut **chicken** into lengthwise strips, about ½ inch wide; place in wide shallow baking dish. Pour 2 cups of Cabernet over chicken breasts. If possible, marinate chicken for *two hours.*

Preheat oven to 325° F.

Prepare the **green beans.** Boil them in pot of water in which 1 slice of bacon and sea salt have been added. Let green beans cook for approximately 25 minutes.

Cook **chicken**, still in marinate, in oven for about 15-20 minutes. Turn chicken in marinate at least once while cooking. Place cooked chicken under broiler for a couple of minutes. The chicken will lose its red coloring during this process.

Meanwhile prepare **rice** according to package directions.

While rice cooks, proceed to prepare the **wine sauce**. Sauté onions in ¼ cup oil until opaque. Add 1 cup Cabernet, sugar and vinegar; simmer on low flame until liquid is reduced. Set aside.

Serve with cooked rice and green beans.

BELL PEPPER SPAGHETTI

with French Bread and Tossed Salad

1 lb. ground meat
½ onion, chopped
1 cup red bell pepper, chopped
1 cup celery, chopped
1 teaspoon thyme leaves
1 can Cheddar cheese soup
½ lb. spaghetti, uncooked

Tossed Salad Ingredients:
- **iceberg lettuce**
- **green leaf lettuce**
- **cucumber**
- **radishes**
- **tomato**
- **ripe olives**
- **croutons**

French bread

If you're having the **fresh bread** cook it first. Preheat the oven to 400° F.

While the oven heats, prepare the **spaghetti sauce.** In saucepan, brown meat and onions until meat loses redness. Add remaining ingredients: chopped red bell pepper, chopped celery, thyme and Cheddar cheese soup. Cover and simmer slowly for about 30 minutes.

Meanwhile, when the oven is heated, insert the **fresh bread**.

While bread cooks, prepare the **tossed salad.** Wash and dry all vegetables. Tear the lettuces into bite-size pieces. Slice the cucumber and radishes. Cut the tomatoes into wedges. Toss all together. If there's time we suggest you put this in the refrigerator to cool for a few moments then add the ripe olives and the croutons.

Cook **spaghetti** in a pot of boiling water. Cook according to package directions; drain. Serve sauce over the spaghetti.

INDIAN STYLE SHRIMP

with Curried Rice and Green Salad

¼ cup ketchup
2 Tbsps. soy sauce
1 Tbsp. dry sherry or white wine
½ teaspoon sugar
½ teaspoon ginger, grated
¼ teaspoon red pepper, flakes
Vegetable or wok oil
½ lb. shrimp, shelled and deveined
1 Tbsp. kosher salt
3 cloves garlic, finely chopped
¼ cup green onions, cut in ¼ inch pieces

Curried Rice Ingredients:
Converted Rice
1 Tbsp. onion, minced
2 Tbsps. butter
½ tsp. curry powder
¼ teaspoon salt

Green Salad Ingredients:
iceberg lettuce
green leaf lettuce
cucumber
celery stalk, julienned
parsley

Make the **green salad** first. Wash, dry and tear the lettuces into bite-size pieces. Slice cucumber thinly, julienne the celery stalk into 2-inch lengths, the size of match sticks. Add parsley as a garnish. Place the salad in a large bowl and refrigerate until mealtime.

Cook Converted rice following package directions, before proceeding.

Meanwhile, *salt-leach* the **shrimp.** Peel shrimp, then wash and remove vein if present. Sprinkle kosher salt over shrimp, coating evenly. Let shrimp sit for one minute. Rinse and drain. Repeat salting again, let sit for another minute, rinse and drain well. Set aside. Make ketchup mixture. Combine ketchup, soy sauce, sherry or white wine, sugar, ginger and red pepper flakes. Set aside. Heat wok or heavy skillet to high temperature. Pour in the small amount of wok oil, twirling pan to coat. Add shrimp, cook stirring constantly for a minute or two. Remove shrimp to heated plate. Add garlic to oil remaining in pan; stir-fry a few seconds. Stir in green onions, adding more oil as needed; stir-fry a minute or two. Add ketchup mixture. Cook stirring constantly over MEDIUM heat until bubbly.

Prepare the **Curried Rice**. Cook onions in margarine or butter until onion is tender. Stir in the curry powder, salt and pepper. Stir this mixture into the hot rice. Mix well.

RICE AND AVOCADO SALAD

with Tomato Wedges

Salad Ingredients:
- **1 cup cooked chicken**
- **1 cup cooked rice**
- **1 cup sliced celery**
- **½ ripe avocado, cut in wedges**
- **½ green pepper, cut into thin slices**
- **¼ cup minced onion**

Converted Rice

Avocado Dressing:
- **2 Tbsps. lemon juice**
- **1 Tbsp. vegetable oil**
- **1 clove garlic minced**
- **Dash red pepper sauce**
- **Dash white pepper**
- **Lettuce leaves**

½ avocado, in wedges
2 tomatoes cut in wedges

Cook **rice** according to package directions.

For the **avocado dressing**, combine lemon juice and next four ingredients in a jar: vegetable oil, garlic, hot sauce, and white pepper. Cover tightly and shake vigorously. Pour dressing over rice mixture; toss gently. Cover. *Chill at least 2 hours.*

To prepare the **chicken**, first, pound the chicken to achieve an even thickness. Cook chicken in boiling water until done, about 20 minutes.

Combine first six ingredients in a large bowl: chicken, rice, celery, avocado, green pepper and onion.

Serve on a bed of lettuce with tomato wedges and avocado slices.

NUTTY NOODLE CASSEROLE

with Easy Tomato Slices and Fresh Bread

½ pkg. egg noodles
1 teaspoon salt
¼ cup butter or margarine
½ cup chopped pecans
2 Tbsps. dried parsley
2 cloves garlic, chopped
3 crackers, crushed
Salt and pepper to taste
Grated Parmesan cheese
½ cup half and half cream

Easy Tomato Slices:
2 whole ripe tomatoes
2 green onions, chopped
2 Tbsps. red wine vinegar or Marsala wine vinegar
Salt and pepper to taste

Fresh bread

Preheat oven to 350° F for the bread and the casserole.

While oven heats prepare the **easy tomato slices**. Cut tomatoes into thick slices. Place them on salad plate in the manner of toppled dominoes. Chop the green onions and sprinkle about. Pour the red wine over the tomatoes and sprinkle with salt and pepper to taste.

If having the **fresh bread,** bake it before the casserole and allow it to cool while the casserole bakes.

Prepare the **noodles** following package directions. Add salt to water for noodles. Drain noodles when cooked and rinse with cold water. Sauté the pecans, parsley, garlic and cracker crumbs in melted butter for 2 - 3 minutes.

In a casserole dish, make a layer of noodles and top with nutty sauce. Season with salt and pepper and Parmesan cheese. Repeat this layering; lay in more noodles, topping and cheese.

Pour the half and half over the casserole.

Bake the nutty noodle casserole in oven for 40-45 minutes or until it begins to brown.

POACHED TROUT IN WINE

with Corkscrew Noodles and Greek Salad

2 trout fillets
1 cup white wine
1 cup water
2 carrots, peeled and sliced
1 sprig parsley
¼ teaspoon thyme
1 bay leaf
1 whole clove
½ teaspoon salt
6 peppercorns, crushed
2 teaspoons cornstarch
3 Tbsps. butter, softened
1 Tbsp. parsley, chopped
Greek Salad Ingredients:
- **green leaf lettuce**
- **iceberg lettuce**
- **carrot**
- **cucumber**
- **ripe olives**
- **radishes**
- **feta cheese**

½ lb. corkscrew noodles

Prepare a **Greek salad** using lettuces, julienne cut carrot, sliced cucumber, sliced black olives, sliced radishes and topped with feta cheese. Serve as a first course.

This **fish** calls for a wine-based poaching liquid. Pour **wine** into a pan and add water, carrots, parsley, thyme, bay leaf, clove, salt and peppercorns. Bring to a boil then lower heat to simmer mixture for about 30 minutes. *Without the fish!*

Meanwhile, prepare **corkscrew noodles** according to package directions.

Add trout to poaching mixture, bring to boil again, reduce heat and simmer for 10 minutes. Remove trout and place on a warm serving dish. Strain poaching broth; cook over high heat and reduce broth to 1 cup. Thicken broth with cornstarch dissolved in 2 tablespoons cold water. Add butter and beat with a wire whisk until butter is melted. Pour sauce over the trout and sprinkle with parsley.

Serve with the corkscrew noodles and the Greek salad.

BEEF TENDERLOIN WITH WINE SAUCE

with Mashed Potatoes and Green Beans

Whole, peeled beef tenderloin
(about 2 pounds for 4 servings)
3 Tbsps. of olive oil
Salt and pepper to taste
2 mushrooms
10-12 cherry tomatoes

3 potatoes
½ stick margarine
¼ cup milk

Wine Sauce:
1 Tbsp. onions, chopped
2 Tbsps. flour
2 Tbsps. butter
1 Tbsp. fresh parsley
¼ teaspoon each of dried thyme, salt, pepper
1 ¼ cups beef broth
¼ cup red wine
1 lb. green beans
1 slice bacon, uncooked

Select from a whole, peeled tenderloin.

Preheat oven to 450° F.

Heat oil in a heavy skillet. Sear **tenderloin** quickly on all sides. Place tenderloin in shallow roasting pan. Salt, pepper and insert thermometer. DO NOT COVER! Cook tenderloin until done. 150° F for medium rare and 160° F for well done.

While tenderloin cooks, prepare **mashed potatoes**. Wash and peel potatoes and quarter into smaller pieces. Heat a pot of water and insert the potato pieces. Salt the water to your taste. Cook for approximately 20 minutes; drain. Into hot potatoes, place ½ stick of margarine, ¼ cup of milk and whip to the desired smoothness.

Meanwhile, prepare **green beans** by the boiling method. Cut off ends of beans and cut in half to make smaller pieces or leave long. Barely cover them with water; add one slice of bacon and sprinkle with salt. Cook until they are tender: 20 minutes for *al dente.*

For the final touch, make the **sauce**. Melt butter over low heat; add flour and cook 1 minute, stirring often, Add next five ingredients, stirring constantly. Gradually, add beef broth and wine. Cook over medium heat, stirring constantly until thick.

Garnish beef tenderloin with mushrooms, parsley and cherry tomatoes.

Third week JULY

Sunday	*Monday*	*Tuesday*	*Wednesday*	*Thursday*	*Friday*	*Saturday*
Char-donnay Chicken Snow Peas, Baked Potatoes	**Jalisco Salad** Buttered Tortillas	*Plan ahead* **Sweet Curry Shrimp Salad**	**Fettuccine Pork Chops** Tomato. Green Salad	**Real Manicotti** Fresh Bread Broccoli Salad	**Baked Salmon w/ Sauce** Herbed Rice, Mustard Greens	**Garlic Stuffed Sirloin** Baked Potatoes Green Peas

Fresh Vegetables \ Fruits		*Herbs \ Spices*	*Basics*
lemons - 4 parsley bunch snow peas - ¼ lb. potatoes - 8 tomatoes - 5 white onion - 1 iceberg lettuce - 1 red leaf lettuce - 1 mustard green bundle	garlic pod - 1 fresh basil bunch broccoli bunch potatoes - 4 green onions - 12 avocados - 2 celery bundle	bay leaf chili powder curry powder ground chili powder red pepper sauce	sea salt brown sugar olive oil peanut oil flour extra-virgin olive oil white vinegar sugar cornstarch Dijon mustard mayonnaise

Entrée Food	*Dairy*	*Miscellaneous*	*Cans \ Jars*
skinless, boneless chicken breasts 4 ground sirloin 1 lb. cooked shrimp ½ lb butterfly pork chops - 2 salmon steaks - 2 boneless beef sirloin - 1 ½ lbs. **Frozen** green peas or green beans pkg.	milk - 1 C Cheddar cheese 2 oz butter - 4 T bacon - 11 slices Ricotta cheese - ½ lb Mozzarella cheese - ½ lb Parmesan cheese 2 oz. **Wine** white wine - ¼ cup	Thousand Island dressing - 4 oz. Doritos® - 6 ¼ oz. corn tortillas - 12 hot rolls - 12 fettuccini noodles ½ lb. large sea shell pasta 1 lb. raisins - 1 cup fresh bread - 1 loaf herbed seasoned rice - pkg orange marmalade - ½ C	chicken broth - 2 8 oz. pineapple chunks - 1 whole tomatoes - 2 kidney beans - 1 2 oz. pimentos - 1 water chestnuts - 3 oz. prepared horseradish - 2 tsp.

CHARDONNAY CHICKEN

with Snow Peas and Baked Potatoes

2 boneless, skinless, chicken breasts
¼ teaspoon ground pepper
¼ cup white wine
½ cup chicken broth
2 Tbsps. lemon juice
1 bay leaf
1 cup low fat milk
2 Tbsps. cornstarch
1 Tbsp. Dijon mustard
2 Tbsps. fresh, minced parsley
¼ lb. snow peas
1 slice bacon
4 potatoes, for baking
1 tomato, in wedges

This chicken calls for a Chardonnay wine as part of the poaching liquid. We choose one with a lemony flavor and accent it with lemon juice.

Season **chicken** with pepper. Prepare the poaching liquid. Combine wine, broth, lemon juice, lemon peel and bay leaf in your largest skillet. Heat until the liquid begins to boil; carefully add in chicken and reduce heat to a simmer. Cover and cook in simmering liquid for about 15 minutes or until the chicken is fully cooked.

Meanwhile, prepare **baked potatoes.** We typically use the microwave to completely bake or to at least partially bake the potatoes. Wash the potatoes and pierce with fork. Place potatoes in the microwave and cook on HIGH for 4 minutes per potato per side, turning once. (3 or 4 potatoes will cook in 24 minutes.)

Prepare the **snow peas**. Boil them with slice of bacon for about 20 minutes; drain.

When chicken is done, remove from poaching liquid and keep warm. We place chicken on a plate that has been heated slightly.

A **sauce** can be made to compliment this meal. In a small bowl, blend milk, cornstarch, and mustard until smooth; stir into simmering liquid in skillet. Increase heat to medium, cook until mixture boils and thickens, stirring constantly. Return chicken to skillet; coat well with sauce. Sprinkle with parsley.

When ready to serve, cut **tomato** into wedges; add to dish as garnish.

JALISCO SALAD, NORTH AMERICAN STYLE

with Buttered Tortillas

Jalisco Salad Ingredients:

1 medium onion, chopped
2 medium tomatoes, sliced
¼ head lettuce, shredded
2 oz. sharp Cheddar cheese, grated
Thousand Island dressing, about 3 oz.
Red pepper sauce, to taste

1 (6 ¼ oz.) bag Doritos®
1 avocado, sliced
1 lb. ground sirloin
2 Tbsps. peanut oil
1 (15 oz.) can kidney beans, drained
¼ teaspoon sea salt
Chili powder, to taste
12 corn tortillas

Brown **ground sirloin** in peanut oil, drain off grease and toss with beans, sea salt and chili powder. Simmer 20 minutes then add to salad bowl and mix well.

Prepare the **Jalisco salad** next. Chop the onions, and tomatoes; place in large salad mixing bowl. Shred the lettuce and add to bowl. Grate the cheddar cheese and add to mixture. Add the Thousand Island salad dressing and mix well. Shake in a few drops of red pepper sauce and stir well again.

Into the same large bowl, hand crush a desired amount of Doritos. Forget any diets for tonight. Set a few slices of avocado aside and toss remaining into salad.

Garnish salad with remaining slices of avocado, whole Dorito chips and tomato slices.

Serve with hot **buttered tortillas**, rolled into tubes to be eaten like rolls. The buttered tortillas can be heated in the microwave in a dampened towel.

2 hours - Plan ahead

SWEET CURRY SHRIMP SALAD

with Lemon, Avocado Wedges and Hot Rolls

1 (8 oz.) can pineapple chunks, drained
¼ cup mayonnaise
1 teaspoon lemon juice
1 teaspoon curry powder
1 teaspoon brown sugar
½ lb. cooked shrimp, rinsed and drained
½ (2 oz.) jar pimentos, drained
½ (3 oz.) sliced water chestnuts
¼ cup thinly sliced celery
4 green onions, chopped

Red leaf lettuce, leaves separated and washed
1 lemon, cut into 6 wedges
1 small avocado
1 dozen hot rolls

Prepare the **sweet curry salad**. In a large bowl, pour in the pineapple chunks. R*eserve 1 tablespoon juice***.** Blend the mayonnaise with the reserved pineapple juice, lemon juice, curry and sugar. Stir in ½ of the pineapple, shrimp, pimentos, water chestnuts, celery and onions. ***Chill at least 2 hours.***

Preheat the oven for the **hot rolls.**

Cook rolls according to package directions.

Arrange lettuce on plates; top with shrimp and remaining chestnuts.

Garnish with **lemon** and **avocado wedges.**

FETTUCCINE PORK CHOPS

with Lemon-Herb Sauce, Tomato and Green Salad

2 Tbsps. peanut oil
2 butterfly pork chops
Lemon-Herb Sauce Ingredients:
- **4 Tbsps. butter**
- **1 teaspoon olive oil**
- **1 Tbsp. flour**
- **1 cup chicken broth, divided**
- **2 Tbsps. fresh basil**
- **1 Tbsp. cornstarch**
- **1 lemon, juiced**

Green Salad Ingredients:
- **iceberg lettuce**
- **red leaf lettuce**
- **celery stalk, julienned**
- **tomato**

½ pkg. fettuccine noddles
½ teaspoon salt

This menu uses the pan-poaching technique for the **pork chops**. Brown the pork chops in a minimum of peanut oil; sprinkle with salt. Add a tad bit of water; you may need to check the water from time to time. When the water boils, reduce the heat and simmer the chops for about 40 minutes. We flip the chops after twenty minutes.

While the pork chops cook, prepare the **green salad.** Wash and dry lettuce leaves, julienne the celery and toss with the leaves. Place this in refrigerator until ready to serve.

When the pork chops are about ready to serve, prepare the **fettucine** following package directions. While the fettucine cooks, prepare the **lemon-herb** sauce. Into a skillet**,** melt the butter, add the olive oil and flour, mixing well. Cook this for a couple of minutes. Add the remaining chicken stock, herb and lemon juice. Simmer for a few minutes more. Add cornstarch to thicken if desired. Add this sauce to the fettuccini and toss well.

You can top the green salad with wedges of **tomato** to add a nice red color.

REAL MANICOTTI

with Fresh Bread and Broccoli Salad

3 Tbsps. extra-virgin olive oil
1 clove garlic, chopped
2 (14 oz.) cans whole tomatoes
Dash of chili powder
Salt to taste
¼ lb. Mozzarella cheese
1 lb. large sea shell pasta
¼ lb. Ricotta cheese
Parmesan or Romano cheese

1 bunch broccoli
10 slices bacon
5 green onions, sliced
½ cup raisins
½ cup mayonnaise
3 Tbsps. vinegar
2 Tbsps. sugar
Lettuce leaves
Fresh bread

If you're having **fresh bread**, preheat oven to temperature stated on package directions. Bake bread.

Make the **Italian sauce.** Heat olive oil in pan over medium heat. Add garlic and sauté for about a minute or two. Drain the juice from two cans of tomatoes and cut tomatoes into chunks, and add to saucepan. Add a dash of ground chili powder and salt to taste. Cook over low heat until the liquid is reduced, about 15 minutes.

At the same time, prepare the **broccoli salad**. Wash and cut broccoli into bite-size pieces. Cook bacon until crisp; crumble. Add bacon, onions and raisins to broccoli. Combine the rest of ingredients and add to broccoli mixture, tossing gently. Serve broccoli in a glass bowl on individual lettuce leaves. *We serve this salad as a first course.*

Grate the Mozzarella cheese.

Cook the pasta shells in a very large pot of water to which you add a tablespoon of olive oil. Cook until they are just *al dente* then drain and rinse with cold water to halt the cooking process. To prepare the **manicotti,** pour the sea shells in a large baking dish and add the ricotta and mozzarella cheese. Stir to mix the cheeses and sea shells. Place the baking dish in the oven to melt the cheese; pour the tomato sauce over shells and serve immediately. The guests can top the manicotti with Parmesan or Romano cheese.

A nice Chianti wine adds to this Italian speciality.

BAKED SALMON

with Sauce, Herbed Rice and Mustard Greens

¼ cup orange marmalade
2 teaspoons prepared horseradish
1 teaspoon cider or distilled white vinegar
2 salmon steaks, 6 ounces each

Herb-seasoned rice*

Mustard greens

** Herb-seasoned rice can be found with the white and brown rices. Several companies make the seasoned variety of rice. If unavailable, make white rice and add a dash of several herbs along with chopped onions and parsley.*

Preheat oven to 375° F.

Prepare **Herb-seasoned rice** according to package directions.

Meanwhile, in a small bowl stir orange marmalade, horseradish and vinegar.

Rinse **salmon steaks** and pat dry. Lay steaks on a baking pan that has been sprayed with a vegetable oil. Spread the horseradish sauce top of steaks.

Bake steaks until opaque in center, about 8 to 10 minutes.

While the fish bakes, steam the **mustard greens**. In a pot over boiling water place the greens. Cover and simmer for about 5 minutes.

GARLIC STUFFED SIRLOIN

with Baked Potatoes and Green Peas

4 garlic cloves, finely chopped
½ Tbsp. olive oil
6 green onions, sliced
1 ½ lbs. boneless beef sirloin, 2 inches thick

Salt and pepper to taste

4 potatoes, for baking

1 pkg. frozen green beans or peas

A grill recipe!

Cook garlic in oil over low-heat until tender, about 2 minutes. Add onions; increase heat to medium-low and continue cooking until onions are crisp tender, about 5 minutes.

Bake **potatoes** according to your favorite method. We typically use the microwave to completely bake or to at least partially bake the potatoes. Wash the potatoes and pierce with fork. Place potatoes in the microwave and cook on HIGH for 4 minutes per potato per side, turning once. (3 or 4 potatoes will cook in 24 minutes.)

Cut pocket in **steak.** Make a horizontal cut through the center of the steak, parallel to the surface of the meat, about 1 inch from each side. Stuff garlic and onion mixture into pocket; secure opening with toothpicks.

Place steak on grill over medium-low coals. Cover and grill until done to your likeness.

You can prepare **frozen green beans** or **peas** to compliment the steak.

***Testing the Heat*:**

This is a good tip, courtesy of the beef industry. To check the temperature of coals on a grill, cautiously hold the palm of your hand 4 to 6 inches above the coals. The length of time you can hold your hand in that position until the heat forces you to pull back will tell you the heat of the coals.

2 seconds = hot (high)
3 seconds = medium-high
4 seconds = medium
5 seconds = low

Fourth week JULY

Sunday	Monday	Tuesday	Wednesday	Thursday	Friday	Saturday
Chicken Enchiladas Rice Avocado Salad Black Beans	**Slicer's Sand-wiches** Potato Wedges, Beer	**Shrimp & Avocado Salad** Rice	**Barbecued Pork Chops** Potato Salad	**Italian Tetrazzini** Green Wedge Salad, Tomato, Fresh Bread	**Grilled Salmon** Snow Peas, New Potatoes	*Plan ahead* **Marinated Beef** w/ Tomato Chutney, Baked Potatoes

Fresh Vegetables \ Fruits		*Herbs \ Spices*	*Basics*
white onion - 2 iceberg lettuce - 2 butter lettuce head 1 avocado - 2 cilantro bunch red onion - 1 potatoes - 6 new potatoes - 10 tomatoes - 4 endive bunch carrot bundle snow peas ¼ lb. orange	garlic pod jalapeño pepper - 1 collard greens head or mustard greens green bell pepper - 1 lemon - 1 limes - 3 cucumbers - 2 radish bunch celery bundle green onions - 6 jicama - 1	Italian seasoning bay leaf Paprika celery seed nutmeg dry mustard chives ground coriander	cooking spray olive oil sugar white vinegar ketchup Marsala red wine vinegar Balsamic vinegar extra-virgin olive oil Dijon mustard mayonnaise, mustard Converted rice peanut oil sea salt

Entrée Food	*Dairy*	*Miscellaneous*	*Cans \ Jars*
skinless, boneless chicken breast - 3 cod, orange roughy, fish fillets - 2 cooked shrimp 20-24 pork chops - 4 salmon fillets - 2 4 oz beef fillets - 4 ham slices - 4	sour cream - 8 oz. Monterey Jack cheese 4 oz. Cheddar cheese - 4 slices. Swiss cheese slices 4 Parmesan cheese - 4 oz bacon - 1 slice feta cheese- 2 oz. milk - ½ cup	corn tortillas - 12 black beans - 1 C whole wheat buns-4 fresh bread pkg. macaroni - 1 lb. honey - 4 T French dressing - 4 oz	cream chicken soup 1 cream mushroom - 1 cream of celery - 1 chicken broth - 2 ripe olives - 4 oz. chili sauce - 1 Tbsp. tomato paste - 1 dill pickles. - 2 oz. sliced mushrooms 4 oz.

CHICKEN ENCHILADAS

with Rice, Avocado Salad and Black Beans

1 boneless, skinless chicken breast
2 Tbsps. butter
1 small onion, chopped
2 Tbsps. peanut oil
1 jalapeño, sliced to taste
1 can cream of chicken soup
1 (8 oz.) sour cream
½ cup chicken broth
1 cup grated Monterey Jack or Cheddar cheese
Corn tortillas

Tossed Avocado Salad:
lettuce
avocado
½ cup French dressing
1 Tbsp. chili sauce

Converted Rice

1 cup black beans
4 cups water
1 slice bacon, uncooked
Cilantro

In a medium size pot, combine water, **black beans**. Bring water to a boil and cook for two minutes; remove from heat. Let the beans soak for 1 hour. Drain the beans, refill the pot with fresh water, a strip of bacon, salt to taste and bring to a simmer. Let cook for about 1 hour. Black beans for this menu should be mashed and mixed with pieces of cilantro.

Preheat oven to 350° F.

Flatten **chicken breast** to an even thickness. In skillet with 2 tablespoons of butter, cook chicken until almost done, about 5 minutes each side; remove and place on baking dish.

For the **chicken enchiladas,** sauté onion in small amount of peanut oil until clear. Add chopped jalapeño pepper, soup, sour cream and broth. Simmer. In large casserole dish, layer cooked chicken, corn tortillas and soup mixture. Repeat, putting cheese on top. Bake for 30 minutes.

While the chicken bakes, prepare the **rice** following package directions.

At the same time, prepare the **tossed avocado salad**. Tear lettuce into bite-size pieces. Cut avocado lengthwise into halves; cut halves into slices. Make the dressing, mixing ½ cup French dressing with 1 tablespoon chili sauce. Pour sauce over the avocados and mix well.

SLICER'S SANDWICHES

with Potato Wedges and Beer

2 potatoes, for baking
1 Tbsp. olive oil
Pepper and salt, to taste
Cooking spray
4 whole wheat buns
Mustard
Mayonnaise
4 slices ham, shredded
4 slices Cheddar cheese, shredded
4 slices Swiss cheese, shredded
Pickles
Lettuce, grated
Red onions, sliced
1 tomato, quartered

Preheat the oven to 350° F.

Prepare the **potato wedges** first. Cut potatoes, with skin, into thin wedges. Set the wedges in cold water for a minimum of 15 - 20 minutes. Dry the potatoes after soaking, using paper towels. Transfer to a large bowl and mix with 1 Tbsp. vegetable oil, pepper and salt. Arrange the seasoned potatoes on a baking dish that has been sprayed with vegetable cooking spray.

Bake the potatoes for about 20 minutes or until they are golden brown. Turn them after about 10 minutes.

For the **Slicer sandwiches,** heat rolls; spread with mustard and/or mayonnaise. Fill with the ham, cheeses and top with pickles, lettuce, onion slices and tomato quarters.

Serve with beer and potato wedges.

SHRIMP AND AVOCADO SALAD

with Rice

20-24 cooked shrimp*
2 oz. crumbled feta cheese
¼ cup chopped onion
¼ cup fresh cilantro, chopped
2 Tbsps. olive oil
1 lemon, juiced
¼ teaspoon pepper

1 avocado, peeled, pitted and thinly chopped
1 head of assorted greens (collard, mustard)

Converted Rice

* *We purchase medium-size cooked shrimp for this menu.*

Prepare **rice** according to package directions.

Meanwhile, combine the **cooked shrimp**, cheese, onion and cilantro in a bowl.

In another bowl, mix together the olive oil, lemon juice and pepper; pour half of sauce over the cooked shrimp. Toss the shrimp with the sauce to coat evenly.

Add the **avocado** to the remaining dressing and stir gently to coat; pour avocado and dressing on top of shrimp sauce mixture.

When buying greens, look for those without brown edges. Greens can be stored unwashed in the refrigerator for only a few days, so plan ahead. To prepare the **greens**, wash thoroughly, drain and pat dry with paper towels. Remove any pulpy stems and discolored leaves. For a salad, tear into bite-size pieces.

Arrange salad greens on plates, spoon shrimp salad and avocado on top.

BARBECUED PORK CHOPS

with Potato Salad

4 lean pork chops
2 Tbsps. peanut oil
BBQ sauce: *
½ cup ketchup
1 clove garlic, crushed
1 teaspoon salt
1 teaspoon celery seed
½ teaspoon nutmeg
¼ cup white vinegar
1 cup water
1 bay leaf
Dash dry mustard

Potato Salad Ingredients:
6 medium-size red potatoes
½ cup finely-diced red onions
3 Tbsps. extra-virgin olive oil
¼ cup balsamic vinegar
½ cup chicken broth
2 Tbsps. sliced green onions
Black pepper, to taste
1 Tbsp. Dijon mustard

* *This home-made barbecue sauce is very mild, allowing the flavor of the pork to come through. Try it at least once. At other times select a bottled BBQ sauce from the grocery shelf.*

Preheat oven to 350° F.

Brown **pork chops** in hot peanut oil. Transfer pork chops to a baking dish. Pour over combined remaining ingredients: the ketchup, garlic, salt, celery seed, nutmeg, white vinegar, water, bay leaf and dry mustard. Cover and bake in moderate oven 1 ½ hours.

While pork chops bake, prepare **potato salad**. Boil potatoes for 30 minutes. Set aside to cool; peel and cube to desired size. Combine rest of ingredients: the red onions, olive oil, balsamic vinegar, chicken broth, green onions, black pepper and Dijon mustard in a separate bowl to make the dressing. Pour over the potatoes.

Serve potato salad warm or chilled. *We like ours chilled.*

ITALIAN TETRAZZINI

with Green Wedge Salad, Tomato and Fresh Bread

1 skinless, boneless chicken breast
½ green bell pepper, chopped
1 Tbsp. chopped onion
Paprika
1 (10 oz.) can cream of mushroom soup
1 (10 oz.) can cream of celery soup
2 ½ cups cooked macaroni
½ cup milk
1 (4 oz.) can sliced mushrooms
¼ cup chopped ripe olives
¼ cup grated Parmesan cheese

Green Wedge Salad:
½ head iceberg lettuce
½ cucumber in thick slices
2 radishes, in thin slices
2 celery stalks, julienned

Fresh bread

1 tomato, in wedges

Preheat the oven temperature as stated on **bread** package.

While oven heats, prepare the ingredients for the chicken tetrazzini. Chop and slice as indicated in the ingredient list.

Bake bread according to timing and temperature indicated on package.

Make the **Italian Tetrazzini**. Pound the chicken breast to achieve an even thickness. Boil in water for 15 minutes; remove and cool. When chicken has cooled, cut into small pieces.

Meanwhile, combine the green pepper, onion and paprika. Cook this mixture in the microwave on HIGH for about 2-3 minutes. Add remaining ingredients: the soups, cooked macaroni, milk, cooked chicken, mushrooms, ripe olives and Parmesan cheese. Mix thoroughly. Cook in microwave on HIGH for five minutes. Stir the ingredients and cook for another five minutes.

While tetrazzini cooks, prepare the **green wedge salad.** Cut the iceberg lettuce into wide wedges. Remove center portion and chop, spreading on salad plate. Cut the cucumber and place in the remaining curved portion of lettuce wedge. Slice the radishes and place on cucumbers. Julienne the celery and place on top of and around the wedge. Add tomato wedges as garnish.

GRILLED SALMON

with Snow Peas and New Potatoes

2 Tbsps. minced fresh green onions
1 Tbsp. olive oil
1 Tbsp. Balsamic wine vinegar
½ teaspoon black pepper, fresh
2 salmon fillets
4 small red potatoes, cooked
Sea salt, to taste
¼ lb. snow peas

Chive Vinaigrette:
¼ cup olive oil
¼ cup Balsamic vinegar
1 Tbsp. dried chives
1 Tbsp. water
Dash black pepper
¼ teaspoon salt

Prepare the outdoor grill (or indoor oven broiler).

While charcoal briquets are heating, prepare the **marinade** using left side ingredients. Combine green onions, oil, vinegar and pepper in a large baking dish. Rinse salmon and pat dry. Add fish to pan and turn to coat both sides; set aside.

Next, prepare the **new potatoes.** Wash the skins but do not peel. Add new potatoes to pot of boiling water and add sea salt depending on the number of potatoes. Try 1 tablespoon for four potatoes. Let the potatoes boil 15-20 minutes. Test for softness. Drain and set aside. Cut cooked potatoes, at room temperature, lengthwise into four wedges each; place in a bowl. Set aside.

Add partially-cooked potato wedges to remaining marinade; turn to coat sides. Place potato wedges around **salmon.** Grill about 3 minutes; flip salmon and potatoes and continue grilling until salmon turns opaque in center.

While salmon cooks, prepare the **snow peas.** Sauté peas in olive oil for two minutes over medium-high heat.

Prepare **Chive Vinaigrette dressing.** In a small jar with a tight-fitting lid, combine all ingredients on right side and shake well. Makes ½ cup.

MARINATED BEEF

with Tomato Chutney and Baked Potato

½ teaspoon minced garlic
½ onion sliced
4 Tbsps. honey
¼ cup olive oil
½ teaspoon ground coriander
1 teaspoon balsamic vinegar
3 limes
4 beef fillets, 4 oz. each

Tomato Chutney:
1 clove garlic, minced
2 Tbsps. chopped onion
½ teaspoon salt
1 ½ Tbsps. tomato paste
1 orange
2 large tomatoes, chopped
¼ cup chopped jicama
4 potatoes

To marinate **beef**, combine garlic, onion, honey, olive oil, ground coriander, balsamic vinegar and lime juice in a large, covered baking dish. Add beef fillets, turning to coat; cover and place flat in refrigerator for up to 16 hours. Turn the fillets when the thought strikes you, occasionally.

Prepare **Tomato Chutney.** In a glass bowl, combine garlic, onion and salt, lightly mashing them together. Blend in tomato paste and the juice from 1 orange and mix thoroughly. Fold in tomatoes and jicama. Cover and refrigerate until meat is ready.

Bake **potatoes** according to your favorite method. We typically use the microwave to completely bake or to at least partially bake the potatoes. Wash the potatoes and pierce with fork. Place potatoes in the microwave and cook on HIGH for 4 minutes per potato per side, turning once. (3 or 4 potatoes will cook in 24 minutes.)

Remove beef from the marinade; put marinade in a small saucepan. Cook marinade over medium-low heat until reduced; about 15 minutes. Meanwhile, place the beef fillet in a hot skillet and cook until brown on both sides, approximately 5 minutes each side for medium-rare. Remove from heat and set aside.

When serving, drizzle the reduced marinade over beef and arrange Tomato Chutney on top.

Fifth week JULY

Sunday	*Monday*	*Tuesday*	*Wednesday*	*Thursday*	*Friday*	*Saturday*
Italian Chicken Italian Salad	*Plan ahead* **Pasta Marinara** Italian Salad, Hot Garlic Bread	**Fish in Sour Cream** Baked Potato Green Wedge Salad	**Fettuccine Delight** Tossed Salad, Fresh Bread	**Salmon in Ribbon Pasta** Italian Bread, Celery Salad, Wine	*Plan ahead* **Citrus Char-broiled Swordfish** Saffron Rice Baby Carrots	**Beef Cubes in Sour Cream** Mashed Potatoes, Broccoli

Fresh Vegetables \ Fruits		*Herbs \ Spices*	*Basics*
white onion - 4 red onion - 1 iceberg lettuce - 2 green leaf lettuce - 2 carrot bundle red cabbage head tomato - 3 orange - 1 red grapefruit - 1 red bell pepper - 1 green bell pepper - 1 yellow bell pepper 1	garlic pod - 1 jalapeño pepper - 1 mushrooms - 2 parsley bunch lemon - 3 lime - 1 potatoes - 7 cucumber -4 radish bunch celery bundle broccoli - ¾ lb.	Italian seasoning bay leaf paprika dry mustard celery salt dried mint	olive oil extra-virgin olive oil peanut oil sugar white vinegar mayonnaise flour

Entrée Food	*Dairy*	*Miscellaneous*	*Cans \ Jars*
skinless, boneless chicken breast - 2 cod, orange roughy fillets - 2 swordfish steaks - 2 boneless beef chuck cubes - 1 ½ lb. **Wines** sauterne wine rum ½ oz. red wine - bottle vermouth ¼ cup	Cheddar cheese 1 ½ C Parmesan cheese 4 oz. American cheese 1 T sour cream - 2 cups Romano cheese ¼ cup plain yogurt - 8 oz. margarine - 1 stick milk ¼ cup	spaghetti - ½ lb. baked croutons pkg. garlic bread pkg. fresh bread pkg. Italian bread loaf fettuccini pasta ½ lb. Tagliatelle (ribbon) pasta - 1 lb. saffron rice pkg angel hair pasta 1 lb. baby carrots bundle	cream mushroom soup - 1 chicken broth - 1 diced pimientos 4 oz. ripe olives - 4 oz. salad pepper - 8 whole tomatoes - 1 tomato sauce - 1 tomato paste - 1 mushrooms - 4 oz. red salmon - 7 oz. instant chicken bouillon - 1 Tbsp.

ITALIAN CHICKEN

with Italian Salad

2 whole chicken breasts
3 Tbsps. olive oil
2 garlic cloves, minced
½ pkg. spaghetti, quartered
1 cup Cheddar cheese, grated
2 Tbsps. Parmesan cheese
½ cup green peppers, julienned
¼ onion, minced
½ can cream of mushroom soup
¼ cup chicken broth
¼ cup vermouth
½ (2 oz.) can diced pimentos
Salt and pepper to taste
Dash Italian seasoning

Italian Salad Ingredients:
- **iceberg lettuce**
- **green leaf lettuce**
- **tomato, in wedges**
- **red cabbage, julienned**
- **ripe olives**
- **carrot, shredded**
- **salad pepper**
- **croutons (optional)**

Pound the **chicken breasts** to an even thickness. Mince the garlic cloves. Into a skillet of olive oil, sauté the garlic. Add the chicken breasts and sauté for 4 minutes each side; remove and cool.

Preheat oven to 350° F.

Cook **spaghetti** *al dente* according to package directions; drain.

Combine 1 cup Cheddar cheese, 2 tablespoons Parmesan cheese and all remaining ingredients: the green peppers, onion, cream of mushroom soup, chicken broth, vermouth, diced pimentos, salt, pepper and Italian seasoning. Cut the chicken halves into pieces and add to ingredients. Toss with the spaghetti. Place in greased casserole dish and sprinkle with additional Parmesan cheese. Cook, covered, for 30 minutes.

While spaghetti bakes, prepare the **Italian salad**. Tear lettuces into bite-size pieces. Cut tomato into wedges in desired thickness. Cut red cabbage into julienne strips. Add a few ripe olives. Shred the carrot on top. Toss well. Add a salad pepper to top and spread croutons around.

PASTA MARINARA

with Angel Hair Pasta, Italian Salad and Hot Garlic Bread

2 cloves garlic, minced
1 onion, chopped
3 Tbsps. olive oil
1 (16 oz.) can whole tomatoes
1 (8 oz.) can tomato sauce
1 (6 oz.) can tomato paste
1 (4 oz.) can mushrooms
1 teaspoon salt
2 teaspoons sugar
2 cups water
¼ cup chopped parsley
1 ½ teaspoons Italian seasoning
1 bay leaf

Italian Salad Ingredients:
iceberg lettuce
green leaf lettuce
tomato, in wedges
red cabbage, julienned
ripe olives
carrot, shredded
salad pepper
croutons (optional)
Garlic bread
1 lb. angel hair pasta

Red wine

For the **marinara sauce,** cook and stir garlic and onions in olive oil in large saucepan over low heat until they become clear. Add remaining ingredients: the whole tomatoes, tomato sauce, tomato paste, mushrooms, salt, sugar, water, parsley, Italian seasoning and bay leaf. Cover and simmer for 2 hours or longer. *Occasionally, we use the slow cooker and let sauce simmer for the entire day.*

Sometime before the meal, prepare the **garlic bread**. If using packaged bread, follow the directions to prepare. *Sometimes we make our own by spreading a garlic mix on toast bread and placing under the oven broiler.*

When you are ready to eat, prepare the **Italian salad.** Tear lettuces into bite-size pieces. Cut tomato into wedges in desired thickness. Cut red cabbage into julienne strips. Add a few ripe olives. Shred the carrot on top. Toss well. Add a salad pepper to top and spread croutons around.

Prepare a large pot of water to cook the **angel hair pasta**. Cook according to the package directions. Serve a red wine with this menu.

FISH IN SOUR CREAM

with Baked Potato and Green Wedge Salad

Fish fillets
(sole, orange roughy, cod, snapper)
1 oz. sauterne wine *
1 cup sour cream
¼ cup Romano cheese
1 lemon, juiced
1 Tbsp. onion, grated
½ teaspoon salt
Paprika

4 potatoes, for baking

Green Wedge Salad Ingredients:
½ head iceberg lettuce
½ cucumber in thick slices
2 radishes, in thin slices
2 celery stalks, julienned

* *Substitute sherry or vermouth for a change.*

This is a guaranteed-to-please menu!

Pre-heat oven to 350° F.

While oven heats, bake **potatoes**. We typically use the microwave to completely bake or to at least partially bake the potatoes. Wash the potatoes and pierce with fork. Place potatoes in the microwave and cook on HIGH for 4 minutes per potato per side, turning once. (3 or 4 potatoes will cook in 24 minutes.)

Place **fish fillets** in baking dish and sprinkle with sauterne. Combine 1 cup sour cream with grated Romano cheese, lemon juice and chopped onion. Add salt to taste. Bake until fish flakes, about 12 minutes.

While the fish bakes, prepare the **green wedge salad:** cut the iceberg lettuce in half and then into wide wedges. Remove center portion and chop, spreading on salad plate. Cut the cucumber and place in the remaining curved portion of lettuce wedge. Slice the radishes and place on cucumbers. Julienne the celery and place on top of and around the wedge.

FETTUCCINE DELIGHT

with Tossed Salad and Fresh Bread

1 pkg. Fettuccine pasta
2 Tbsps. olive oil
1 cup shredded carrots
1 cup sliced celery
2 cups sliced cucumbers
1 cup shredded red cabbage
1 small (8 oz.) pkg. plain yogurt
¼ cup mayonnaise
2 Tbsps. vinegar
1 teaspoon dry mustard
Salt and pepper to taste
Paprika

Tossed Salad Ingredients:
green leaf lettuce
iceberg lettuce
cucumber
radishes
tomato
ripe olives
croutons

Fresh bread

Prepare the **tossed salad.** Wash and dry all vegetables. Tear the lettuces into bite-size pieces. Slice the cucumber and radishes. Cut the tomato into wedges. Toss all together, then add the ripe olives and the croutons. Place in refrigerator while you proceed.

For the **fettuccine delight,** in a large pot of boiling water, add 2 tablespoons of olive oil and as much fettuccine as the package directs for the number you are serving. Allow the fettuccine to cook until fully done, then drain and rinse with cold water to halt the cooking process. Place pasta in a large salad bowl and add the ingredients: carrots, celery, cucumbers, cabbage; stir to mix. Next, add the yogurt, mayonnaise, vinegar and dry mustard. Season with salt and pepper to taste. Add a dash of paprika. Place in refrigerator to chill.

While the pasta chills, prepare the **fresh bread** following package directions.

SALMON IN RIBBON PASTA

with Italian Bread, Sautéed Celery Salad and Wine

¼ onion cut into paper-thin slices
1 lemon, juiced
Freshly ground pepper
1 lb. Tagliatelle (pasta ribbons ⅛ ")*
1 (7 ½ oz.) can red salmon, drained
6 Tbsps. extra-virgin olive oil
Salt to taste

Red wine

Italian bread sticks
Sautéed Celery Salad:
5 celery stalks
1 Tbsp. peanut oil
1 Tbsp. instant chicken bouillon
½ teaspoon salt
Dash celery salt
2 Tbsps. diced pimentos

** Linguine will substitute.*

To prepare the **sautéed celery**, cut the stalks of celery diagonally. Cook and stir celery slices in skillet with 1 tablespoon peanut oil. Add the instant bouillon, salt, celery salt and cook over medium heat, turning often until the celery is tender, about 8 minutes. Toss in the pimentos to heat before serving.

While the celery cooks, begin the pasta. In a large pot bring 6 qt. salted water to a boil.

Meanwhile, cut onion into paper-thin slices, place in a bowl, sprinkle with lemon juice and season to taste with pepper. Toss well and set aside.

Cook the **Tagliatelle pasta** according to package directions. Drain the pasta and transfer to a warm platter.

Scatter the salmon and onion over the pasta, then sprinkle with olive oil. Season with salt and pepper and gently toss.

Serve immediately with the **Italian bread sticks, celery salad** and **wine.**

2-4 hours - Plan ahead

CITRUS CHARBROILED SWORDFISH

with Saffron Rice, and Baby Carrots

2 swordfish steaks
Peanut oil
Salt and pepper to taste

Saffron rice
6-12 baby carrots, or
3 sticks regular size

Citrus Salsa

1 lemon, peeled and quartered
1 orange, peeled and quartered
½ red grapefruit, peeled and cut into wedges
1 lime, peeled and quartered

¼ red bell pepper, julienned
¼ green bell pepper, julienned
¼ yellow bell pepper, julienned
1 small red onion, chopped
1 teaspoon dried mint
½ oz. rum (optional)

This menu is based on one from the Four Seasons Hotel in Austin, Texas.

For the **citrus salsa**, peel and section all of the fruit. If grapefruit sections are too large, cut again in half. Combine all salsa ingredients into a bowl: the fruit, peppers and onion. Add an ounce of rum, if you desire, and allow this mixture to marinate in the refrigerator for at least a couple of hours.

Prepare the grill with coals and let it heat.

Prepare the **rice** according to package directions. Steam the **carrots** in a steamer or in the microwave if you prefer.

When the coals are hot, brush the **swordfish** with the peanut oil. Season with salt and pepper. Grill about 6-7 inches from the coals. Grill for about 7 minutes on each side or until the steak is done. Place steak on a serving plate and cover the fish with the salsa. Add the baby carrots on the side.

BEEF CUBES IN SOUR CREAM

with Mashed Potatoes, Broccoli, and Salad

1 ½ lb. boneless beef chuck, cut into 1-inch cubes
Flour
2 Tbsps. olive oil
1 medium-sized onion, sliced
½ cup sour cream
½ cup water
1 Tbsp. grated American cheese
Salt and Pepper to taste

3 potatoes
½ stick margarine
¼ cup milk
Green Salad Ingredients:
green leaf lettuce
iceberg lettuce
1 celery stalk
cucumber
¾ lb. broccoli
2 oz. shredded Cheddar cheese

Prepare the **beef cubes**. Roll meat in flour and brown in olive oil. Add onion. Combine remaining ingredients: sour cream, water, grated American cheese, salt and pepper to taste; pour over meat. Cover tightly and cook slowly for about 2 hours.

Prepare **mashed potatoes.** Wash and peel potatoes and cut into halves, then quarter into smaller pieces. Heat a pot of water and insert the potatoes pieces. Salt the water to your taste. Cook for approximately 20 minutes; drain. Into hot potatoes, place ½ stick of margarine, ¼ cup of milk and whip to desired smoothness.

Prepare **green salad** as first course. Wash and dry lettuce leaves, tear lettuce into bite-size. Cut celery julienne style. Cut cucumber into thin slices.

Serve with a green vegetable of choice. We enjoy **broccoli**. Steam the broccoli for a minute or two. Sprinkle Cheddar cheese over it.

A Perfect Summer Night

The perfect summer night begins when the sun rises. It ends with finger foods and gazing at the stars.

We take time during the day to make the snack below for the star gazing. Sausage balls, ribbon sandwiches, stuffed Romas, fingertip vegetables and a relish tray. As dusk approaches we carry the goodies outside and lay out the blankets facing the north. If you happen to own or have access to a telescope, this night can be a memory maker.

Sausage Balls

1 lb. hot sausage (Jimmy Dean® or Owens®)
1 lb. Cheddar cheese
3 cups Bisquick® mix
Mix ingredients together.
Roll into small balls, about 1 teaspoon size.
Cook in 300 ° F oven for about 20 minutes.

Stuffed Romas

6 - 8 Roma Tomatoes
4 oz. cream cheese
parsley flakes
Cut Roma tomatoes in half. Remove seeds and ribs.
Stuff small amount of cream cheese into each cavity.
Garnish with parsley leaves.

Fingertip Vegetables

½ lb. broccoli florets
4 carrots, cut in wedges
1 bunch cauliflower
4 stalks celery, cut in 2-inch lengths

Ribbons sandwiches

See page **2**-410

Vegetable Dip

2 eggs
2 Tbsps. sugar
2 Tbsps. white vinegar
1 chopped onion
½ cup diced green pepper
2 (3 oz.) pkg cream cheese

For the vegetable dip: Beat the eggs. In medium saucepan, heat the eggs, sugar and vinegar and cook until it begins to thicken, stirring constantly. Remove from heat and blend in the cream cheese until smooth. Mix in green peppers and chopped onions. Chill for a few hours.

August

The best of the Pork Menus!

August is known as the dog days of summer for its extreme heat but you'll come to remember August for the truly great pork menus you find in *More Than Recipes*. We have pork cooked the very best way: by braising it. *Pork Tenderloin*, if you can find it, will become, like beef tenderloin, your favorite cut. We try some toppings for pork and you'll enjoy *Pork with White Crowns,* which has a sour cream topping, and *Pork Chop Chutney* which features a tomato chutney sauce of raisins, capers, ginger, sugar, vinegar that will delight your taste buds. Finally, we serve the *Pork Cutlets with Cheese Sauce* that features tomato sauce and cheddar cheese and a spice of cayenne pepper. By the end of August, you'll know why the Pork industry is sold on the variety offered by the new low-fat pork.

Each of the pork menus are cooked inside, so we go outside to grill chicken in a *Southwestern Cookout*. Everyone knows that Texas makes the best barbecue sauce, but you'll be impressed with this chicken that is marinated in beer and molasses, enhancing the chicken flavor. Grilling keeps the chicken juicy and tangy. We'll also grill Salmon again but this time marinate it first in oil and red wine vinegar. We think you'll like the taste.

In August you'll explore the use of the microwave when making fish and you'll prepare another meat loaf but this time on the stove top.

You'll get your monthly dosage of Mexican food with *Easy Flatboat Chalupas*, an Interior Mexico meal.

To close the month out you'll have *Italian Fried Chicken* which has a coating of Italian bread crumbs and is served with peas and mashed potatoes that the kids will love. You'll enjoy a *Poor Boy Sandwich*, an easy to make meal, in these hot days. Next, we throw in a *Minestrone Soup* to show you that soup can be serve any time of the year.

August Menus

Chicken

Orange Tarragon Chicken w/ Noodles, Apple Slices, Green Wedge Salad
Chicken in Dijon Sauce with Baked Potato and Broccoli
Grilled Chicken with Sherry w/ New Potatoes and Roasted Carrots
Southwestern Chicken Cookout with Potato Salad and Green Beans
Italian Fried Chicken with Mashed Potatoes, Italian Salad and Green Peas

Quick & Easy

Corned Beef and Cabbage with Spinach and Mashed Potatoes
The Original Hash with French Bread, Italian Salad and Red Wine
Quick BBQ Sandwiches and Ranch Style Beans® and Cole Slaw
Baked Meat Loaf with Rice, Corn and Tossed Salad
Poor Boy Sandwiches with Soup and Salad
Marinated Beef and Noodles with Garlic Bread and Salad

Shrimp

Fiery Shrimp with Red Sauce with Rice and Italian Salad
Shrimp Stroganoff with Rice and 3-C Salad
Triple Stuffed Baked Potatoes with Shrimp, Apple Wedges and Carrots

Pork

Braised Pork Chops with Spinach and Fried Tomatoes
Pork Chops w/ White Crowns with Cheddar Macaroni and Green Salad
Pork Chop Chutney with Corn and Celery Salad
Pork Tenderloin with Mashed Potatoes and Steamed Spinach
Pork Cutlets w/ Cheese Sauce with Rice and Spinach

Pasta / Soup

Black Bean Confetti Salad with Fresh Bread and Red Wine
Macaroni Salad with Fresh Bread and Cheese Assortment
Grilled Chicken Caesar Salad
Quick Fish and Pasta with Italian Bread and Green Salad
Oven Roasted Italian Vegetables with Pasta, French Bread and Red Wine

Fish

Fillet of Sole Veronique with Baked Potato and Herbed Tomatoes
Microwave Snapper with New Potatoes, Steamed Broccoli and Carrots
Spiced Orange Roughy with Baked Potato and Tossed Salad
Grilled Salmon in Vinaigrette with Baked Potatoes and Grilled Vegetables
Broiled Fish in Caper Sauce with Steamed Broccoli and New Potatoes
Seafood Caesar Salad with Rice and Garlic Bread Loaves

Red Meats

Pepper Steak with Rice, Tossed Salad and Sake
Braised Beef Roast with Mashed Potatoes, Carrots and Tomato Wedges
Easy Flatboat Chalupas with Rice and Margarita
Mushroom Steak with Mashed Potatoes and Broccoli
Shish Kabob with Rice

AUGUST

Sunday	Monday	Tuesday	Wednesday	Thursday	Friday	Saturday
Plan Ahead **Orange Tarragon Chicken** Noodles, Apple Slices, Green Wedge Salad	**Corned Beef & Cabbage** Spinach, Mashed Potatoes	**Fiery Shrimp in Red Sauce** Rice, Italian Salad	**Braised Pork Chops** Fried Tomatoes & Spinach	**Black Bean Confetti Salad** Fresh Bread, Red Wine	**Micro-wave Snapper** New Potatoes, Steamed Broccoli, Carrots	**Pepper Steak** Rice, Tossed Salad, Sake
Chicken in Dijon Sauce Baked Potato, Broccoli	**Quick BBQ Sand-wiches** Ranch Style Beans®, Cole Slaw	**Shrimp Stroganoff** Rice, 3-C Salad	**Pork Chops w/ White Crowns** Cheddar Macaroni, Green Salad	**Macaroni Salad** Fresh Bread, Cheese Assortment	**Fillet of Sole Veronique** Baked Potatoes, Herbed Tomatoes	**Easy Flatboat Chalupas** Rice, Margaritas
Grilled Sherry Chicken New Potatoes, Roasted Carrots	**The Original Hash** French Bread Red Wine Italian Salad	**Seafood Caesar Salad** Rice, Garlic Bread Loaves	**Pork Tenderloin** Mashed Potatoes, Steamed Spinach	*Plan Ahead* **Marinated Beef and Noodles** Garlic Bread And Salad	**Triple Stuffed Baked Potatoes** Shrimp, Apple Wedges, Carrots	**Braised Beef Roast** Mashed Potatoes, Carrots, Tomato Wedges
Plan Ahead **South-western Cookout** Potato Salad, Green Beans	**Baked Meat Loaf** Rice, Tossed Salad, Corn	**Quick Fish and Pasta** Italian Bread Green Salad	**Pork Chop Chutney** Corn, Celery Salad	**Grilled Chicken Caesar Salad**	**Spiced Orange Roughy** Baked Potato, Tossed Salad	*Plan Ahead* **Shish Kabob** Rice
Italian Fried Chicken Mashed Potatoes, Italian Salad, Green Peas	**Poor Boy Sand-wiches** Soup, Salad	**Broiled Fish in Caper Sauce** Broccoli, New Potatoes	**Pork Cutlets w/ Cheese Sauce** Rice, Spinach	**Oven Roasted Italian Vegetables** Pasta, French Bread, Red Wine	**Grilled Salmon in Vinai-grette** Baked Potatoes, Grilled Vegetables	**Mushroom Steak** Mashed Potatoes, Broccoli

First week AUGUST

Sunday	*Monday*	*Tuesday*	*Wednesday*	*Thursday*	*Friday*	*Saturday*
Plan Ahead **Orange Tarragon Chicken** Noodles, Apple Slices, Green Wedge Salad	**Corned Beef & Cabbage** Spinach, Mashed Potatoes	**Fiery Shrimp in Red Sauce** Rice, Italian Salad	**Braised Pork Chops** Fried Tomatoes & Spinach	**Black Bean Confetti Salad** Fresh Bread, Red Wine	**Microwave Snapper** New Potatoes, Steamed Broccoli, Carrots	**Pepper Steak** Rice, Tossed Salad, Sake

Fresh Vegetables \ Fruits		*Herbs \ Spices*	*Basics*
apples - 2	red cabbage head	tarragon	Worcestershire sauce
iceberg lettuce - 2	garlic pod - 1	dry mustard	cornstarch
cucumber - 2	red bell pepper - 1	Acćent® meat tenderizer	flour
radish bunch	green bell pepper - 1	onion flakes	balsamic vinegar
celery bundle	red onion - 1	red pepper sauce	Dijon mustard
parsley bunch	Boston lettuce head		honey
carrot bundle	green leaf lettuce - 1		kosher salt
white onions - 2	cilantro - bunch		peanut oil
potatoes - 3	new, red potatoes - 6		olive oil
spinach - 2 bunches	broccoli bunch		Converted Rice
orange - 1	tomatoes - 4		white vinegar

Entrée Food	*Dairy*	*Miscellaneous*	*Cans \ Jars*
skinless, boneless chicken breasts - 2	Cheddar cheese - 2 oz.	extra wide noodles - pkg.	ripe olives - 4 oz.
raw shrimp - ½ lb	process cheese -1/4 lb.	baked croutons pkg	black beans -15 oz
butterfly pork chops - 2	margarine - ¾ stick	liquid smoke - 2 oz.	whole corn - 12 oz.
large smoked or raw shrimp 16-20	butter - 4 Tbsps	apple juice - 1 Tbsp	6 oz. tomato paste 1
snapper fillets - 2	milk - ¼ cup	fresh bread loaf - 1	salad peppers - 4 oz. (vlasic® Pepperoncini)
round steak - 1 lb	**Wine**	dill lemon dressing - 1 C	
corn beef - 3 slices	Sake - bottle	honey - ¼ cup	
	red wine - bottle		

ORANGE TARRAGON CHICKEN

with Noodles, Apple Slices and Green Wedge Salad

2 whole skinless, boneless chicken breasts
1 Tbsp. orange rind
¼ cup orange juice
¼ cup honey
2 Tbsps. Worcestershire sauce
1 teaspoon tarragon
1 teaspoon dry mustard
Salt to taste
2 teaspoons cornstarch

½ lb. extra wide noodles

2 apples

Green Wedge Salad:
- **½ head iceberg lettuce**
- **½ cucumber, sliced**
- **2 radishes, in thin slices**
- **2 celery stalks, julienned**

For the **chicken,** combine orange rind, juices, honey, Worcestershire sauce, tarragon, mustard and salt. Pour over chicken breasts and marinate for *2 hours* in refrigerator.

When ready to eat, transfer chicken and marinade to a large flat baking dish; preheat oven to 350° F.

Prepare the **green wedge salad** while the oven heats. Cut the iceberg lettuce into large wedges. Remove center portion and chop into small pieces onto salad plate. Cut the cucumber and place in the curved portion of lettuce wedge. Slice the radishes and place on cucumbers. Julienne the celery and place on top of and around the wedge.

Bake chicken, covered, at 350° F for 30 minutes, turning once.

Just before the chicken is finished prepare the **extra wide noodles** according to package directions. Quarter **apples** at this time.

When chicken is done, thicken the sauce with cornstarch, dissolved in 1 tablespoon of water. Ladle sauce over chicken when serving.

CORNED BEEF AND CABBAGE

with Spinach and Mashed Potatoes

¼ cup parsley
3 slices cooked corned beef, chopped
1 cup red cabbage, chopped
1 cup process cheese, shredded
½ cup shredded carrot
¼ cup onion, shredded

3 potatoes
½ stick margarine
¼ cup milk

½ cup vinegar
1 bunch spinach

Prepare **mashed potatoes**. Wash and peel potatoes and cut into halves then quarter into smaller pieces. Heat a pot of water and insert the potato pieces. Salt the water to your taste. Cook for approximately 20 minutes; drain. Into hot potatoes, place ½ stick of margarine, ¼ cup of milk and whip to desired smoothness.

While potatoes cook, preheat the oven to 350° F. (Skip if you're using a microwave!)

For the **casserole,** mix together the potatoes and ¼ cup of chopped parsley and place in 2 quart casserole baking dish (with cover). Mix together the cooked corned beef, chopped cabbage, cheese, carrots and onion and fold over the potatoes.

If using conventional oven, bake casserole for 30 minutes. If using microwave, cook on HIGH about 10 minutes or until heated through.

Prepare **spinach.** We wash fresh spinach in a basin of water mixed with ½ cup of vinegar. Thoroughly rinse the spinach after washing. We then steam the fresh spinach using a small steamer basket over boiling water. You can just as well place the spinach in a pot with a minimum of water and let the spinach steam for a few minutes.

FIERY SHRIMP IN RED SAUCE

with Rice and Italian Salad

½ lb. peeled, deveined raw shrimp
1 - 2 Tbsps. kosher salt
1 Tbsp. onion flakes
¼ stick butter
1 teaspoon salt
½ teaspoon pepper
2- 3 drops red pepper sauce

Converted Rice

Italian Salad Ingredients:
iceberg lettuce
green leaf lettuce
tomato, in wedges
red cabbage, julienned
ripe olives
carrot stalk
salad pepper
croutons (optional)

Cook **rice** before proceeding, following package directions.

Make **Italian salad** next. Tear lettuce into bite-size pieces. Cut tomato into wedges of desired thickness. Cut red cabbage into julienne strips. Add a few ripe olives. Shred the carrot on top. Toss well. Add a salad pepper to top and spread croutons around.

Peel the **shrimp** and wash clean. Salt-leach the shrimp: Sprinkle with kosher salt, coating evenly. Let sit for one minute. Rinse and drain. Repeat salting again, let sit for another minute, rinse and drain well then set aside.

In skillet, sauté onion flakes, salt-leached shrimp, salt, pepper and Tabasco sauce in the butter for less than 1 minute to coat shrimp evenly. Cover the pan, turn the heat to High and steam for about 3 minutes. Remove from heat and serve shrimp over the rice.

BRAISED PORK CHOPS

with Spinach and Fried Tomatoes

2 butterfly pork chops,
1 clove garlic, crushed
Salt and pepper
2 Tbsps. peanut oil
½ cup hot water
1 Tbsp. olive oil
Garlic

2 tomatoes (ripe or green)
Flour

½ cup vinegar
Spinach

Converted Rice (optional)

Rub garlic on both sides of **pork chops** and sprinkle with salt and pepper. Brown on both sides in oil. Use low heat to avoid overcooking. When barest brown, add ½ cup of hot water. Cover and simmer for thirty minutes.

If you would like a fuller meal, you can prepare **rice.** Cook according to package directions.

While chops cook, prepare **fried tomatoes.** Cut tomatoes into ½ inch thickness.

- If using *green* tomatoes, dip into flour and season with salt and pepper. In a skillet, add peanut oil and heat to medium hot. Fry the tomato slices until brown on both sides.
- If using *ripe* tomatoes, dip slices into egg mixture and teaspoon of water, fry in hot oil and season with salt and pepper

When tomatoes are fried, cook **spinach** by steaming for a few minutes. If using fresh spinach you may want to consider cleaning the spinach in the sink full of water in which you have added ½ cup of vinegar. If using frozen spinach, cook according to package directions.

BLACK BEAN CONFETTI SALAD

with Fresh Bread and Red Wine

1 (15 oz.) can black beans, drained
1 (12 oz.) can whole kernel corn, drained
½ red bell pepper, chopped
1 small red onion, chopped
4 Tbsps. cilantro or parsley, chopped
Boston lettuce
Large smoked shrimp or large raw shrimp (16-20)
Liquid smoke (optional)

Cilantro Dressing Ingredients:
3 Tbsps. cilantro, chopped
1 clove garlic, chopped
1 Tbsp. apple juice
2 Tbsps. Dijon mustard
1 cup balsamic vinegar
Salt and pepper, to taste

Fresh bread
Red wine

Preheat the oven to 400° F for the **fresh bread**. Cook according to package directions.
This menu calls for large smoked shrimp. If unavailable, you can make your own by frying in a pan of olive oil. Add liquid smoke to create the illusion of smoked shrimp.

Meanwhile, prepare **cilantro dressing.** Mix together the 3 tablespoons of cilantro, garlic, apple juice, Dijon mustard and balsamic vinegar. Whisk and season with salt and pepper to taste. Set aside. If cilantro is not available or you do not like the taste of this Mexican herb then substitute parsley.

For the **salad,** mix together the black beans, corn, red pepper and red onion and the 4 tablespoons of cilantro or parsley. Toss with cilantro dressing. Serve on Boston lettuce.

Place about three large smoked shrimp on top of salad.

Serve with a **red wine**.

MICROWAVE SNAPPER

with New Potatoes, Steamed Broccoli and Carrots

6 new, red potatoes
5 Tbsps. Dill-Lemon dressing*
2 snapper fillets

Broccoli spears
Cheddar cheese
Fresh carrots

** Dill-Lemon dressing can be found in most supermarkets. If unavailable, select any dressing you find appealing.*

Wash **new potatoes** and cut in half. Put potatoes in a microwave-safe bowl; cover bowl with plastic wrap and leave open at one corner. Microwave on HIGH (100%) until potatoes are tender but firm when pierced, about 4-6 minutes, depending on number.

While potatoes cook, pour 2 tablespoons **dressing** into a shallow microwave-safe baking dish. Lower in the fish and turn to coat both sides. Cover dish with a plastic wrap, leaving one corner loose. Set fish aside for the moment.

When potatoes finish cooking, remove and stir in remaining dressing; cover tightly and let potatoes stand until ready to serve.

Prepare the **broccoli spears**. Remove any large leaves from the broccoli bunch. Cut the stalks lengthwise from end to broccoli head to make spears. Cook by steaming over boiling water for about five minutes. When serving, sprinkle with Cheddar cheese.

Microwave **snapper** on MEDIUM until fish flakes when prodded with a fork, about 5-6 minutes. Rotate baking dish halfway through the cooking. Remove dish from microwave and allow it to finish cooking while you serve the meal.

Stir potatoes to coat with dressing. Divide the potatoes and fish between the plates.

We usually serve the **carrots** raw, cutting them lengthwise into halves.

PEPPER STEAK

with Rice, Tossed Salad and Sake

1 lb. round steak
1 medium onion, sliced round
1 green bell pepper, sliced round
1 (6 oz.) can tomato paste
2 teaspoons salt
2 teaspoons black pepper
1 teaspoon Aćcent®

Sake
Converted Rice
Tossed Salad Ingredients:
- **iceberg lettuce**
- **cucumber**
- **radishes**
- **tomato, in wedges**
- **ripe olives**
- **croutons**

Serve warm **sake** as appetizer for this meal.

Brown **steak** on both sides in clean, hot skillet. Pour off fat. Brown onion and add pepper. Add the tomato paste, and a teaspoon of Aćcent® and about 1 ½ cups of water. Simmer, just under the boiling point, until meat is tender, 40 minutes or more.

Meanwhile prepare **rice,** following package directions. At this point you may also prepare a T**ossed Salad.** Wash and dry all vegetables. Tear the lettuce into bite-size pieces. Slice the cucumber and radishes. Cut the tomato into wedges. Toss all together, then add the ripe olives and the croutons.

When steak is done, cut meat into strips. Spoon over cooked rice.

Second week AUGUST

Sunday	*Monday*	*Tuesday*	*Wednesday*	*Thursday*	*Friday*	*Saturday*
Chicken in Dijon Sauce Baked Potatoes, Broccoli	**Quick BBQ Sand-wiches** Ranch Style Beans®, Cole Slaw	**Shrimp Stroganoff** Rice, 3-C Salad	**Pork Chops w/ White Crowns** Cheddar Macaroni, Green Salad	**Macaroni Salad** Fresh Bread, Cheese Assortment	**Fillet of Sole Veronique** Baked Potatoes, Herbed Tomatoes	**Easy Flatboat Chalupas** Rice, Margarita

Fresh Vegetables \ Fruits		*Herbs \ Spices*	*Basics*
mushrooms - 4 parsley bunch potatoes - 8 broccoli - ½ lb. white onions - 3 green bell pepper - 1 cabbage head carrot bundle celery bundle cucumbers - 2 parsley bunch	garlic pod - 1 shallot pod - 1 fresh basil iceberg lettuce - 1 tomatoes - 7 yellow pepper - 1 snow peas - ½ cup green beans - ¼ lb. green onions - 4 zucchini - 1 lemon - 2 seedless grapes 1 C	marjoram dill weed paprika ground cumin dry mustard celery seeds	olive oil ketchup Worcestershire sauce sugar sea salt white vinegar flour peanut oil Marsala red wine vinegar Converted rice Dijon mustard mustard

Entrée Food	*Dairy*	*Miscellaneous*	*Cans \ Jars*
skinless, boneless chicken breasts - 2 raw shrimp - ½ lb butterfly pork chops 2 sole fish fillets - 2 ground chuck - 1 lb. cooked beef slices - ½ lb. **Wine** white wine - 2 C Rum - 6 oz.	sour cream - 1 cup butter - 2 sticks milk ½ cup white cheddar cheese ¼ lb. Parmesan cheese 2 oz. Cheddar cheese 1 cup cheese assortment - 3	walnuts - ¼ cup hamburger buns - 8 macaroni - ½ lb. fusilli pasta - 1 lb. golden raisins - 2 T fresh bread loaf corn tortillas - 12 Bacardi® Margarita Mixer - 1 can chicken bouillon cubes - 2	chicken broth - 2 Ranch style beans - 23 oz. beef broth - 1 sliced mushrooms 4.5 oz. 16 oz refried beans Rotel tomatoes - 1 barbecue sauce 8 oz. diced pimentos 2 oz. olives - 2 oz. ripe olives - 2 oz.

CHICKEN IN DIJON SAUCE

with Baked Potatoes and Broccoli

2 chicken breasts, skinless, boneless
6 Tbsps. olive oil, divided
2 mushrooms, sliced
1 Tbsp. minced shallot
Pepper, to taste
2 Tbsps. fresh parsley, minced
½ cup chicken broth
¼ cup white wine
1 Tbsp. Dijon mustard
Dash marjoram
4 potatoes, for baking
½ lb. broccoli

Bake **potatoes** according to your favorite method. We typically use the microwave to completely bake or to at least partially bake the potatoes. Wash the potatoes and pierce with fork. Place potatoes in the microwave and cook on HIGH for 4 minutes per potato per side, turning once. (3 or 4 potatoes will cook in 24 minutes.)

Pound **chicken** to achieve an even thickness. In a large skillet, over medium-high, heat 2-3 tablespoons olive oil. Add chicken breasts and cook for 6 minutes per side or until golden brown and cooked through. Set aside and keep warm. We use a warmed plate and cover the chicken.

Prepare the **Dijon sauce**. Heat 3 tablespoons of olive oil. Add mushrooms, shallot, pepper and parsley. Sauté for a couple of minutes. Stir in broth and wine, bring to a boil and cook until liquid is reduced by half. Reduce heat to low; stir in mustard until well blended. Lastly, add a dash of marjoram. Place chicken back into sauce and coat well before serving.

Cook **broccoli** using your favorite technique. We like to cook ours in a steamer for a couple of minutes but you can just as easily place the broccoli in a pot with the minimum of water, turn the heat up and cover the pan.

QUICK BBQ SANDWICHES

with Ranch Style Beans® and Cole Slaw

1 (8 oz.) jar Barbecue sauce
½ lb. sliced cooked beef
Hamburger buns

1 can Ranch Style Beans®

Cole slaw (Bottom of Page)

For a fuller meal prepare the **cole slaw** salad described below.

Purchase one of many barbecue sauce brands in whatever flavor suits you.

Heat all sauce ingredients together, bring to boil over medium-high heat. Add the cooked beef and when it begins to boil, stirring constantly, reduce heat. Simmer uncovered, stirring occasionally, 15 minutes.

Meanwhile, heat the **Ranch Style Beans®** and prepare the sandwiches.

COLE SLAW

1 teaspoon salt
¼ teaspoon pepper
½ teaspoon dry mustard
Scant teaspoon celery seeds
½ Tbsp. sugar
¼ cup chopped green bell pepper
1 Tbsp. chopped pimento

1 tsp. grated onion
3 Tbsps. olive oil
¼ cup white vinegar
3 cups julienned cabbage
¼ cup chopped olives

In a salad bowl, mix salt, pepper, dry mustard, celery seeds and ½ tablespoon of sugar. Add chopped bell pepper and pimentos . Add onion, olive oil and white vinegar. Mix well. Cover and refrigerate until ready to serve.

Before serving add the julienned cabbage and the chopped olives.

SHRIMP STROGANOFF

with Rice and 3-C Salad

8 Tbsps. butter
2 mushrooms, sliced
1 Tbsp. onions, chopped
1 clove garlic, minced
2 chicken bouillon cubes
1 Tbsp. flour
¼ cup milk
¼ cup white wine
Dash Worcestershire
Dash ketchup

¼ cup sour cream
1 teaspoon dill weed
½ lb. peeled, raw shrimp

Converted Rice
3-C Salad Ingredients:
carrot
celery
cucumber
red wine vinegar

Cook **rice** according to package directions now.

Fifteen minutes into the rice, make the **3-C salad** by slicing the carrot, celery and cucumber. Place in a serving dish. A red-wine vinegar will do the trick for the topping. Let this salad marinate for about ten minutes before serving.

Begin **shrimp sauce.** Sauté sliced mushrooms in 4 tablespoons of butter. Add onion and garlic; stir until tender. Make chicken broth using two chicken bouillon cubes and water; add flour, milk and wine. Cook until thickened. Add Worcestershire and ketchup. Remove mixture from heat and blend in sour cream and dill weed. Season to taste.

When sauce is made, in separate skillet, cook **shrimp** in balance of butter. Pour shrimp into mixture from above.

To serve, pour mixture over rice.

PORK CHOPS WITH WHITE CROWNS

with Cheddar Macaroni and Green Salad

2 Tbsps. peanut oil
2 butterfly pork chops
1 (10 oz.) can beef broth
1 (4.5 oz.) jar, sliced mushrooms
1 Tbsp. prepared mustard
2 Tbsps. chopped parsley
1 teaspoon paprika
Salt and pepper, to taste

1 onion, sliced
½ cup sour cream
Cheddar Macaroni
(Facing Page==>)
Green Salad Ingredients:
lettuce, cucumber
celery, julienned
parsley

Brown **pork chops** in peanut oil in skillet.

In a small bowl, mix the can of beef broth with the small jar of sliced mushrooms. Add 1 tablespoon of prepared mustard, 2 tablespoons of chopped parsley, and 1 teaspoon of paprika. Add salt and pepper to taste.

Cut half an onion into thin slices and place the circles on each of the pork chops.

Pour beef broth mixture over chops. Simmer for 45 minutes.

While the chops cook, make the **green salad.** Wash, dry and tear the lettuce into bite-size pieces. Slice cucumber thinly, cut the celery stalk into 2-inch lengths, the size of match sticks. Add parsley as a garnish. Place the salad in a large bowl and refrigerate until mealtime.

After the salad is made, prepare **Cheddar macaroni** according to recipe on facing page==>.

After 45 minutes, add sour cream to pork chops and cook for another 10 minutes.

CHEDDAR MACARONI

1 Tbsp. olive oil
Sea salt to taste
2 cups uncooked macaroni
2 Tbsps. butter, melted
¼ lb. white Cheddar cheese
¼ cup milk

Preheat oven to 350° F .

In a large pot heat a generous amount of water to a full boil. You can add olive oil and some salt if you like. Measure and slowly lay in the **macaroni pasta**. Cook till *al dente* according to the package directions. Drain the pasta.

Melt 2 tablespoons of butter; have ready.

Cut thin slices of **cheese** to spread over macaroni.

In a deep baking dish, layer cooked macaroni, cheese slices, portions of the milk, ½ of the butter. Make at least two layers. Sprinkle with salt and pepper.

Bake , covered, until the cheese is melted, about 10-15 minutes.

MACARONI SALAD

with Fresh Bread and Cheese Assortment

1 Tbsp. Dijon-style mustard
¼ cup red-wine vinegar
1 teaspoon garlic, minced
½ teaspoon sugar
½ cup olive oil
Salt and pepper to taste
3 cups fusilli (or other pasta)
3 ripe tomatoes, chopped
½ yellow bell pepper, diced
¼ cup coarsely chopped walnuts
½ cup snow peas, blanched
¼ lb. green beans, blanched
3 green onions, thinly sliced
½ zucchini, ¼ inch dice
¼ cup pitted black olives
½ cup fresh basil, chopped
2 Tbsps. golden raisins
2 Tbsps. Parmesan, grated
Fresh bread
Cheese assortment

Lots of ingredients, we know, but also lots of taste. It's worth it!.

Preheat the oven for baking the **fresh bread**; follow package directions.

Prepare the **dressing** first. In a large bowl, whisk together the Dijon mustard, red-wine vinegar, garlic and sugar. Slowly drizzle in the olive oil, whisking constantly. Season with salt and pepper and set on dinner table for at *least one hour*.

While the dressing marinates, prepare other ingredients. Chop, slice and blanch vegetables as instructed on the ingredient list.

Twenty minutes before serving, blanch the **snow peas** and **green beans** together.

Cut the **various cheeses** into a variety of shapes.

Bring to boil a large pot of salted water. Cook **fusilli pasta** until just tender (*al dente*). Drain, rinse with cold water, drain again. Place in bowl and toss with ¾ of dressing made above. Add tomatoes, yellow pepper and walnuts. Add snow peas, green beans, green onions, zucchini, black olives and the basil leaves. Toss together and adjust seasoning. Add raisins when you serve.

Toss pasta and other ingredients again and set aside. Top with Parmesan cheese.

FILLET OF SOLE VERONIQUE

with Baked Potatoes and Herbed Tomatoes

1 Tbsp. olive oil, or butter
2 Tbsps. minced green onions
1 clove garlic, minced
1 cup dry white wine
1 teaspoon fresh lemon juice
1 or 2 fish fillet of sole
Salt and pepper, to taste
½ tsp. grated lemon peel

2 tomatoes
1 clove garlic, minced
Fresh-ground pepper, to taste
Marsala wine vinegar

4 potatoes, for baking
1 cup seedless grapes
1 lemon, sliced for garnish
Sprig of fresh herb

For the **Herbed Tomatoes** slice the tomatoes into ¼ inch slices. Sprinkle minced garlic on top as well as fresh ground black pepper. Pour some Marsala wine vinegar over the slices. Place in refrigerator to marinate.

Prepare **baked potatoes** by micro waving on HIGH for 4 minutes per side, turning once. (3 or 4 potatoes will cook in 24 minutes.) If using conventional oven, preheat to 350° F and cover with aluminum foil. Bake for about an hour and a half.

For the **fish:** prepare all ingredients first. Heat olive oil or butter in a 10 to 12-inch frying pan over medium-high heat. Add minced green onions and garlic; stir about 30 seconds. Pour in wine and lemon juice. Add fillets and spoon liquid over fillets. Sprinkle fish with salt, pepper and lemon peels then green onion slices. Cover and simmer until fish is done, about 5 to 7 minutes. Transfer fish to a platter to keep warm.

Place grapes in liquid and simmer 2 to 3 minutes. Remove grapes and spoon over fish. Increase heat to high and boil liquid until reduced to 2 to 3 tablespoons. Pour sauce over fish and grapes. Garnish with a lemon slice and a sprig of fresh herb.

EASY FLATBOAT CHALUPAS

with Rice and Margarita

1 lb. ground chuck
½ teaspoon ground cummin
2 tsps. sea salt
½ teaspoon pepper
1 (10 oz.) can Rotel tomatoes
1 (16 oz.) can refried beans
1 package (12) corn tortillas
¼ cup peanut oil

1 onion, chopped
¼ head of lettuce, shredded
2 large tomatoes, diced
1 cup grated Cheddar cheese

Converted Rice
Barcardi® Margarita Mixer
Rum

Chalupas are Mexico City's antojitos, hence their oval, canoe shape.

Brown **ground chuck** in peanut oil in heavy skillet until meat turns brown. Drain any excess fat. Add cumin, salt and pepper to taste. Add Rotel tomatoes and continue to cook the meat while you proceed as follows:

While meat browns, prepare **rice** following package directions.

Before rice is done, heat **refried beans** in a separate pan.
Heat **corn tortillas** in the microwave for 30 seconds or until thoroughly warmed. We wrap the tortillas in a dampened towel.

Spread hot beans on each tortilla. Spread meat over the beans then add chopped onion, shredded lettuce and diced tomatoes to suit the guests. For spice, add more Rotel tomatoes and sprinkle generously with Cheddar cheese.

If you would like a **margarita** with this meal, we suggest you try the Barcardi® Mixer of margarita. Simply follow directions on the frozen can for a perfect margarita.

Third week AUGUST

Sunday	*Monday*	*Tuesday*	*Wednesday*	*Thursday*	*Friday*	*Saturday*
Grilled Sherry Chicken New Potatoes, Roasted Carrots	**The Original Hash** French Bread Red Wine. Italian Salad	**Seafood Caesar Salad** Rice Garlic Loaves	**Pork Tenderloin** Mashed Potatoes Steamed Spinach	*Plan Ahead* **Marinated Beef and Noodles** Garlic Bread And Salad	**Triple Stuffed Baked Potatoes** Shrimp, Apple Wedges, Carrots	**Braised Beef Roast** Mashed Potatoes, Carrots, Tomato Wedges

Fresh Vegetables \ Fruits		*Herbs \ Spices*	*Basics*
new potatoes - 6 carrots - 2 bunches white onion - 1 yellow onions - 2 iceberg lettuce - 2 red tip lettuce - 1 red cabbage head lemons - 2 apples - 2	garlic pod - 1 potatoes - 10 fresh spinach - 1 bag tomatoes - 5 parsley - bunch cucumber - 1 celery bunch green onions - 6	paprika ground cumin red pepper sauce dried thyme dry dill weed	sugar white vinegar peanut oil olive oil flour mayonnaise vegetable oil Converted Rice

Entrée Food	*Dairy*	*Miscellaneous*	*Cans \ Jars*
boneless chicken breasts -2 ground steak - 1 lb scallops - ¼ lb. pork tenderloin - 1 lean beef round 1 lb small cooked shrimp - ½ lb beef rib eye - 2 lb **Frozen** chopped broccoli pkg	Parmesan cheese ¼ C milk - 1 C margarine - 1 stick sour cream - ½ cup Cheddar cheese ½ C low fat yogurt - ½ C **Wine/Beer** beer - 1 dry sherry wine ½ C Chianti wine bottle	charcoal briquets - bag spaghetti - 1 C croutons - pkg. French bread loaf garlic bread loaves tomato juice - ½ C egg noodles - ½ pkg	whole tomatoes - 1 black olives - 4 oz salad pepper - 4 oz vlasic® Pepperoncini boneless, skinless salmon - 1 can tomato juice - 4 oz. beef bouillon cubes - 5

Grocery List

Grocery List

GRILLED SHERRY CHICKEN

with New Potatoes and Roasted Carrots

2 boneless chicken breasts, with skin
2 teaspoons paprika
2 teaspoons ground cumin
2 teaspoons sugar
2 teaspoons white vinegar
1 clove garlic, minced
½ cup dry sherry wine
Salt and pepper, to taste

1 bag charcoal briquets

6 new potatoes

¼ bunch of carrots

To prepare **chicken** for grilling, pound the chicken to achieve an even thickness.

In a shallow dish, large enough to hold the chicken pieces, mix together all of the ingredients on the left side. Add chicken to this mixture and allow to marinate in refrigerator for about an hour, or for the time it takes to prepare the outdoor grill.

When you light the grill, prepare the **new potatoes** by boiling them in water for about 30 minutes.

After coals are white hot, place the chicken on the grill and use the marinade for basting several times during cooking.

As for the **carrots**, we like to put them on the grill with the chicken, so that they can be served together.

Serve the new potatoes in halves.

THE ORIGINAL HASH

with French Bread, Italian Salad and Red Wine

1 small onion, chopped
3 Tbsps. peanut oil
1 clove garlic, crushed
1 lb. ground steak
1 (14 oz.) can whole tomatoes
1 teaspoon salt
½ teaspoon pepper
1 cup uncooked spaghetti

Italian Salad Ingredients:
iceberg, red tip lettuce
tomato wedges
red cabbage, julienned
pitted black olives
carrots, shredded
salad pepper
croutons (opt.)
French bread
Red wine, Chianti

Preheat oven to 400° F for the **fresh French bread**.

For the **hash:** in a large skillet, cook onions in peanut oil until they become clear. Add crushed garlic. Add meat and cook until meat is light brown. Add ½ cup water. Add tomatoes with liquid, salt and pepper and simmer for one hour.

While the hash simmers, cook the bread following package directions.

Meanwhile, prepare the **Italian salad.** Tear lettuces into bite-size pieces. Cut tomato into wedges in desired thickness. Cut red cabbage into julienne strips. Add a few ripe olives. Shred the carrot on top. Toss well. Add a salad pepper to top and spread croutons around.

Minutes before serving, prepare **spaghetti** according to package directions.

A good **red wine**, such as a Chianti, will elevate this meal.

SEAFOOD CAESAR SALAD

with Rice and Garlic Bread Loaves

Caesar Dressing Ingredients:

- **1 can salmon, boneless and skinless**
- **1 clove garlic, peeled and minced**
- **2 Tbsps. olive oil**
- **1 lemon, juiced**
- **¼ teaspoon freshly-ground black pepper**
- **¼ cup grated Parmesan cheese**

¼ pound scallops
2 teaspoons olive oil
1 head red tip lettuce

Converted Rice
Garlic bread loaves

Cook **rice** according to package directions.

While rice cooks, prepare the **garlic bread loaves**. If using fresh loaves follow package directions for baking.

Meanwhile, wash lettuce, pat dry and remove damaged leaves. Tear leaves into bite-size pieces or slice crosswise into ½ inch-wide strips. Put lettuce into a large bowl.

Make Caesar dressing. Mince **salmon** and garlic. Combine with oil, lemon juice and pepper. Mix well. Pour dressing over lettuce and toss to coat evenly. Sprinkle generous amount of cheese over salad.

Scallops should be about ½-inch round. Slice to make them this size if needed. Heat a small frying pan or wok over high heat. Add 2 teaspoons olive oil and swirl to coat pan. Add scallops and cook, stirring occasionally, until scallops are opaque in middle, about 1 minute. Spoon on top of salad.

PORK TENDERLOINS

with Mashed Potatoes and Steamed Spinach

1 pork tenderloin, cut into ½ inch pieces
½ cup milk
½ cup sour cream
½ cup tomato juice
Dash Tabasco® sauce

3 potatoes
½ stick margarine
¼ cup milk
½ lb. fresh spinach
½ cup vinegar
Tomato Wedge Salad:
½ head lettuce
1 tomato

Have the butcher cut the pork tenderloins into ½ inch thickness.

Cook **pork tenderloin** in olive oil over medium-hot skillet until browned on both sides. Add milk, sour cream, tomato juice and Tabasco® sauce. Cover and simmer 30 minutes.

Meanwhile prepare **mashed potatoes**. Skin and cut potatoes into small pieces. Add to salted water and bring to a boil. Boil the potatoes for about 20 minutes; remove from heat and drain. Add ½ stick margarine and ¼ cup milk and whip to texture you desire.

At the same time that the potatoes are cooking, prepare the **spinach** in a steamer for just a couple of minutes. If using fresh spinach, soak it in a tub of water with ½ cup of vinegar, then rinse thoroughly.

Also, at the same time, prepare the **tomato wedge salad**. Cut lettuce head in half and then into quarters. Add thick slice of tomato to each wedge. Drizzle with your choice of dressing.

Overnight - Plan ahead

MARINATED BEEF AND NOODLES

with Garlic Bread and Green Salad

4 Tbsps. olive oil
2 yellow onions, peeled and thickly sliced
½ Tbsp. sugar
½ cup all-purpose flour
1 teaspoon black pepper
½ teaspoon salt
1 Tbsp. dried thyme
1 lb. lean beef round cut into 1 inch cubes
1 can or bottled beer
2 beef bouillon cubes
½ cup water

2 carrots, in 2" rounds

Green Salad Ingredients:
iceberg lettuce
red tip lettuce
cucumber
celery, julienned
parsley

½ pkg. egg noodles, cooked

¼ cup chopped parsley
1 garlic bread loaf

The night before, prepare the beef stew. Heat 2 tablespoons oil in skillet. Add onions; lightly brown over low-heat, about 15 minutes, stirring occasionally. Sprinkle with sugar; cook 3 minutes to caramelize. Remove to an oven-proof casserole bowl.

On wax paper, mix flour, pepper, salt and ½ tablespoon thyme. Dredge **beef** in mixture. Heat 2 tablespoons oil in skillet and brown beef on all sides over medium-high heat; pour off remaining oil.

Add beer, bouillon and water to skillet. Cook over medium heat, scraping up any brown bits. Return beef and onions to skillet; add carrots and remaining thyme. Bring to a boil. Remove from heat. Pour back into oven-proof casserole. Let cool and *refrigerate overnight.*

When ready for the meal, preheat oven to 350° F. Place the beef, covered, in oven to bake for 1 hour.

Make the **green salad** next. Wash, dry and tear the lettuces into bite-size pieces. Slice cucumber thinly, julienne the celery stalk into 2-inch lengths, the size of match sticks. Add parsley as a garnish.

After an hour, uncover beef and bake another 15 minutes. Cook noodles during this time. When beef is done, stir in parsley. Serve over the hot noodles. Serve the bread.

TRIPLE-STUFFED BAKED POTATOES

with Shrimp, Apple Wedges and Carrot Sticks

4 large potatoes
½ lb. tiny cooked and peeled shrimp
½ (10 oz.) package frozen chopped broccoli, thawed
½ cup shredded Cheddar cheese
½ cup plain low-fat yogurt
¼ cup mayonnaise
¼ cup chopped green onions
1 teaspoon dry dill weed
Salt and pepper, to taste
Apple wedges
Carrot sticks

Wash **potatoes** and prick with a fork to allow steam to escape while they are cooking. Microwave for 10 minutes on HIGH (100%). Turn potatoes over and microwave for another 10 minutes or until tender, but still slightly firm in center when pierced with a fork. Remove potatoes from the microwave and wrap in foil and let stand until very tender in center, about 10 minutes.

While the potatoes stand, rinse the cooked **shrimp** and pat dry. Run frozen broccoli under running water to thaw; break apart and drain well. In a bowl, combine shrimp, broccoli, cheese, yogurt, mayonnaise, onion and dill.

Unwrap potatoes and cut in half lengthwise. Scoop potato meat from skin, leaving about ¼ inch all around. Add potato meat to shrimp mixture and stir well. Add salt and pepper to taste. Spoon the mixture into potato shells. Any stuffing left over can be placed on the side of the potatoes. Set stuffed potatoes on a plate and microwave on HIGH (100%) until heated thoroughly, about 3 minutes.

While the potatoes reheat, prepare the **apple wedges** and the **carrot sticks**. Cut the apple into wedges; steam the carrot sticks.

BRAISED BEEF ROAST

with Mashed Potatoes, Carrots and Tomato Wedges

2 lb. beef rib eye, roast or top round
1 Tbsp. vegetable oil
1 Tbsp. cracked pepper
2 cups water
3 beef bouillon cubes

3 potatoes
½ stick margarine
¼ cup milk
Carrots
½ cup cold water
¼ cup all-purpose flour
2 tomatoes

Cook **beef roast** in peanut oil in large, covered saucepan over medium to low heat until brown; sprinkle with cracked pepper. Add 2 cups of water and the bouillon cubes. Heat to boiling; reduce heat. Cover; simmer on stove top until tender, about 1 ½ hours.

Before the beef is done, prepare the **mashed potatoes** following your favorite method. Simply skin and cut potatoes into small pieces, add to salted water and let cook for about twenty minutes. Remove and strain. Add margarine, milk and beat to the texture you desire.

Dice the **carrots** and steam. Mix into the potatoes; or simply slice raw carrots into sticks if you do not like to mix the vegetables.

Remove beef to warm platter and make gravy. Reserve 1 ½ cups of drippings in the saucepan. Remove excess fat. In a small bowl, thoroughly mix ½ cup of cold water and the flour. Slowly stir this mixture into the reserved liquid. While stirring, heat to boiling and cook 1 minute.

When serving, cut **tomatoes** into wedges as garnish.

Fourth week AUGUST

Sunday	*Monday*	*Tuesday*	*Wednesday*	*Thursday*	*Friday*	*Saturday*
Plan Ahead **South-western Cookout** Potato Salad, Green Beans	**Baked Meat Loaf** Rice Tossed Salad, Corn	**Quick Fish and Pasta** Italian Bread Green Salad	**Pork Chop Chutney** Corn, Celery Salad	**Grilled Chicken Caesar Salad**	**Spiced Orange Roughy** Baked Potato, Tossed Salad	*Plan Ahead* **Shish Kabob** Rice

Fresh Vegetables \ Fruits		*Herbs \ Spices*	*Basics*
white onions - 4 lemons - 5 green beans - 1 lb. red potatoes - 6 baking potatoes - 4 celery - bunch green onions - 3 tomatoes - 8 iceberg lettuce- 2 green leaf lettuce - 1 green bell pepper -1	garlic pod - 1 fresh ginger radishes - bunch corn - 4 ears parsley - bunch romaine lettuce - 1 lime - 1 cucumber - 2 cherry tomatoes 12-20	dry mustard paprika cayenne pepper ground allspice dried chives dried marjoram red pepper flakes oregano	ketchup mayonnaise sugar mustard olive oil sea salt white wine vinegar peanut oil extra-virgin olive oil Worcestershire sauce Converted Rice

Entrée Food	*Dairy*	*Miscellaneous*	*Cans \ Jars*
chicken breasts - 2 skinless, boneless chicken breasts -2 ground chuck - 1 lb cod fillets 2-4 pork chops - 4 orange roughy fillets - 2 sirloin steak 2-3 lb **Frozen** corn - pkg	eggs - 5 Parmesan cheese ¼ C bacon- 3 slices butter - 1 stick **Wine/Beer** red wine - bottle white wine - ½ cup beer (1)	dark molasses - 1 T charcoal briquets pkg bread crumbs 1 C croutons - pkg. spaghetti - ½ lb Italian bread loaf golden raisins ¼ C	tomato sauce - 1 stuffed olives - 4 oz ripe black olives 8 oz. spaghetti sauce- 14 oz capers - 2 oz.

SOUTHWESTERN COOKOUT

with Potato Salad and Green Beans

2 whole chicken breasts, with skin
1 bottle beer
1 Tbsp. dark molasses
2 Tbsps. onion, minced
2 Tbsps. lemon juice
½ cup ketchup
1 clove garlic, pressed
¼ teaspoon dry mustard
Salt, to taste
Charcoal briquets
1 lb. green beans
1 slice bacon, uncooked
Potato Salad
(Facing Page===>)

The day before this meal, make the **potato salad** using the instructions on the facing page===>.

Prepare the **chicken marinade** first. Select a bowl large enough to hold the chicken pieces or two bowls if needed. Combine beer, molasses, minced onions, lemon juice, ketchup, garlic, dry mustard and salt. Add chicken, cover and refrigerate in marinade *for about 2 hours.*

An hour before eating, prepare outdoor grill. *If weather is bad, opt for the oven broiler. You'll lose a bit of the grill taste but the meal can take it.*

Grill chicken 5 to 6 inches above medium-hot coals about 30 minutes or until cooked through. Remember to turn and baste with marinade every 10-15 minutes.

Meanwhile, prepare the **green beans** by the boiling method. Cut ends off beans and cut in half or leave long. Barely cover them with water and add one slice of bacon; sprinkle with salt. Cook until they are tender, 20 minutes for *al dente.*

POTATO SALAD

6 medium size red potatoes
2 bacon strips
¾ cup chopped white onions
1 cup chopped celery
1 tsp. salt
1 tsp. pepper
Sprinkle of sugar
1 Tbsp. mustard
¼ cup mayonnaise
2 eggs, hard-boiled
Paprika

Boil potatoes for 30 minutes. Set aside to cool, then peel and cube to desired size.

Fry bacon in frying pan until crisp. Save the grease.

Sauté the white onions in the bacon grease.

Mix celery, onions, salt, pepper, sugar and potatoes.

Add mustard and mayonnaise and mix again.

For topping, slice hard-boiled eggs and sprinkle with paprika.

BAKED MEAT LOAF

with Rice, Tossed Salad and Corn

1 lb. ground chuck or lean ground beef
1 (8 oz.) can tomato sauce
6 pimiento-stuffed olives, sliced
½ cup chopped onion
1 cup bread crumbs
1 egg, beaten
1 teaspoon salt
¼ teaspoon pepper
1 tomato, sliced

Tossed Salad Ingredients:
iceberg lettuce
cucumber
radishes
tomato
ripe olives
croutons
4 ears of corn

Converted Rice

Preheat oven to 350° F.

In a large bowl, mix **beef**, ½ of tomato sauce, sliced olives, onion, bread crumbs, egg and seasoning. Shape into a loaf and place in a baking dish. Cover with remaining tomato sauce. Top with slices of the tomato. Bake 1 hour.

After thirty minutes, prepare the **rice** following package directions for servings and time.

If having a **tossed salad**, prepare it now while everything is cooking. Wash and dry all vegetables. Tear the lettuce into bite-size pieces. Slice the cucumber and radishes. Cut the tomatoes into wedges. Toss all together, then add the ripe olives and the croutons.

Prepare the **corn**. In boiling water, let corn cook for ten minutes. Remove and cover with margarine.

When meat loaf is done, cut the meat loaf into slices to serve.

QUICK FISH AND PASTA

with Italian Bread and Green Salad

2-4 cod fillets
½ lb. spaghetti
10-12 capers
12-20 ripe black olives
1 (14 oz.) jar spaghetti sauce
Dash cayenne pepper
Olive oil
Sea salt, to taste

Green Salad Ingredients:
iceberg lettuce
green leaf lettuce
cucumber
celery, julienned
parsley

Italian bread

Preheat oven to temperature needed for the **Italian bread,** if you would like it heated.

Make the **green salad** first. Wash, dry and tear the lettuces into bite-size pieces. Slice cucumber thinly, cut the celery stalk into 2-inch lengths, the size of match sticks. Add parsley as a garnish. Place the salad in a large bowl and refrigerate until mealtime.

Place Italian bread in the oven to heat.

For the **pasta:** boil a large amount of water. Add 1 tablespoon of olive oil and sea salt to taste When water is fully boiling, lay in the spaghetti and cook until *al dente*, according to package directions.

When you add the spaghetti above, rinse the **fish** and pat dry; cut into ½ inch cubes. Drain and chop capers and coarsely chop olives. While pasta cooks, combine spaghetti sauce, capers, black olives and cayenne pepper in a saucepan. Cover and bring to a boil, over medium-high heat. Reduce to a simmer and stir in fish cubes. Simmer and stir gently until fish flakes when prodded with a fork, about 3-4 minutes.

Drain pasta. Pour caper sauce over the pasta. Don't forget the green salad!

PORK CHOP CHUTNEY

with Corn and Celery Salad

2 tomatoes, chopped
¼ cup golden raisins
1 Tbsp. small capers, minced
1 teaspoon garlic, minced
1 teaspoon ground ginger
Dash sugar
¼ cup white wine vinegar
Pinch of ground allspice

1 Tbsp. peanut oil
4 pork chops

Frozen corn

Celery Salad Ingredients:
- **iceberg lettuce**
- **celery, julienned**
- **cucumber**

To braise the **pork chops**, simply brown them in a medium-hot skillet with peanut oil for a couple of minutes. Add a minimum of water and cover. Allow the pork to simmer for 30 minutes, turning once. With this method of cooking, you will have to pay close attention to the chops. Add water as needed.

While watching the chops, make the **celery salad.** Wash the outer layer of the lettuce. If outer layer is damaged, remove it. Shred the lettuce using a grater or by thinly slicing it. Do the shredding over the salad plate. Next, cut the celery stalk into 2-inch lengths, the size of match sticks. Toss over the lettuce. Slice cucumber thickly then quarter. Scatter about the lettuce.

For the **tomato chutney sauce,** combine the tomatoes, raisins, capers, garlic, ginger, sugar, vinegar and allspice in a microwave-safe casserole bowl. Cook in microwave on full power, uncovered for 6 minutes; stir. Cook an additional 8 minutes or until mixture thickens. Allow to cool.

While the sauce cools, prepare the **frozen corn** according to package directions.
Serve the tomato chutney over the pork chops.

GRILLED CHICKEN CAESAR SALAD

a One-dish Meal

Baked croutons
1 clove garlic, cut into halves
2 boneless, skinless chicken breasts
1 stick butter
1 teaspoon Worcestershire sauce
½ teaspoon dry mustard
Freshly ground pepper
1 large bunch romaine lettuce torn into bite-size pieces
1 lemon, cut into halves
¼ cup grated Parmesan cheese
2 tomatoes, cut into wedges
Ripe olives
2 hard-cooked eggs, sliced

We usually purchase the **croutons** for this meal but you can also bake your own. Cut the crust from bread slices. Cube the bread; dip into melted butter and sprinkle with an herb, such as parsley. Toast in an 350° F oven for about 10 minutes.

Grill the **chicken breast.** Pound the chicken breasts to an even thickness. Brush margarine or extra-virgin olive oil over the chicken. Place chicken under the broiler and cook about 5 minutes each side or until done. Remove the chicken and when it cools, cut it into chunks or thinly julienne the pieces.

Mix together in a large bowl, the Worcestershire sauce, dry mustard, ground pepper, romaine lettuce, lemon, Parmesan cheese, tomato wedges and ripe olives. Toss well and add the chicken pieces. Top the salad with slices of egg.

SPICED ORANGE ROUGHY

with Baked Potato and Tossed Salad

Olive oil
1 clove garlic, minced
½ Tbsp. chives
½ Tbsp. marjoram
½ cup white wine
1 lemon, squeezed
2 orange roughy, cod or sole fish fillets
2 green onions, sliced
1 lime, peeled

4 potatoes, for baking

Tossed Salad Ingredients:
iceberg lettuce
green leaf lettuce
cucumber
radishes
tomato
ripe olives
croutons

Begin by preparing the **tossed salad**. Wash and dry all vegetables. Tear the lettuces into bite-size pieces. Slice the cucumber and radishes. Cut the tomatoes into wedges. Toss all together, then add the ripe olives and the croutons. Refrigerate until served.

Bake **potatoes** according to your favorite method. We typically use the microwave to completely bake or to at least partially bake the potatoes. Wash the potatoes and pierce with fork. Place potatoes in the microwave and cook on HIGH for 4 minutes per potato per side, turning once. (3 or 4 potatoes will cook in 24 minutes.)

The **orange roughy** is cooked by the pan-poaching technique. In a skillet, large enough to contain the fish, heat the olive oil and sauté the garlic and fresh herbs for about a minute or two. Add the wine and the lemon juice. Add the fish and coat with the liquid. Add the green onions and the peelings from the lime. Cover and poach for about 7 minutes or until the fish flakes under pressure when prodded with a fork.

Garnish with slices from the peeled lime.

Overnight - Plan ahead

SHISH KABOB

with Rice

1 cup olive oil
2-3 cups red wine
1 clove garlic, minced
1 onion, sliced
Sea salt and pepper to taste
1 lemon, juiced
Dash red pepper flakes
Dash of oregano
2-3 lb. sirloin steak, cut into 1-inch cubes
Green bell pepper
Onion, in wedges
12-20 cherry tomatoes
Converted Rice

The **sirloin** used in this menu needs to be marinated for several hours or overnight. Place sirloin in shallow, covered baking dish. Combine oil, wine, garlic, onion slices, sea salt, pepper, juice from one lemon, red pepper flakes and oregano. Pour mixture over sirloin.

Cover and refrigerate *4-5 hours or overnight.*

If cooking outside, prepare the grill with coals. If broiling in oven, preheat the broiler.

Thread sirloin cubes, green pepper, onion and cherry tomatoes on each skewer.

Grill to desired doneness.

While the kabob cooks, prepare **rice** according to package directions.

Fifth week AUGUST

Sunday	*Monday*	*Tuesday*	*Wednesday*	*Thursday*	*Friday*	*Saturday*
Italian Fried Chicken Mashed Potatoes, Italian Salad, Green Peas	**Poor Boy Sand-wiches** Soup and Salad	**Broiled Fish in Caper Sauce** Broccoli, New Potatoes	**Pork Cutlets w/ Cheese Sauce** Rice, Spinach	**Oven Roasted Italian Vegetables** Pasta, French Bread, Red Wine	**Grilled Salmon in Vinaigrette** Baked Potatoes, Grilled Vegetables	**Mushroom Steak** Mashed Potatoes, Broccoli

Fresh Vegetables \ Fruits		*Herbs \ Spices*	*Basics*
potatoes - 10 iceberg lettuce - 2 red leaf lettuce - 1 tomatoes - 6 red cabbage head red onion - 1 cucumber - 2 radishes-bunch zucchini - 2 eggplant - 1 green onions - 3	white onion - 3 carrots - bundle celery - bundle green beans - ½ lb. new potatoes - 4 broccoli - 1 lb. parsley-bunch lemon - 1 red bell peppers - 3 green bell pepper - 1	paprika white pepper cayenne pepper onion powder minced onions	vegetable oil extra-virgin olive oil flour olive oil red wine vinegar mayonnaise peanut oil Converted rice

Entrée Food	*Dairy*	*Miscellaneous*	*Cans \ Jars*
skinless, boneless chicken breasts - 2 ham slices - 2 orange roughy fillets 2-3 butterfly pork chops - 2 salmon fillet - 1 top round steak - 1 ½ lb **Frozen** green peas - pkg spinach - pkg	Swiss cheese slices 2 Cheddar cheese slices - 2 Cheddar cheese - 1 C Parmesan cheese 1½ C butter - ½ cup. egg - 1 milk 2 cups margarine - 1 stick **Wine** dry sherry - ½ cup white wine - 1 cup red wine - 1 bottle	Italian bread crumbs ½ cup wheat bread loaf bread crumbs ½ C potato chips - pkg. dill pickles - 1 oz. corkscrew pasta 2 C kidney beans ½ C fettucine pasta 1 lb. French bread pkg. croutons - pkg	ripe olives - 4 oz. salad pepper vlasic® Pepperoncini - 4 oz. stewed tomatoes - 1 chicken broth - 2 capers - 1 oz. tomato sauce - 1 cream of mushroom soup - 1 sliced mushrooms 4 oz instant beef bouillon - 2 T

ITALIAN FRIED CHICKEN

with Mashed Potatoes, Green Peas and Italian Salad

3 cups vegetable oil
2 chicken breasts, boneless, skinless
½ cup Italian bread crumbs
Salt and pepper, to taste

3 potatoes
½ stick margarine
¼ cup milk

Italian Salad Ingredients:
iceberg lettuce
red leaf lettuce
tomato in wedges
red cabbage, julienned
ripe olives
carrot, shredded
salad pepper
1 (10 oz.) pkg. frozen green peas

Make the **Italian salad** as a first course. Tear the lettuces into bite-size pieces. Cut the tomato into wedges of desired thickness. Cut red cabbage into julienne strips. Add a few ripe olives. Shred the carrot on top. Toss well. Add a salad pepper to top.

Next prepare the **chicken.** Pound the chicken lightly. Mix Italian bread crumbs, salt and pepper. Cut the chicken breasts in half. Dredge the chicken pieces through the bread crumbs, coating well. Set aside.

Make **mashed potatoes**. Wash and peel potatoes and cut into halves then quarter into smaller pieces. Heat a pot of water and add in the potato pieces. Salt the water to your taste. Cook for approximately 20 minutes; drain. Into hot potatoes place ½ stick margarine, ¼ cup milk and whip to desired smoothness.

In skillet over medium heat, cook chicken in hot oil 10 minutes, turning once.

While the chicken cooks, prepare the frozen **green peas** according to package directions.

POOR BOY SANDWICHES

with Soup and Salad

Wheat bread
Mayonnaise
2 slices each of:
Swiss cheese
Cheddar cheese
Ham
Lettuce
Red onion
1 tomato, chopped
Potato chips
Dill pickle

Minestrone soup
(Facing Page ----->)
or any canned soup

Tossed Salad Ingredients:
iceberg lettuce
cucumber
radishes
ripe olives

Prepare the **tossed salad**. Wash and dry all vegetables. Tear the lettuce into bite-size pieces. Slice the cucumber and radishes. Toss all together, then add the ripe olives.

Make four **Poor Boy sandwiches**. Coat wheat bread with mayonnaise. Slice cheeses and ham into thin strips; mix together. Lay meats and cheese on wheat slices. Top with shredded lettuce and red onion. Add chopped tomato. Garnish with potato chips and a pickle.

For a delightful **soup** you can try the minestrone on the facing page; otherwise, try any favorite.

MINESTRONE SOUP

2 cups corkscrew pasta
3 cups chicken broth
½ cup dry sherry
1 teaspoon salt, to taste
⅛ teaspoon ground pepper
½ cup onions, sliced
1 cup carrots, julienned
1 cup celery, julienned
1 cup fresh or frozen green beans
1 can stewed tomatoes
½ cup cooked kidney beans
½ cup grated Parmesan cheese

Cook corkscrew-shaped pasta (fusilli) according to package directions; drain, rinse under cold water and set aside.

In a large saucepan over medium-high heat, bring broth and sherry to a boil. Season with salt and pepper.

Cut ½ of onion into thin slices, then halve the slices and separate the half-rings. Cut the carrots and celery in small julienned strips. Add onion, celery and carrots to the broth above.

Stir in green beans and heat **soup** to boiling. Pour the liquid from the stewed tomatoes into the broth; chop the tomatoes roughly and add to broth. Add kidney beans and pasta; simmer 1 minute longer or until vegetables are as tender as you like.

Add ½ cup grated Parmesan cheese just before serving.

BROILED FISH IN CAPER SAUCE

with Broccoli and New Potatoes

2-3 orange roughy fillets
Salt and pepper
White wine

4 new potatoes
½ lb. broccoli florets

Caper Sauce Ingredients:
¼ cup butter
2 Tbsps. extra-virgin olive oil
2 Tbsps. chopped parsley
1 lemon, juiced
2 Tbsps. capers

Prepare **boiled new potatoes**. Place whole potatoes in boiling water and let cook for about 15 minutes or until done.

While the new potatoes cook, prepare the **caper sauce.** In a small saucepan, melt the butter. Add extra-virgin olive oil, chopped parsley and the juice from one lemon. Add 2 tablespoons of capers. Set aside until the fish is about done, then heat slowly.

Rinse **fish** and pat dry. Place fish on a baking sheet lined with foil for easy cleanup; sprinkle fish with salt and pepper. You may add a few drops of wine to keep the fish moist. Broil under low heat 4 to 5 inches from heat source for 6 to 8 minutes until top is lightly browned and flakes in middle when prodded with a fork.

To microwave fish, cook on HIGH/FULL POWER for 2 minutes then let rest 2 minutes before cooking again on HIGH for 3 to 5 minutes.

While fish cooks, prepare the **broccoli**. Place broccoli in a steamer basket over boiling water. If you have no steamer, lay the broccoli in a pot with a minimum of water. Steam the broccoli for a couple of minutes.

When fish is done, pour warmed caper sauce over fish and serve.

PORK CUTLETS WITH CHEESE SAUCE

with Rice and Spinach

2 butterfly pork chops
Salt and pepper, to taste
1 egg
½ cup bread crumbs
2 Tbsps. peanut oil

Converted Rice
1 (10 oz.) pkg. frozen spinach

Cheese Sauce Ingredients:
2 Tbsps. butter
2 Tbsps. flour
1 cup milk
Paprika
2 dashes cayenne pepper
1 cup grated Cheddar cheese

1 (8 oz.) can tomato sauce
1 tomato, cut into wedges

Pound the **pork chops** to make them thinner. Cut into halves. Season with salt and pepper. In a small bowl, beat egg. On wax paper, spread the bread crumbs. Dip pork into egg, then dredge through the crumbs.

Heat peanut oil in a heavy skillet till medium-hot. Lay in the coated chops and cook until they become golden brown on both sides. This should take about 4 minutes per side. Reduce heat, add small amount of water. Cover tightly and braise until tender, about 30 minutes. Watch this closely unless you have a pressure cooker because the water will steam away quickly. Add water as needed.

While pork cooks, prepare the **rice** according to package directions. Minutes before the pork is done, prepare the frozen **spinach** by following package directions.

When pork is done, remove steaks and set aside. In the same pan, make **cheese sauce**. Melt butter over low heat. Stir in flour until well blended. Cook over low heat until mixture is smooth and bubbly. Remove from heat and gradually stir in the cup of milk, paprika and the cayenne pepper. Bring to boil and stir constantly for 1 minute. Stir in grated Cheddar. Pour in the tomato sauce and heat.

Place pork cutlets over the sauce. Heat thoroughly.

Serve with rice and spinach on opposite sides of the meat. Garnish with tomato wedges.

OVEN ROASTED ITALIAN VEGETABLES

with Pasta, French Bread, and Red Wine

2 zucchini, cut into thick slices
1 eggplant, thinly sliced
2 onions, cut into wedges
2 red bell peppers, julienned
4 Tbsps. extra-virgin olive oil

1 lb. linguine or fettucine pasta
French bread

Tossed Salad Ingredients:
iceberg lettuce
red leaf lettuce
cucumber
radishes
tomato
ripe olives
croutons
Red wine, Valpolicella

Preheat the oven to 425° F.

Begin this light meal with a **tossed salad.** Wash and dry all vegetables. Tear the lettuces into bite-size pieces. Slice the cucumber and radishes. Cut the tomato into wedges. Toss all together, then add the ripe olives and the croutons. You can refrigerate the salad while you wait for the vegetables or serve the salad as a first course.

When oven is heated, put in the **French bread,** if you are making fresh bread. Follow package directions.

While the bread cooks, prepare the **vegetables:** zucchini, eggplant, onion, red peppers, chopping or slicing them as indicated. In a shallow baking dish, place all vegetables. Coat with olive oil and roast in oven until they are to your liking. We let this meal cook for about 15 minutes. Watch and decide for yourselves.

Two or three minutes before the vegetables are ready, fix the **pasta** according to package directions.

We serve a **red wine** like a Valpolicella with this meal.

GRILLED SALMON IN VINAIGRETTE

with Baked Potatoes and Grilled Vegetables

¼ cup olive oil
¼ cup red wine vinegar
Black pepper to taste
2 Tbsps. green onions
1 salmon fillet
4 potatoes, for baking

1 green bell pepper
1 red bell pepper

2 carrots
1 tomato, cut in half

Prepare the grill with coals. While charcoal briquets are heating, prepare the salmon vinaigrette marinade. Combine oil, red wine vinegar and pepper in a glass baking dish. Add green onions. Rinse salmon and pat dry. Add **salmon** to baking dish and turn to coat both sides; set aside to marinate.

Bake **potatoes** according to your favorite method. We normally use the microwave to completely bake or to at least partially bake the potatoes. Wash the potatoes and pierce with fork. Place potatoes in the microwave and cook on HIGH for 4 minutes per potato per side, turning once. (3 or 4 potatoes will cook in 24 minutes.)

When grill charcoals are ready, grill the **vegetables** until the skin begins to blister; add the tomato a minute or two after the bell peppers and carrots. Grill until the tomato just begins to turn limp. Remove peppers, carrots, and tomato from grill and allow to cool.

After vegetables are done, add **salmon** to grill. Turn salmon after about 3 minutes; continue grilling until salmon turns opaque in center.

MUSHROOM STEAK

with Mashed Potatoes and Broccoli

1 ½ lb. top round steak, ½ " thick
¼ teaspoon salt
Dash pepper
2 Tbsps. flour
2 Tbsps. peanut oil
Steak Sauce Ingredients:
1 (8 oz.) can cream of mushroom soup
1 (4 oz.) can sliced mushrooms
½ cup water
¼ cup dried minced onions
2 Tbsps. instant beef bouillon
½ teaspoon onion powder

3 potatoes
½ stick margarine
¼ cup milk

½ lb. broccoli
2 oz. Cheddar cheese, shredded

Prepare the **steak**. Cut beef into 2 or 3 servings. On wax paper, mix together the salt, pepper and flour. Press both sides of steak into this flour mixture. Heat peanut oil in a heavy skillet to a medium-high temperature. When hot, add the steak and brown meat.

While the steak browns, prepare the sauce. Mix condensed cream of mushroom soup, sliced mushrooms, ½ cup of water, the instant minced onions, the beef bouillon and the onion powder. Pour over cooking beef. Heat to boiling and reduce heat; cover and simmer until beef is tender, about 30 minutes.

As the meat cooks, prepare the **mashed potatoes.** Wash and peel potatoes and cut into halves then quarter into smaller pieces. Heat a pot of water and insert the potato pieces. Salt the water to your taste. Cook for approximately 20 minutes; drain. Into hot potatoes, place ½ stick of margarine, ¼ cup of milk and whip to desired smoothness.

Cook the **broccoli** in a steamer, or cook in a small amount of water in a covered pan for about five minutes. Top broccoli with shredded Cheddar cheese.

September

The Month of New Brides

September is the month of new brides according to the people in the wedding industry. So to celebrate the new unions, *More Than Recipes* offers the traditional *Ribbon Sandwiches*. It always amazes the two of us how finger foods such as crust-less sandwiches can raise the appetite of everyone, old and young alike. There are many choices for ingredients for ribbon sandwiches. We decided on Philadelphia cream cheese, pimento cheese with chopped olives, pickled beets layered on a bread spread with vegetarian pâté. This combination of ingredients is our favorite.

***Chicken with Dijon* sauce shows its stuff again, served this time with new potatoes and broccoli, a combination that will bring everyone to the table. Other easy chicken menus include the best *Tex-Mex Quesadillas.* We have two unusual chicken meals: *Asian Chicken Broccoli* with Noodles and a celery Salad and *Chicken Breasts Diane* also with noodles.**

The meat eaters in the family will consider September on a par with May for the best beef menus. There's *Old-fashioned BBQ* sandwiches with beans, a juicy *English Rib Eye*, *Steak with Brandy and Whipping Cream* (Leonard's favorite) and we end the month with Kathy's favorite, the *Apple Cider Roast Beef*.

We have four different pork recipes for September. We have pork done Chinese-style in *Pork Teriyaki*, an Italian version called *Sweet Italian Sausage* which uses ground pork for an excellent meal with bread and wine. There is a *Mushroom Stuffed Pork Chop* with herbed rice and apple slices that will take your breath away, it is that good.

In September, we're taking a step up the taste staircase. The fish menus offer salmon with a different taste: *Broiled Salmon with Mustard-Dill* with rice and *Salmon with Avocado Glaze* also with rice. You can decide for yourselves if the step up is a real step up or a misstep. But try it before you decide.

September Menus

Chicken

Chicken á la King with Rice, Hot Buttered Toast and Green Salad

Dijon Sauce Chicken with New Potatoes and Broccoli Spears

Grilled Chicken Steak with Rice Guacamole Salad and Roasted Peppers

Chicken Breasts Diane with Noodles and Cucumber Salad

TexMex Chicken Quesadillas with Guacamole Salad and Black Beans

Chicken in Wine Sauce with Baked Potatoes and Green Peas

Asian Chicken Broccoli with Noodles and Sautéed Celery Salad

Quick & Easy

Chef's Ribbon Sandwiches with Relish Dish and Zesty Deviled Eggs

Hamburger Cookout with Potato Salad and Ranch Style Beans®

American Zucchini Beef with Green Salad and French Bread

Meat Loaf in a Tube with Rice & Corn

Old-Fashioned BBQ Sandwiches with Ranch Style Beans®

Shrimp

Onion Rockefeller with Rice and Tossed Salad

Stir Fried Shrimp with Snow Peas and Rice

Australian Shrimp with Rice, Broccoli and Tossed Salad

Shrimp & Macaroni with Tossed Salad

Sherry Sautéed Shrimp with Curried Rice and Sake

Pork

Baked Pork w/ Zucchini with Rice Pineapple Salad and Spinach

Pork Teriyaki with Rice and Tossed Salad

Sweet Salerno Sausage with Tomatoes, Cabbage, Italian Bread, Red Wine

Mushroom Stuffed Pork Chops with Herbed Rice and Apple Slices

The Sicilian Sunset with Shredded Mound Salad and French Bread

Pasta / Soup

Fish with Pasta with Green Wedge Salad

Chicken and Bell Peppers with Italian Salad and French Bread

Oven Baked Broccoli with Rice and Cheese Assortment

Oriental Smoked Chicken Salad with Rice and Egg Rolls

Fish

Salmon w/ Avocado Glaze with Rice and Chopped Tomatoes

Sole with Red Pepper Sauce and Baked Potato

Broiled Salmon Mustard-Dill with Fresh Spinach and Rice

Grilled Halibut Salad with Baked Potatoes and Tossed Salad

Pan-Fried Halibut Chunks with Baked Potatoes and House Salad

Red Meats

English Rib Eye Steak with Baked Potatoes and Green Beans

Beef Stroganoff with Rice and Tossed Salad

Steak in Brandy and Whipping Cream with Potato Rounds, Green Beans

Apple Cider Roast Beef with Mashed Potatoes, Green Peas and Carrots

SEPTEMBER

Sunday	Monday	Tuesday	Wednesday	Thursday	Friday	Saturday
Chicken á la King Rice, Hot Buttered Toast, Green Salad	**Chef's Ribbon Sand-wiches** Relishes, Zesty Deviled Eggs	**Onion Rockefeller Shrimp** Rice, Tossed Salad	*Plan Ahead* **Grilled Chicken Steak** Rice, Guacamole Salad, Roasted Peppers	**Fish with Pasta** Green Wedge Salad	**Salmon with Avocado Glaze** Rice, Chopped Tomatoes	**English Rib Eye Steak** Baked Potatoes, Green Beans
Dijon Sauce Chicken New Potatoes, Broccoli Spears	*Plan Ahead* **Ham-burger Cookout** Potato Salad Ranch Style Beans	**Stir-Fried Shrimp** Snow Peas, Rice	*Plan Ahead* **Pork Teriyaki** Rice, Tossed Salad	**Oriental Smoked Chicken Salad** Rice, Egg Rolls	**Sole w/ Red Pepper Sauce** Baked Potato	**Beef Stroganoff** Rice, Tossed Salad
Chicken Breasts Diane Noodles, Cucumber Salad	**American Zucchini Beef** Green Salad, French Bread	**Australian Shrimp** Rice, Broccoli, Tossed Salad	**Sweet Salerno Sausage** Tomatoes, Cabbage, Italian Bread, Red Wine	*Plan Ahead* **TexMex Chicken Quesa-dillas** Guacamole Salad, Black Beans	**Broiled Salmon Mustard-Dill** Rice, Fresh Spinach	**Steak in Brandy & Cream** Potato Rounds, Green Beans
Meat Loaf in a Tube Rice, Corn	**Chicken in Wine Sauce** Baked Potatoes, Green Peas	**Shrimp and Macaroni** Tossed Salad	**Baked Pork w/ Zucchini** Rice, Pineapple Slices, Spinach	**Chicken and Bell Peppers** Italian Salad French Bread	**Grilled Halibut Steaks** Baked Potatoes, Tossed Salad	**The Sicilian Sunset** Shredded Mound Salad, French Bread
Asian Chicken Broccoli Noodles, Sautéed Celery Salad	**Old-Fashioned BBQ Sand-wiches** Ranch Style Beans	**Sherry Sautéed Shrimp** Curried Rice, Sake	**Mushroom Stuffed Pork Chops** Rice, Apple Slices	**Oven Baked Broccoli** Rice, Cheese Assortment	**Pan-Fried Halibut Chunks** Baked Potatoes House Salad	*Plan Ahead* **Apple Cider Roast Beef** Mashed Potatoes Green Peas Carrots

First week SEPTEMBER

Sunday	*Monday*	*Tuesday*	*Wednesday*	*Thursday*	*Friday*	*Saturday*
Chicken á la King Rice, Hot Buttered Toast, Green Salad	**Chef's Ribbon Sandwich** Relishes, Zesty Deviled Eggs	**Onion Rockefeller Shrimp** Rice, Tossed Salad	Plan Ahead **Grilled Chicken Steak** Rice, Guacamole Salad, Roasted Peppers	**Fish with Pasta** Green Wedge Salad	**Salmon with Avocado Glaze** Rice, Chopped Tomatoes	**English Rib Eye Steak** Baked Potatoes, Green Beans

Fresh Vegetables \ Fruits		*Herbs \ Spices*	*Basics*
celery bundle carrot bundle fresh mushrooms - 2 green bell pepper - 1 red bell peppers - 2 iceberg lettuce - 2 cucumbers - 2 parsley bunch radishes-bunch lemons - 4 orange - 1	garlic pod - 1 green onions - 9 tomatoes - 4 snow peas - ¼ lb. avocados - 2 white onion - 1 sweet onion - 1 lime - 1 cilantro-small bunch potatoes - 4 green beans - 1 lb.	red pepper flakes red pepper sauce dry mustard paprika ground cumin white pepper thyme cayenne pepper chives bacon bits	flour mayonnaise extra-virgin olive oil Worcestershire sauce olive oil peanut oil mustard Dijon mustard soy sauce Converted Rice

Entrée Food	*Dairy*	*Miscellaneous*	*Cans \ Jars*
whole chicken - 1 fresh jumbo shrimp 12-20 skinless, boneless chicken breasts - 2 orange roughy fillets - 2 salmon fillets - 1 rib eye steaks - 2	butter - 2 sticks margarine - 2 sticks low fat milk - pint eggs - 8 Philadelphia cream cheese - 8 oz. pimento cheese with ripe olives - 6 oz. nonfat yogurt ¾ cup sour cream - 1 cup bacon - 1 slice	thick bread loaf white bread loaf wheat bread loaf croutons - pkg. bread crumbs 6 oz. thin spaghetti 1 lb. sun-dried tomatoes pkg. 4 oz white wine- ½ cup brandy - 1 oz. dry sherry - 1 oz	pimentos - 2 oz. vegetarian paté 7 oz pickled beets - 8 oz. olives 6 oz. ripe olives - 4 oz. green chilies - 4 oz.

CHICKEN Á LA KING

with Rice, Hot Buttered Toast and Green Salad

1 whole chicken, cut up
2 celery stalks
3 carrot sticks
2 fresh mushrooms, sliced
¼ cup green bell pepper, diced
¼ cup butter or margarine
3 Tbsps. flour
2 cups low-fat milk
Salt and pepper
1 egg yolk, beaten
2 Tbsps. pimentos, diced

Converted Rice

Thick bread (for toast)

Green Salad Ingredients:
iceberg lettuce
cucumber
celery, julienned
parsley

Boil the **chicken** in a large pot. Add roughly-chopped celery and carrot sticks. Boil for about 17 minutes, remove from water and let cool. Discard cooking stock.

While the chicken cooks, prepare the **salad**. Wash, dry and tear the lettuce into bite-size pieces. Slice cucumber thinly, julienne the celery stalk into 2-inch lengths, the size of match sticks. Add parsley as a garnish. Place the salad in a large bowl and refrigerate until mealtime.

Make **rice** in desired amount according to package directions.

When the chicken has cooled enough to handle, remove meat from the bones and chop the meat into small pieces. Set aside.

In a saucepan, sauté the mushrooms and the green pepper in a small amount of butter or margarine; add flour and blend till smooth. Add the low fat milk, the salt and pepper. Cook until it begins to thicken, stirring constantly; stir some of this mixture into the beaten egg yolk then return to mixture. Cook for about 8 minutes more. Add the diced chicken and pimentos.

Just before chicken is done, place the **bread** into a toaster or oven and brown.

CHEF'S RIBBON SANDWICHES

with Zesty Deviled Eggs and Relishes

½ loaf white bread
½ loaf whole wheat bread
1 (4 oz.) vegetarian patê
1 (6 oz.) Philadelphia Cream Cheese
1 (6 oz.) pimento cheese with chopped ripe olives
1 jar pickled beets
Relishes:
carrots, cucumbers
radishes, celery sticks

Zesty Deviled Eggs Ingredients:
4 hard-cooked eggs
2 oz. cream cheese
Dash red pepper flakes
1 Tbsp. mayonnaise
1 Tbsp. prepared mustard
¼ teaspoon salt
2 dashes dry mustard
4 green olives (optional)

Make the **zesty deviled eggs** first. Place 4 eggs in boiling water for 10 minutes, cut off the heat and let eggs sit in hot water for another ten minutes. Halve the eggs and remove yolks. Mix together the yolks, 2 ounces soft cream cheese, a dash of red pepper, 1 tablespoon mayonnaise, 1 tablespoon prepared mustard, ¼ teaspoon salt, and dashes of dry mustard. Blend until smooth; season to taste.

Stuff mixture into egg whites. Garnish with parsley leaves, or you can top with slices of olives.

Ribbon sandwiches are crust less, thin sandwiches with three contrasting fillings. To make the ribbon sandwiches, remove crust from bread. Coat the bread slices with butter or margarine or use a vegetarian paté. Top the slices with cream cheese, pimento cheese with ripe olives and pickled beets. Stack the bread together and cut into four thin pieces.

For future reference : Another variety to include could be, honey and peanut butter. Yet another sandwich could have crab meat and mayonnaise with a second of finely-chopped pickled beets and the third as hard-cooked eggs.

To compliment the sandwiches, toss together **relish dish** of carrots, cucumbers, radishes and celery.

ONION ROCKEFELLER SHRIMP

with Rice & Tossed Salad

1 sweet onion
2 Tbsps. extra-virgin olive oil
1 teaspoon extra-virgin olive oil
Jumbo shrimp (12-20, or amount to please)
2 Tbsps. soy sauce
½ teaspoon minced garlic
2 Tbsps. lemon juice
1 teaspoon lemon peelings
Pinch cayenne pepper

Tossed Salad Ingredients:
iceberg lettuce
cucumber
radishes
tomato
ripe olives
croutons

Converted Rice

Have all ingredients measured and cut before beginning this menu.

Cook **rice**, following package directions, for serving sizes. While rice cooks, prepare a **tossed salad**. Wash and dry all vegetables. Tear the lettuce into bite-size pieces. Slice the cucumber and radish. Cut the tomato into wedges. Toss all together, then add the ripe olives and the croutons.

Preheat the oven broiler.

Cut **onion** into thick slices. Brush each onion slice with 1 teaspoon olive oil. Arrange slices on a baking sheet. Broil about 5-6 inches from broiler wire for about 3 minutes. Turn over and repeat. Move baking sheet from beneath heating elements. Meanwhile, peel and butterfly **shrimp**; rinse thoroughly and pat dry.

Lay 2 shrimp on each onion slice then place back under broiler. Bake shrimp 4 to 5 inches from heat, about 2 minutes. Remove and keep warm.

In a small sauce pan heat the 2 tablespoons oil, soy sauce, and garlic until boiling. Remove pan from heat and add lemon juice, lemon peel and cayenne pepper.

Place shrimp on plate with the rice. Drizzle each shrimp serving with the warm lemon sauce.

Serve the tossed salad and rice.

1 hour - Plan ahead

GRILLED CHICKEN STEAK

with Guacamole Salad, Rice and Roasted Peppers

2 whole boneless, skinless chicken breasts
3 Tbsps. butter or margarine
1 ½ teaspoons Worcestershire sauce
¼ teaspoon paprika
Salt and pepper, to taste
2 red bell peppers, halved
Lettuce leaves

Converted Rice

1 avocado, skinned, cut up
¼ cup chopped white onions
1 green chili pepper
1 teaspoon lemon juice
½ teaspoon salt
¼ teaspoon pepper
¼ teaspoon orange juice
1 Tbsp. mayonnaise
½ tomato, finely chopped
1 small clove garlic, minced

Make the **guacamole salad**. Use all ingredients on right side. Beat avocados, onions, chili pepper, lemon juice, salt, pepper, orange juice, mayonnaise until creamy. Stir in tomato bits and garlic. Cover and refrigerate *at least 1 hour.*

Prepare the outdoor grill with charcoal, or use your oven grill if you prefer. When grill is ready, prepare the **rice** according to package directions.

For the **grilled chicken,** pound the breasts to achieve a uniform thickness. In a small bowl combine the sauce materials: butter, Worcestershire sauce, paprika, salt and pepper. Brush the sauce over the chicken pieces. Place chicken pieces on the preheated grill or on a baking sheet in the oven at about 5 inches from the heat source. Cook for about 5 minutes, turn and coat with more of the marinade.

For the last five minutes of grilling, add the **red bell peppers** so they can roast to a golden tinge.

When ready to serve, arrange lettuce leaves on salad plate and spoon on the guacamole salad.

FISH WITH PASTA

with Green Wedge Salad

2 orange roughy fillets
¼ cup olive oil
2 cloves garlic
1 teaspoon thyme
½ cup white wine
1 lemon, juiced
2 green onions, minced
½ cup extra-virgin olive oil
6 oz. bread crumbs, plain
Salt and pepper, to taste
Parsley sprig
Green Wedge Salad Ingredients:
- **½ head iceberg lettuce**
- **½ cucumber, in thick slices**
- **2 radishes, in thin slices**
- **2 celery stalks, julienned**

1 lb. thin spaghetti pasta

To prepare the **Green Wedge Salad**, cut the iceberg lettuce into large wedges. Remove inner core and chop onto the salad plate. Cut the cucumber and place in the curved portion of lettuce wedge. Slice the radishes and place on cucumbers. Julienne the celery and place on top of and around the wedge. This can be stored in refrigerator or can be served as first course.

This menu uses the pan-poaching technique. We recommend that you begin the fish poaching at the same time that you place the spaghetti into boiling water, unless you are using fresh pasta which will take only a minute or two.

Cook **pasta** according to package directions.

For the **fish:** heat olive oil or butter in a 10 to 12 inch frying pan over medium-high heat. Add 1 clove of garlic and herbs and stir about 30 seconds. Pour in wine and juice from one lemon. Add fillets and spoon liquid over them. Sprinkle fish with pepper and lemon peels then green onion slices. Cover and simmer until fish is done; about 7 to 9 minutes. There is no need to turn fillets. Remove fish and keep warm.

In another frying pan, prepare **bread crumb topping.** Heat the olive oil and toss in the other clove of garlic to sauté for a moment or two. Add the bread crumbs and continue to sauté for a couple of minutes. Keep warm.

Drain the pasta and arrange on serving platter. Pour the bread crumb mixture over the top; season to taste with salt and pepper. Place fish on serving dish. You can add a sprig of parsley to garnish.

SALMON WITH AVOCADO GLAZE

with Rice and Chopped Tomatoes

1 salmon fillet
1 Tbsp. olive oil
1 ripe avocado
¾ cup sour cream
½ can diced green chilies
1 teaspoon hot pepper sauce
1 teaspoon lime juice
1 teaspoon ground cumin
½ teaspoon salt
Pinch white pepper
2 chopped tomatoes
2 Tbsps. fresh cilantro (opt.)
Converted Rice

The avocado dressing on the salmon makes for a very different taste, exciting to some, repulsive to others, especially the young. We serve the dressing on the side to give everyone a taste.

Prepare grill with coals if cooking out-of-doors. Otherwise, pre-heat oven to 375° F.

Prepare **rice** in desired amount, following package directions.

Remove the **salmon** bones with tweezers; lightly run fingers down center of fillet to locate them. Cut salmon fillet into serving portions and rub skin with olive oil. To grill, place salmon skin side down on a grill 4-6 inches above coals. Cook until just barely translucent in center, about 8 minutes; carefully turn the fish after five minutes. To bake, place salmon on rimmed baking dish and bake about 10 minutes.

While fish grills, prepare the **avocado sauce**. Remove skin and seed from avocado; mash. In a small bowl, mix together the avocado, sour cream, green chilies, hot pepper sauce, lime juice, cumin, salt and pepper.

Chop **tomatoes** into large chunks and store in refrigerator until serving time.

Remove salmon from heat and let stand several minutes to finish cooking. Serve with avocado sauce and tomato chunks, served separately, in bowls. Garnish with fresh cilantro.

Save leftover sour cream for the meal on Friday.

ENGLISH RIB EYE STEAK

with Baked Potatoes and Green Beans

1 lb. green beans
1 bacon slice

2 rib eye steaks
2 Tbsps. peanut oil
Salt and pepper to taste
2 Tbsps. brandy

Potato toppings:
chives, sour cream, bacon bits

2 Tbsps. butter
2 Tbsps. dry sherry wine
1 lemon, juiced
½ tsp. Dijon mustard
1 Tbsp. chopped parsley
1 Tbsp. Worcestershire sauce
1 Tbsp. chopped chives
4 potatoes, for baking

Prepare **green beans** by the boiling method. Cut ends off beans and cut in half or leave long. Barely cover beans with water and add one slice of bacon; sprinkle with salt. Cook until they are tender, 20 minutes for *al dente.*

Bake potatoes according to your favorite method. We typically use the microwave to completely bake or to at least partially bake the potatoes. Wash the potatoes and pierce with fork. Place potatoes in the microwave and cook on HIGH for 4 minutes per potato per side. (3 or 4 potatoes will cook in 24 minutes.)

Sauté **rib eye steaks** in peanut oil over medium-high heat to desired doneness, about 7 minutes each side. Add salt and pepper to taste as the steaks cook. Reduce heat, add brandy. With a match, carefully light the fumes. When flame dies, remove steaks and keep warm in an oven set to lowest setting.

To pan juices, add 2 tablespoons of butter, the dry sherry, the juice from a squeezed lemon. Add the teaspoon of Dijon mustard, the chopped parsley and the Worcestershire sauce. Sprinkle chives into sauce. Heat to boiling. Pour over steaks. Serve immediately.

Serve with green beans and baked potatoes. To spice up the baked potatoes we add chives, sour cream and bacon bits, all optional.

Second week SEPTEMBER

Sunday	*Monday*	*Tuesday*	*Wednesday*	*Thursday*	*Friday*	*Saturday*
Dijon Sauce Chicken New Potatoes Broccoli Spears	*Plan Ahead* **Ham-burger Cookout** Potato Salad, Ranch Style® Beans	**Stir-Fried Shrimp** Snow Peas, Rice	*Plan Ahead* **Pork Teriyaki** Rice, Tossed Salad	**Oriental Smoked Chicken Salad** Rice, Egg Rolls	**Sole w/ Red Pepper Sauce** Baked Potato	**Beef Stroganoff** Rice, Tossed Salad

Fresh Vegetables \ Fruits		*Herbs \ Spices*	*Basics*
new potatoes - 10 red potatoes - 6 baking potatoes - 4 broccoli bunch - ½ lb mushrooms - 5 parsley bunch green onions - 15 celery bundle white onions - 3 tomatoes - 4	garlic pod fresh ginger - 2 oz. iceberg lettuce - 2 green leaf lettuce snow peas - 2 cups cucumber - 2 radishes-bunch red bell pepper - 1 lemon - 2	paprika dry mustard arrowroot white pepper	olive oil Dijon mustard mayonnaise mustard sugar peanut oil honey ketchup pickles kosher salt soy sauce Converted Rice

Entrée Food	*Dairy*	*Miscellaneous*	*Cans \ Jars*
skinless, boneless chicken breasts -2 ground beef - 1 lb. medium-size shrimp ½ lb boneless pork steaks - 1 lb. 1 whole (smoked) chicken or 2 skinless breasts sole fillets - 2 round steak - 2 lb.	Cheddar cheese 2 oz. eggs - 2 butter - 6 T sour cream - 1 cup **Frozen** egg rolls pkg. **Wine** dry white wine - 1 C dry sherry - ¼ cup Sake - 4 cups	croutons - pkg. Chinese noodles pkg apple cider vinegar charcoal bag hickory stick bag	chicken broth - 2 ripe olives - 4 oz. water chestnuts 1 (8 oz.) beef bouillon - 1 teriyaki sauce 1 cup liquid smoke - 4 oz. Ranch Style Beans® 23 oz.

DIJON SAUCE CHICKEN

with New Potatoes and Broccoli Spears

4 new potatoes
½ lb. broccoli
2 oz. Cheddar cheese
2 chicken breasts, skinless, boneless
5 Tbsps. olive oil, divided
2 mushrooms, sliced
2 Tbsps. green onions
Dash pepper
½ cup white wine
2 Tbsps. fresh parsley
½ cup chicken broth
1 Tbsp. Dijon mustard

Cook **new potatoes**. Place potatoes with skins in pot of boiling water. Let the new potatoes cook for about 20 minutes, for medium-size red potatoes. Remove and allow to cool.

Prepare **broccoli spears**. Remove any large leaves from broccoli bunch. Cut stalks lengthwise from end to broccoli head to make spears. Cook by steaming over boiling water for about five minutes. When serving, sprinkle with Cheddar cheese.

Pound **chicken** to an even thickness. Heat 3 tablespoons olive oil in a large skillet over medium-high heat. When hot, add chicken breasts and cook for 5 minutes per side, or until golden brown and cooked through. Set aside and keep warm. We use a warmed plate and cover chicken with a pot lid.

For the **mustard sauce:** heat 2 tablespoons olive oil. Stir in sliced mushrooms, green onions and pepper. Stirring frequently, cook 2 minutes. Stir in white wine, parsley and chicken broth. Bring to a boil and cook until liquid is reduced to about half. Add Dijon mustard and stir until well blended. Pour mustard sauce over chicken pieces when serving.

HAMBURGER COOKOUT

with Potato Salad and Ranch Style Beans®

6 medium-size red potatoes
½ cup chopped white onions
1 cup chopped celery
Dash of salt
1 tsp. pepper
1 tsp. sugar
¼ cup mayonnaise
1 Tbsp. mustard

Cookout supplies: charcoal, hickory sticks etc.

2 eggs, hard-boiled
Paprika
1 lb. lean ground beef
1 small onion
1 tomato
1 head lettuce
Pickles
1 (23 oz.) can Ranch Style Beans®

You can make the **potato salad** the day before if you wish. Boil potatoes for 30 minutes. Set aside to cool, then peel and cube to desired size. Sauté onions in 2 to 3 teaspoons of bacon grease or peanut oil. Mix celery, onion, salt, pepper, sugar and potatoes. Add mayonnaise and mustard; mix again. For topping, slice hard-boiled eggs and sprinkle with paprika.

Prepare the outdoor grill with coals. Allow the coals to burn for at least forty minutes before you cook the hamburgers.

While the grill heats, prepare the hamburger **relishes:** onions, tomato slices, lettuce and pickles.

At the time hamburgers are placed on grill, you can warm the canned **Ranch Style Beans®** in a saucepan over medium heat.

STIR-FRIED SHRIMP

with Snow Peas and Rice

½ lb. medium shrimp, peeled, deveined
1 teaspoon minced ginger
4 Tbsps. peanut oil, divided
Pinch of kosher salt
Pinch of white pepper
½ teaspoon arrowroot
½ cup chicken broth

Marinade Ingredients:
¼ cup dry sherry
1 Tbsp. arrowroot
1 teaspoon minced ginger

Converted Rice
2 cups snow peas

Salt-leach the **shrimp**. Sprinkle peeled shrimp with small amount of kosher salt, tossing shrimp to distribute the salt evenly and let stand only 1 minute. Rinse and drain. Repeat the salting again, rinse and drain well; transfer to a small bowl. The effect of the salt leaching is to remove excess water from the shrimp so that when they are stir-fried they are more firm.

Prepare the **marinade.** In a bowl large enough to hold the marinade and shrimp, combine the dry sherry, arrowroot and the ground ginger. Mix well and add the shrimp. Refrigerate now until you are ready to cook.

Prepare **rice** in desired amount according to package directions.

Prepare the shrimp stir-fry by mincing the ginger, if fresh, and measuring the peanut oil, salt and pepper. Dissolve the arrowroot in the chicken broth and set aside. When rice is about done, drain the shrimp and discard the marinade. Heat a large skillet to high heat. Pour in 2 tablespoons of peanut oil, ginger and salt and pepper. Next, add in the drained shrimp and stir-fry about 1 minute. Transfer to a serving plate for a moment.

Add the remaining 2 tablespoons of oil to the pan, add the **snow peas** and stir-fry until heated through. Stir in the arrowroot from above; return the shrimp to the pan. Cook, stirring, until the sauce thickens.

Serve immediately.

PORK TERIYAKI

with Rice and Tossed Salad

1 lb. pork steaks (boneless)

1 cup Oriental teriyaki sauce*

Converted Rice

Sake

Tossed Salad Ingredients:
iceberg lettuce
green leaf lettuce
cucumber
radishes
tomato
ripe olives
croutons

* *If Oriental sauce is unavailable, make your own. Combine ¼ cup soy sauce, ¼ cup olive oil, ½ teaspoon ground ginger, 1 clove crushed garlic, ½ teaspoon sugar, 3 tablespoons white wine and 1 tablespoon of cornstarch or arrowroot. Mix and marinate for 15 minutes.*

Cut **pork steaks** into thin slices. In a large bowl, add the Oriental teriyaki sauce and the pork and toss to coat. Marinate ***overnight*** covered, in a bowl.

Since this is a light meal, we usually begin it with a nice **tossed salad.** Wash and dry all vegetables. Tear the lettuces into bite-size pieces. Slice the cucumber and radishes. Cut the tomatoes into wedges. Toss all together, then add the ripe olives and the croutons.

Prepare **rice** according to package directions while you enjoy the first course. We recommend a nice warm cup of **sake** to set the mood.

Grill **pork strips** in oven under broiler for about 5 minutes each side or until done.

ORIENTAL SMOKED CHICKEN SALAD

with Rice and Egg Rolls

1 smoked chicken, whole
1 pkg. Chinese noodles
1 head lettuce, shredded
9 green onions, chopped
1 (8 oz.) can water chestnuts, drained and sliced

1 package egg rolls

Oriental Dressing Ingredients:
1 teaspoon dry mustard
¼ cup olive oil
¼ cup soy sauce
2 Tbsps. honey
2 Tbsps. ketchup
Liquid smoke
Sake

This menu calls for a **smoked whole chicken**. We have a supermarket in our neighborhood that has the smoked chicken ready for sale. If you don't have this convenience we suggest that you substitute two chicken breasts and let them marinate in liquid smoke sauce for an hour before broiling in oven for 12 - 15 minutes.

Make Oriental dressing from ingredients on right side. Chill.

Cook **noodles** according to package directions.

Remove chicken from bones and cut into small strips. In a large bowl, mix chicken with noodles, lettuce, onions and water chestnuts. Add liquid smoke if you don't have a smoked chicken. Chill.

Get the **egg rolls** ready. Prepare the egg rolls according to package directions.

While the noodles cook, enjoy a cup of warm **sake**.

Just before serving the chicken, toss with Oriental Dressing.

SOLE WITH RED PEPPER SAUCE

with Baked Potato

1 red bell pepper
2 green onions, chopped
1 clove garlic
2 Tbsps. olive oil
1 teaspoon apple cider vinegar
1 teaspoon lemon juice
Salt and pepper to taste

Pan-poaching Ingredients:
2 Tbsps. olive oil
1 clove garlic, minced
¼ cup dry white wine
1 lemon, juiced
2 sole fillets
4 potatoes, for baking

This menu calls for **baked potatoes**. We use the microwave. Wash potatoes and pierce with fork. Place in microwave and cook on HIGH for 4 minutes per side per potato. Turn them once. (3 or 4 potatoes will cook in 24 minutes.)

While potatoes bake, prepare the **red pepper sauce**. Put red bell pepper, cut into strips, green onions, crushed garlic and oil in a pan and cover. Cook over low heat for about 15-20 minutes, stirring occasionally until all vegetables are soft. Add vinegar, lemon juice, salt and pepper. Blend for a few more seconds. Set aside.

Meanwhile, prepare the **pan-poached fish.** Select a pan large enough to hold the fish. Heat olive oil in this pan over medium-high heat. Add garlic and stir about 30 seconds. Pour in the wine and juice from one lemon. Add fillets and spoon liquid over fillets. Sprinkle fish with pepper.

Cover and simmer until fish is done; about 7 to 9 minutes. Test with a fork to see if the fish flakes in the middle. *There is no need to turn fillets.*

Transfer fish to a platter to keep warm.

BEEF STROGANOFF

with Rice and Tossed Salad

2 lb. any tenderized meat
½ cup flour
¼ cup butter
1 can beef bouillon
1 can water
1 teaspoon salt
2-3 fresh mushrooms
1 onion, chopped
2 Tbsps. butter
1 cup sour cream

Converted Rice

Tossed Salad Ingredients:
iceberg lettuce
green leaf lettuce
cucumber
radishes
tomato
ripe olives
croutons

Prepare the **Tossed Salad.** Wash and dry all vegetables. Tear the lettuces into bite-size pieces. Slice the cucumber and radishes. Cut the tomatoes into wedges. Toss all together, then add the ripe olives and the croutons. Place in refrigerator until ready to serve.

Prepare the **Beef Stroganoff.** Cut steak into ¾ inch wide strips. Dredge in flour to coat. In a saucepan, melt butter. Brown the coated meat then add the beef bouillon, can of water and the salt. Bring to a boil, reduce heat and simmer for about 1 hour, before beginning the rice.

Prepare **rice** according to package directions. Let the beef continue to cook until the rice is done.

When rice is about done, say five minutes before, prepare the **mushroom sauce.** Slice mushrooms lengthwise, stem to head. Chop the onion into small pieces. Sauté mushrooms and onion in 2 tablespoons of butter until the onions become clear.

Minutes before serving, add mushroom sauce to the beef. Add the sour cream at this time and let the mixture heat for a moment before serving.

Roasted Garlic Hint Sheet

2 elephant garlic pods (or 6 normal size)
Extra-virgin olive oil
Salt and pepper
Terra Cotta garlic baker dish

DO NOT PREHEAT OVEN. It's important that the oven not be preheated.

If you are using a terra cotter garlic baker, purchase several whole elephant garlic pods, one per person. Remove some of the wrapping skin around the pod then cut some garlic from the head off so that the garlic is exposed. Place the pods in the baking dish, drizzle them with extra-virgin olive, salt and pepper. Cover and place in cool oven. Set oven temperature control to 350° F. Cook for 45 minutes. Baste again with additional olive oil. Uncover and continue to cook for another 45 minutes or until the garlic is creamy.

An alternate method of producing roasted garlic involves the stove top and avoids the terra cotta cookery. Slice garlic. In a covered frying pan with plenty of butter, cook the garlic slowly for about 20 minutes.

Third week SEPTEMBER

Sunday	*Monday*	*Tuesday*	*Wednesday*	*Thursday*	*Friday*	*Saturday*
Chicken Breasts Diane Noodles, Cucumber Salad	**American Zucchini Beef** Green Salad French Bread	**Australian Shrimp** Rice, Broccoli, Tossed Salad	**Sweet Salerno Sausage** Tomatoes, Cabbage, Italian Bread, Red Wine	*Plan ahead* **TexMex Chicken Quesa-dillas** Guacamole Salad, Black Beans	**Broiled Salmon Mustard-Dill** Rice, Fresh Spinach	**Steak in Brandy & Cream** Potato Rounds, Green Beans

Fresh Vegetables \ Fruits		*Herbs \ Spices*	*Basics*
green onions - 5 lemons - 4 parsley bunch white onions - 4 green bell pepper - 2 red bell pepper - 1 zucchini -1 iceberg lettuce - 2 green leaf lettuce - 1 cucumbers - 3 celery bundle	garlic pod broccoli bunch tomatoes - 4 radishes-bunch red cabbage head avocados - 2 limes - 2 fresh cilantro bunch fresh spinach pkg. baking potatoes - 4 green beans - 1 lb. orange - 1	white pepper sea salt ground cumin dry mustard dill weed	Dijon style mustard olive oil cornstarch sesame oil ketchup rice vinegar tarragon vinegar extra-virgin olive oil mayonnaise prepared mustard peanut oil white vinegar Converted Rice

Entrée Food	*Dairy*	*Miscellaneous*	*Cans \ Jars*
skinless, boneless chicken breasts - 3 ground sirloin 1 lb. medium-sized shrimp ½ lb. sweet Italian sausage ¾ lb. salmon fillets - 1 1 " fillet steaks - 2 **Wines** dry sherry 1 T rum - 8 oz	butter - 4 T Parmesan cheese 2 oz. Monterey Jack cheese - 2 oz. bacon - 2 slices whipping cream 2 T margarine - 2 T sour cream - 4 T **Wines** brandy - 3 T red wine bottle	extra wide noodles 1 lb. French bread loaf croutons - pkg. spiral pasta - 1 lb. Italian bread loaf margarita salt Bacardi® Margarita mix - 1 flour tortillas - 12 black beans - 1 C	chicken broth - 1 tomato sauce 8 oz.- 2 whole tomatoes - 3 hamburger dill slices - 4 oz. chili sauce 1 T ripe olives - 2 oz. green chilies - 4 oz. picante sauce - 4 oz.

CHICKEN BREASTS DIANE

with Noodles and Cucumber Salad

2 whole skinless, boneless chicken breasts
Salt and pepper
2 Tbsps. olive oil, divided
2 Tbsps. butter, divided
3 green onions, chopped
2 Tbsps. brandy
3 Tbsps. chopped parsley
2 teaspoons Dijon-style mustard
¼ cup chicken broth
½ lemon, juiced

Cucumber Salad Ingredients:
1 cucumber
2 green onions, minced
1 teaspoon dill weed spice
4 Tbsps. sour cream
2 Tbsps. tarragon vinegar
Salt and pepper, to taste
½ lb. noodles, cooked
1 Tbsp. olive oil
1 Tbsp. sea salt
2 (8 oz.) cans tomato sauce

Make the **cucumber salad.** Cut cucumber into thick slices. In a small bowl mix 2 green onions, a sprinkle of dill weed, 4 tablespoon of sour cream, 2 tablespoon of tarragon vinegar and salt and pepper to taste. Stir well and pour over the sliced cucumber.

Pound **chicken** halves to an even thickness; sprinkle with salt and pepper. Heat 1 tablespoon each of oil and butter in large skillet. Cook chicken over high heat for 3 minutes on each side. DO NOT cook longer or they will be overcooked. Transfer cooked chicken to warm serving platter.

Make **chive sauce**. Place green onions, brandy, parsley and mustard to skillet. Cook 15 seconds, whisking constantly. Add chicken broth and continue to whisk. Stir until sauce is smooth. Add lemon juice. Add remaining tablespoon of oil and butter. Pour this sauce over chicken.

Prepare **noodles** according to package directions. We add 2 tablespoons of olive oil and some sea salt. Heat **tomato sauce** in separate skillet and pour in cooked noodles.

AMERICAN ZUCCHINI BEEF

with Green Salad and French Bread

1 lb. ground sirloin
1 onion, chopped
1 clove garlic, crushed
1 green bell pepper, chopped
1 (16 oz.) can whole tomatoes
¼ teaspoon sea salt
Dash pepper
½ cup chopped hamburger dills
1 zucchini
Parmesan cheese, grated

Green Salad Ingredients:
iceberg lettuce
green leaf lettuce
cucumber
celery, julienned
parsley

½ lb. extra-wide noodles
Red wine
French bread

If you have fresh **French bread** to bake, do it now, before proceeding.

Make the **green salad** next. Wash, dry and tear the lettuces into bite-size pieces. Slice cucumber thinly, cut the celery stalk into 2 inch lengths. Add parsley as a garnish. Place the completed salad in the refrigerator to chill until ready to serve.

Cook and stir **ground sirloin**, onion and garlic in a large frying pan until meat turns brown. Drain off excess fat. Stir in remaining ingredients: green bell pepper, whole tomatoes, sea salt, pepper and hamburger dills. Cut the tomatoes in the pan. Add ½ cup of water. Heat to boiling; reduce heat. Simmer uncovered for about 25 minutes.

Cut **zucchini** into ¼ inch thickness. Add to sauce. Cover and simmer, stirring occasionally, 15 minutes.

While the meat continues to cook, prepare the extra wide **noodles** following package directions. When the ground beef is finished, sprinkle it with Parmesan cheese. Serve with red wine.

AUSTRALIAN SHRIMP

with Rice, Broccoli and Tossed Salad

2 Tbsps. cornstarch
1 Tbsp. sesame oil
½ teaspoon salt
¼ teaspoon white pepper
½ medium-sized shrimp
2 Tbsps. ketchup
1 teaspoon chili sauce
1 Tbsp. rice vinegar

Converted Rice

1 bunch broccoli
1 Tbsp. olive oil
1 teaspoon minced garlic
1 Tbsp. dry sherry

Tossed Salad Ingredients:
iceberg lettuce
cucumber
radishes
tomato
ripe olives
croutons

Prepare the **tossed salad**. Wash and dry all vegetables. Tear the lettuce into bite-size pieces. Slice the cucumber and radishes. Cut the tomato into wedges. Toss all together, then add the ripe olives and the croutons. We have this salad as a first course to the light meal that follows.

Begin by marinating the **shrimp**. In a dry bowl, combine cornstarch, sesame oil, salt and a pinch of white pepper. Add the washed, cleaned and shelled shrimp and stir to coat. Cover with wrap and marinate in refrigerator for about 30 minutes or while rice cooks.

Cook **rice** before proceeding.

Make **shrimp sauce.** In a small bowl, mix together ketchup, chili sauce and rice vinegar. Set aside.

Steam the **broccoli** following your favorite method.

For the **shrimp,** preheat wok or frying pan to high. Add small amount of olive oil. Add garlic and shrimp and stir fry until shrimp turn pink. Add wine and white pepper. This will make shrimp a customary way. If family likes shrimp with *usual* taste remove some from pan and set aside. To make a different tasting shrimp, add chili sauce, stir to coat; heat through about 1 minute.

SWEET SALERNO SAUSAGE

with Tomatoes, Cabbage, Italian Bread and Red Wine

3 Tbsps. extra-virgin olive oil
1 Tbsp. chopped onion
½ head red cabbage, julienned
2 (15 oz.) cans whole tomatoes, drained
Sea salt and pepper, to taste

3 Tbsps. extra-virgin olive oil
¾ lb. sweet Italian sausage
1 lb. spiral pasta
Italian bread

Red wine

Preheat oven to 400° F.

Prepare the **cabbage-tomato sauce.** Heat 3 tablespoons of olive oil in large frying pan, over medium heat. Sauté the onion until it becomes clear. Next, add the julienned cabbage and sauté for another 2 minutes. Finally, put in the drained tomatoes and cut them up. Season the sauce to taste with salt and pepper. Cover pan lightly, a portion of the lid ajar and simmer over low heat, stirring occasionally, until the liquid is reduced. Cook for 20-30 minutes.

Meanwhile, begin cooking the **fresh bread** according to directions.

Make the sausage. In a separate pan, heat about 3 tablespoons olive oil over medium heat. Add the **ground sausage** and cook for about 7-8 minutes, stirring occasionally.

At the same time, in large pot, bring water to boil. Add 2 tablespoons of olive oil and add the **spiral pasta**; cook until *al dente.*

Drain the pasta and arrange on warm platter. Pour the cabbage sauce over the pasta and toss well. Sprinkle with the Italian sausage and serve piping hot with the Italian bread and red wine.

TEX-MEX CHICKEN QUESADILLAS

Guacamole Salad and Black Beans

1 chicken breast, skinless, boneless
1 clove garlic
1 teaspoon ground cumin
Salt to taste
Ground pepper to taste
1 Tbsp. olive oil
¼ green and red peppers, chopped
½ can green chilies
½ cup picante sauce
2 oz. Monterey Jack cheese

1 avocado
1 chopped tomato
Margarita Ingredients:
- **Bacardi® Margarita Mix**
- **lime**
- **rum**
- **margarita salt**

Flour tortillas

The **black beans** on facing page may be prepared the day before.

The **guacamole salad** for this menu can be made an hour before the meal. See Guacamole Salad on facing page====>.

Pound **chicken breasts** to achieve an even thickness. In large saucepan or Dutch oven, cook chicken and garlic with olive oil, cumin and salt and pepper to taste until about done, about five minutes each side. We cook the bell peppers with the chicken. In strips, they cook for as long as the chicken. When chicken has cooled, chop into small pieces.

Preheat oven to 300° F.

Drain chilies and add to cooked, chopped chicken.

Place tortillas on baking dish and brush lightly with water. Divide the chicken mixture among the tortillas and sprinkle with grated cheese. Add red and green pepper. Top this with another tortilla, pressing down the edges to seal. Brush lightly with water. Bake 15 minutes. Remove from oven and cut into pie-shaped quarters. Pour picante sauce over Quesadillas. Sprinkle with grated Monterey cheese. Top with avocado and tomato.

Serve with **margaritas** for a true Tex-Mex meal. Use 1 can of Bacardi® frozen concentrate mix, 8 oz. rum and fill blender with crushed ice. Blend into frozen mix. To the margarita glass rim, rub the peel from a lime and dip rim into margarita salt. Add margarita liquid and place lime slice on rim.

GUACAMOLE SALAD

1 avocado, skinned, cut up
¼ cup chopped white onions
1 green chili pepper, finely chopped
1 teaspoon lemon juice
½ teaspoon salt
¼ teaspoon pepper, coarsely ground
¼ teaspoon orange juice
1 Tbsp. mayonnaise
½ tomato, finely chopped
1 small clove garlic, chopped

Beat avocados, onions, chili peppers, lemon juice, salt, pepper, orange juice, mayonnaise until creamy. Stir in tomato bits and garlic. Cover guacamole and refrigerate *at least 1 hour*.

BLACK BEANS

4 cups water
1 cup black beans
1 slice bacon, uncooked
Salt to taste
Fresh cilantro

In a medium-size pot, combine water and beans. Bring water to a boil and cook for two minutes then remove from heat.

Let the beans soak for 1 hour. Drain the beans. Refill the pot with fresh water; add bacon, salt to taste and bring to a simmer. Let cook for about 1 hour.

Black beans for this menu should be mashed and mixed with pieces of cilantro.

BROILED SALMON WITH MUSTARD-DILL

with Fresh Spinach and Rice

1 salmon fillet
1 lemon
2 Tbsps. dry mustard
¾ teaspoon dry dill weed

Fresh spinach
½ cup vinegar
Olive oil
Converted Rice

This is another version of the mustard salmon you had the first week of this month.

Prepare **rice** according to package directions.

When rice is cooking, preheat the oven's broiler. Place rack about 4-5 inches below the heat source.

Rinse the **salmon** and pat dry. On a flat baking sheet, lay fish skin down. Do not season.

Prepare the **mustard-dill** sauce. Remove the yellow skin from a lemon. Mince the skin and place in a small mixing bowl or cereal bowl. Squeeze one lemon into the bowl of lemon peel. Next, add the dry mustard and dill weed. Stir to mix well. Because of the sauce's unusual taste, we like to prepare the salmon in a half and half method. Brush the mixture over half of the salmon; the remaining half can be seasoned with lemon zest and lemon.

Broil salmon until center is opaque, about 10-12 minutes.

While the salmon cooks, prepare the **spinach**. We wash fresh spinach in a basin of water mixed with ½ cup of vinegar. Thoroughly rinse the spinach after washing. We then steam the fresh spinach using a small steamer basket over boiling water, or you can place the spinach in a pot with a minimum of water and let the spinach steam for a few minutes. Tear the spinach leaves and mix with a tablespoon of olive oil.

STEAK IN BRANDY AND CREAM

with Potato Rounds and Green Beans

2 1-inch thick fillet steaks, well trimmed
2 Tbsps. butter
Salt and pepper to taste
1 Tbsp. brandy
2 Tbsps. whipping cream
1 teaspoon prepared mustard
Green Salad Ingredients:
- **iceberg lettuce**
- **cucumbers**
- **celery, julienned**
- **parsley**

Potato Rounds:
- **3 baking potatoes**
- **1 Tbsp. peanut oil**
- **½ onion, sliced thinly into rounds**
- **1 teaspoon sea salt**
- **Dash pepper**
- **2 Tbsps. margarine**

1 lb. green beans
1 slice bacon

Make the **green salad** first. Wash, dry and tear the lettuce into bite-size pieces. Slice cucumber thinly, julienne the celery stalk into 2-inch lengths. Add parsley as a garnish. Place the salad in a large bowl and refrigerate until mealtime.

Make the **potato rounds** next. Boil the whole potatoes in boiling water for about 30 minutes; remove and let cool. Slice into rounds, about ¼ inch thick.

Heat the peanut oil in a heavy skillet and place in the rounds, mixing them with the onion rounds. Add the salt and pepper seasoning. Place butter on top of the onion and potato rounds. Cover skillet and reduce heat to medium. Cook 20 minutes undisturbed, then remove cover. Flip the rounds over once and cook for another 15 minutes.

Prepare **green beans** by cutting off ends and cooking in salted water with slice of bacon for approximately 20 minutes.

Sauté **steaks** in butter over medium-high heat to desired doneness, adding salt and pepper as they cook, about 6 minutes each side. Reduce heat and add brandy to rinse pan. Being careful, strike match and light the fumes that rise from the brandy. When flame dies, remove steaks and keep warm. Prepare the sauce by adding whipping cream to pan juices. Stir well and reduce liquid by half.

Just before serving, add prepared mustard and stir well. Pour sauce over steaks.

Fourth week SEPTEMBER

Sunday	*Monday*	*Tuesday*	*Wednesday*	*Thursday*	*Friday*	*Saturday*
Meat Loaf in a Tube Rice, Corn	**Chicken in Wine Sauce** Baked Potatoes, Green Peas	**Shrimp and Macaroni** Tossed Salad	**Baked Pork w/ Zucchini** Rice, Pineapple Slices, Spinach	**Chicken and Bell Peppers** Italian Salad, French Bread	**Grilled Halibut Steaks** Baked Potatoes, Tossed Salad	**The Sicilian Sunset** Shredded Mound Salad, French Bread

Fresh Vegetables \ Fruits		*Herbs \ Spices*	*Basics*
tomatoes - 5 fresh corn - 4 mushrooms - 3 white onion - 2 red onion - 1 potatoes - 8 celery bundle iceberg lettuce - 2 green leaf lettuce - 1 cucumber - 1 radishes-bunch	garlic pod - 1 fresh basil leaves - 5 zucchini - 3 green bell pepper - 1 red bell peppers - 2 carrot bundle red cabbage head lemon - 5 green onions - 3 spinach bunch Roma tomatoes - 3	Italian seasoning garlic salt oregano mint rosemary dried thyme marjoram	ketchup cornstarch sugar honey olive oil peanut oil salad dressing Converted Rice white vinegar

Entrée Food	*Dairy*	*Miscellaneous*	*Cans \ Jars*
ground chuck - 1 lb. skinless, boneless chicken breasts - 3 shrimp - ½ lb. butterfly pork chops - 2 halibut - 1 lb. **Frozen** spinach pkg. - 10 oz green peas pkg	egg - 1 Mozzarella cheese - 2 slices butter - 2 sticks low fat milk - 1 cup Parmesan cheese 2 T bacon - 9 slices **Wine** burgundy 1 T	bread crumbs 4 oz macaroni - ¼ lb. fettucine pasta ½ lb French bread - 2 bow-tie pasta - ½ lb croutons - pkg. brown sugar - ¼ C	chicken broth - 3 ripe olives - 4 oz pineapple chunks - 5 oz salad pepper - 10 oz. (vlasic® Pepperoncini)

MEAT LOAF IN A TUBE

with Rice and Corn

½ pkg. frozen spinach
1 lb. ground chuck or sirloin
1 egg
½ cup soft bread crumbs
1 teaspoon Italian seasoning
2 Tbsps. ketchup
2 Tbsps. milk
¼ teaspoon garlic salt
¼ teaspoon pepper
¼ teaspoon oregano
½ teaspoon salt
2 slices Mozzarella cheese

1 tomato, sliced
4 ears fresh corn
Converted Rice

Preheat oven to 350° F.

Defrost the frozen spinach. Cold running water will loosen the spinach enough to break it into pieces. Drain well.

Make the **meat loaf roll**. Mix ground chuck or ground sirloin, egg, bread crumbs, Italian seasoning, ketchup, milk, garlic salt, pepper, oregano and ½ teaspoon salt. Spread out aluminum foil and form meat into a long, thin rectangle. The meat should be thin enough to roll into a tube.

Spread the spinach on top of the meat and cut the cheese into strips to lay across the meat. Season all with salt.

Roll the meat into a tube using the foil to lift and separate. You can press the ends and edges together to form a finished piece. Place meat tube in a shallow baking pan.

Place tomato slices on top in the manner of toppled dominoes.

Cook uncovered in a 350° F oven about 1 hour.

While meat loaf cooks, prepare **rice** according to package directions.

As rice cooks, prepare the **corn**. For the microwave, wrap in dampened cloth towel and cook on HIGH for 2 minutes, turning once. For stove top, boil the corn for about 10 minutes.

CHICKEN IN WINE SAUCE

with Baked Potatoes and Green Peas

2 Tbsps. butter
1 clove garlic, minced
2 boneless, skinless chicken breasts
1 cup burgundy wine
Salt and pepper to taste
¼ tsp. dried rosemary
¼ tsp. dried thyme
1 onion, sliced into rings
2 fresh mushrooms, sliced
1 Tbsp. cornstarch
¼ cup water

4 potatoes, for baking

1 (10 oz.) pkg. frozen green peas

Prepare the **chicken**. Pound the chicken breasts to achieve an even thickness. In a large, covered pan or Dutch oven, melt butter or margarine over medium-high heat. Add the minced garlic. Add breasts and cook until they are a very light brown, about 5-10 minutes. Add wine, salt, pepper, rosemary and thyme. Slice the onion and scatter the rings about. Cover and simmer until tender, 15-20 minutes.

While the chicken cooks, prepare the **baked potatoes** using the microwave. Wash the potatoes and prick with a fork. Bake on HIGH for 4 minutes per side, turning once. (3 or 4 potatoes will cook in 24 minutes.)

Also prepare the frozen **green peas** following package directions.

When chicken is almost done, add mushrooms and simmer 5 minutes longer or until breast is cooked through. Remove the chicken and mushrooms and pour juices into a small skillet. Straining is optional. Into this liquid, stir in a blend of cornstarch and water. Cook this sauce over medium heat for about a minute.

SHRIMP AND MACARONI

with Tossed Salad

½ lb. fresh shrimp, cleaned, peeled, deveined
3 cloves garlic
2 cans chicken broth
3 Roma tomatoes
5 large basil leaves
¼ lb. macaroni
2 teaspoons sugar (optional)
Low-fat milk (optional)

Tossed Salad Ingredients:
iceberg lettuce
green leaf lettuce
cucumber
radishes
tomato
ripe olives
croutons

This menu comes from Beverly Decarlo who served this meal to us during a teacher appreciation week. It is unforgettably good.

Begin with a **tossed salad**: wash and dry all vegetables. Tear the lettuces into bite-size pieces. Slice the cucumber and radishes. Cut the tomatoes into wedges. Toss all together, then add the ripe olives and the croutons.

For the **main course,** mince garlic. Sauté in 2 tablespoons olive oil. In pot, combine chicken broth, sautéed garlic, and chopped tomato with basil leaves. Cook macaroni in this mixture, and later, add the shrimp to cook. *** *This will vary with the time allowed for the macaroni, whether it is fresh or dried.*

To thicken the broth, you can add cornstarch. Also, to make a cream sauce, add low-fat milk when the mixture is boiling.

BAKED PORK WITH ZUCCHINI

with Rice, Pineapple slices and Spinach

2 butterfly pork chops
2 Tbsps. peanut oil
¼ teaspoon pepper
½ teaspoon salt
½ cup chicken broth
2 zucchini, sliced
¼ cup honey
¼ cup brown sugar
¼ cup butter or margarine

1 (5 ½ oz.) can pineapple chunks

1 bunch fresh spinach
½ cup vinegar

Converted Rice

Preheat oven to 400° F.

Brown **pork chops** in peanut oil over medium heat until barely brown. Season with pepper and salt. Place pork chops in a covered baking dish. Add ½ cup of chicken broth.

Slice the **zucchini** and place on chops in the manner of toppled dominoes. Mix together the honey, brown sugar and melted butter. Pour this mixture over the zucchini. Place pork chops in oven to bake, covered, for about 45 minutes, or until the pork is done to your liking.

While the pork cooks, prepare the **rice** by following package directions.

Before the pork chops are done, prepare **spinach** by steaming. We wash fresh spinach in a basin of water mixed with ½ cup of vinegar. Thoroughly rinse the spinach after washing. We then steam the fresh spinach using a small steamer basket over boiling water, or you can place the spinach in a pot with a minimum of water and let the spinach steam for a few minutes.

When serving food, place **pineapple chunks** around the chops and zucchini.

CHICKEN AND BELL PEPPERS

with Italian Salad and French Bread

1 boneless chicken breast
¼ cup olive oil
½ green pepper, cut into strips
½ red pepper, cut into strips
½ small onion, cut into chunks
1 fresh mushroom, sliced
½ teaspoon marjoram
½ pkg. fettucine pasta
2 Tbsps. grated Parmesan cheese

Italian Salad Ingredients:
iceberg lettuce
green leaf lettuce
tomato, in wedges
red cabbage, julienned
ripe olives
carrot, shredded
salad pepper
croutons (optional)
Salad dressing of choice
French bread

If having fresh **French bread**, preheat oven to 400° F.

Prepare the **Italian salad**. Tear lettuces into bite-size pieces. Cut tomato into wedges in desired thickness. Cut red cabbage into julienne strips. Add a few ripe olives. Shred the carrot on top. Toss well. Add a salad pepper to top and spread croutons around.

When oven is heated, insert the French bread to be cooked. This takes about forty minutes total time but check the package directions.

At a point that will coordinate the timing of the bread, prepare the **chicken.** Pound the chicken breasts to achieve an even thickness. Cut chicken into thin strips. In large skillet, heat olive oil; add chicken strips, peppers, onion, mushrooms and seasoning. Cook and stir over medium heat until chicken is cooked through, about 8 to 10 minutes.

While chicken cooks, prepare **fettuccine pasta** according to package directions; drain, rinse in cold water; drain again. Sprinkle with Parmesan cheese.

GRILLED HALIBUT STEAKS

with Baked Potatoes and Tossed Salad

1 lb. halibut, cut into one-inch cubes
½ cup lemon juice
1 Tbsp. olive oil
2 dashes dried oregano
¼ teaspoon dried mint
1 ½ teaspoons garlic minced
1 red onion, cut in wedges

4 potatoes
Tossed Salad Ingredients:
green leaf lettuce
iceberg lettuce
cucumber
radishes
tomato
ripe olives
croutons

While charcoal briquets are heating, combine lemon juice, oil, oregano, mint and garlic. Place in a 11 x 7 x 2 inch glass baking dish. Rinse **halibut** and pat dry. Add fish to pan and turn to coat both sides; set in refrigerator at least 30 minutes.

Prepare the **tossed salad**. Wash and dry all vegetables. Tear the lettuces into bite-size pieces. Slice the cucumber and radishes. Cut the tomato into wedges. Toss all together, then add the ripe olives and the croutons.

Bake **potatoes** according to your favorite method. We typically use the microwave to completely bake or to at least partially bake the potatoes. Wash the potatoes and pierce with fork. Place potatoes in the microwave and cook on HIGH for 4 minutes per potato per side, turning once. (3 or 4 potatoes will cook in 24 minutes.)

Drain halibut, saving marinade. Thread fish and red onion onto metal skewer. Place on grill and baste occasionally with marinade. Grill about 8-10 minutes.

THE SICILIAN SUNSET

with Shredded Mound Salad and French Bread

9 slices bacon, cut up
3 Tbsp. sliced green onions
1 clove garlic, minced
1 red bell pepper, julienned
1 zucchini, thinly sliced
1 teaspoon basil leaves
½ teaspoon salt
Dash pepper
Bow-tie pasta *

French bread
Shredded Mound Salad:
iceberg lettuce
carrot
celery stalk
tomato

* *Or any substitute*

Prepare the **shredded mound salad**: Wash and dry all vegetables. Halve the tomato and place one on each plate. Using a shredder or grater, on each serving plate, shred the lettuce, carrot, celery into a high mound covering the tomato. Place the salad in the refrigerator until ready to serve.

If you are having **fresh bread**, preheat the oven and cook it now. We like to purchase the ready-to-bake versions.

While the bread cooks, prepare the **pasta** entrée. In large skillet, cook bacon until crisp. Drain, retaining ¼ cup drippings; return to skillet. Add cooked bacon, green onions and garlic; cook 1 minute. Stir in red bell pepper, zucchini, basil, salt and pepper. Simmer 5 minutes.

Prepare Bow-tie pasta according to package directions. Add to mixture; garnish as desired and serve hot.

Fifth week SEPTEMBER

Sunday	*Monday*	*Tuesday*	*Wednesday*	*Thursday*	*Friday*	*Saturday*
Asian Chicken Broccoli Noodles, Sautéed Celery Salad	**Old-Fashioned BBQ Sand-wiches** Ranch Style Beans ®	**Sherry Sautéed Shrimp** Curried Rice, Sake	**Mushroom Stuffed Pork Chops** Rice, Apple Slices	**Oven Baked Broccoli** Rice, Cheese Assortment	**Pan-Fried Halibut Chunks** Baked Potatoes, House Salad	*Plan Ahead* **Apple Cider Roast Beef** Mashed Potatoes, Green Peas, Carrots

Fresh Vegetables \ Fruits		*Herbs \ Spices*	*Basics*
white onions - 2 red bell pepper - 1 celery bundle - 2 green bell pepper - 1 green onions - 3 lemons - 2 fresh mushrooms -2 parsley bunch	garlic pod - 1 broccoli - 1 lb. cucumber - 1 carrot bundle -1 radish - bunch iceberg lettuce - 1 potatoes - 7 red apple - 1	celery salt kosher salt hot pepper sauce garlic salt curry powder minced onions	olive oil soy sauce ketchup Worcestershire sauce extra-virgin olive oil peanut oil flour corn oil Converted Rice Marsala red wine

Entrée Food	*Dairy*	*Miscellaneous*	*Cans \ Jars*
skinless, boneless chicken breasts - 2 ground beef - 1 lb. raw shrimp - ½ lb. butterfly pork chops - 2 ham - ¼ lb. halibut fillets - 2 rump roast - 3 lbs.	Parmesan cheese - 2 oz butter - 2 tsp. margarine - 2 sticks cheese assortment - 3 Swiss cheese- 4 oz. milk - ½ cup **Wine** sherry wine - 4 T Sake - ½ bottle **Frozen** green peas pkg	chicken flavor Ramen noodle soup 3 oz. - 2 hamburger buns - 8 croutons - pkg. apple cider - 2 C instant chicken bouillon - 1 T instant beef bouillon - 2 T	cream of broccoli soup - 2 can of mushroom stems and pieces 1 Franco-American beef gravy - 1 French fried onions - 1 chicken broth - 1 ripe olives - 4 oz. Ranch Style Beans® 1 capers - 4 oz. sliced pimentos - 2 T

ASIAN CHICKEN BROCCOLI

with Noodles and Sautéed Celery Salad

2 chicken breasts, boneless, skinless
2 Tbsps. olive oil
1 small onion, cut in 1" cubes
1 red bell pepper, cut into 1" squares
1 can cream of broccoli soup
3 Tbsps. water
1 Tbsp. soy sauce
2 (3 oz.) pkg. chicken flavor Ramen noodle soup

Sautéed Celery Salad:
5 stalks of celery
1 Tbsp. peanut oil
1 Tbsp. instant chicken bouillon
½ teaspoon salt
Dash celery salt
2 Tbsps. sliced pimentos

Pound **chicken** to achieve an even thickness. Heat the 2 tablespoons of olive oil in a medium-size skillet until hot. Cook chicken until browned on both sides, about 5 - 6 minutes per side. Remove chicken and allow to cool for a few minutes.

You can make the salad as first course at this point. To prepare the **sautéed celery**, slice the celery into diagonal cuts. Cook and stir celery slices in skillet with 1 tablespoon peanut oil. Add the instant bouillon, salt, celery salt and cook over medium heat, turning often until the celery is tender, about 8 minutes. Toss in the pimentos to heat before serving.

Now, back to the chicken. To the chicken in the skillet, add onion and red bell pepper; cook until tender-crisp. Stir in cream of **broccoli soup**, water and soy sauce. Heat to boiling. Reduce heat and cover to simmer about 5 minutes.

Meanwhile, prepare **Ramen noodle soup** according to package directions. Add seasoning packet; drain noodles. If you cannot find the Campbell® soup package, substitute any brand of noodles and add chicken broth as needed liquid.

Serve chicken over noodles.

OLD-FASHIONED BBQ SANDWICHES

with Ranch Style Beans®

1 lb. ground beef meat
2 Tbsps. peanut oil
½ cup onion, chopped
1 clove garlic, crushed
¼ cup chopped celery
¼ cup chopped green bell peppers
¼ cup ketchup *
¼ cup water *

1 Tbsp. Worcestershire sauce *
Red pepper sauce, to taste *
1 teaspoon salt

Hamburger buns, toasted

1 can Ranch Style beans®

** In a pinch you can leave out the starred ingredients and purchase any brand of prepared barbecue sauce.*

Cook and stir the **ground beef** in a skillet with a bit of peanut oil. Immediately, add the onion and the garlic; cook until the redness of the meat disappears. Excess fat should be removed.

Stir in garlic, celery, green peppers, ketchup, water, Worcestershire sauce, red pepper sauce and salt. Heat to boiling; reduce heat. Cover and simmer, stirring occasionally, about 45 minutes.

Before the meat has finished cooking, heat the **Ranch Style Beans®**.

At the same time, brown the **hamburger buns** in a toaster or under the oven's broiler. Spoon the meat mixture onto the hamburger buns.

Serve with iced tea or a good American beer.

SHERRY SAUTÉED SHRIMP

with Curried Rice and Sake

½ lb. raw shrimp
2 Tbsps. kosher salt
2 green onions
3 Tbsps. extra-virgin olive oil
Garlic salt
4 Tbsps. sherry wine
1 lemon, juiced
2 fresh mushrooms, sliced
Grated Parmesan cheese

Converted Rice
1 Tbsp. minced onions
2 Tbsps. margarine
1 teaspoon curry powder
¼ teaspoon salt
¼ teaspoon pepper

Sake

Cook **rice** following package directions. When rice is fully cooked, prepare the curry ingredients. Sauté 1 tablespoon onion in 2 tablespoons of butter until yellow. Gently stir in the cooked rice; add curry powder, salt and pepper.

Salt-leach the **shrimp**. Peel the shrimp and wash clean. Sprinkle with kosher salt, coating evenly. Let sit for one minute. Rinse and drain. Repeat salting again, let sit for another minute, rinse; drain well and set aside.

In skillet, sauté onions. Season with garlic salt. Add sherry, lemon juice, shrimp and mushrooms. Sprinkle with Parmesan cheese. Simmer until shrimp are done.

Serve the shrimp poured over the rice with a cup of warm **sake** on the side.

MUSHROOM - STUFFED PORK CHOPS

with Rice and Apple Slices

2 butterfly pork chops
1 (3 oz.) can mushroom stems and pieces, drained
4 oz. Swiss cheese, chopped
¼ cup parsley, chopped

2 Tbsps. peanut oil
1 can Franco-American gravy
1 Tbsp. Marsala wine
1 red apple, sliced
Parsley sprigs
Converted Rice

Slit **butterfly pork chops** to make a pocket. Stuff with mushrooms, cheese and chopped parsley; fasten with metal skewers or toothpicks.

In skillet large enough to hold the pork chops, pour in 2 tablespoons of peanut oil and heat. Brown chops on both sides. Add the beef gravy and wine. Cover and cook over low heat for about 1 hour, stirring occasionally. If you like a thick gravy, you can continue to cook the gravy after removing the pork chops. Cook uncovered for up to 15 minutes.

While the chops cook, prepare **rice** according to package directions.

We like to add the sweetness of **apple slices** to this menu. Cut sweet red apple into thin wedges and arrange on serving platter or plate. Sprinkle some **fresh parsley** over the top of the apple slices.

OVEN - BAKED BROCCOLI

with Ham or Chicken, Rice and Cheese Assortment

1 lb. fresh broccoli
1 Tbsp. peanut oil
1 can cream of broccoli soup
½ cup milk
1 teaspoon soy sauce
Dash pepper
1 (2.8 oz.) can French fried onions

Converted Rice

¼ lb. ham, in cubes or pan-fried chicken

Cheese assortment

Preheat oven to 350° F.

Prepare **oven-baked broccoli.** Slice the broccoli into florets, saving one stalk which should be diced. Sauté the broccoli pieces in a minimum of peanut oil for five minutes. In a large casserole dish, combine cream of broccoli soup, milk, soy sauce and black pepper. Stir in the sautéed broccoli and about ¼ can of fried onions.

When oven is heated, insert the broccoli casserole and bake, covered, for about 25 minutes.

While the broccoli bakes, prepare **rice** according to package directions.

For those who find this menu on the light side, we suggest you have **thick ham slices** cut into cubes. For those who prefer chicken, fry a whole boneless **chicken breast**. To prepare the chicken, first pound it to achieve an even thickness then season it with salt and pepper and fry it in a skillet until brown, about 6 minutes on each side.

When broccoli bake is done, uncover and bake another 15 minutes to brown. At this time, prepare an **assortment of cheeses**, hard and soft.

PAN-FRIED HALIBUT CHUNKS

with Baked Potatoes and House Salad

¼ cup chicken broth
4 teaspoons drained capers
1 teaspoon lemon juice
2 halibut fillet or steaks
2 Tbsps. all-purpose flour
½ teaspoon each salt and pepper
2 Tbsps. olive oil
2 teaspoons margarine or butter

House Salad Ingredients:
iceberg lettuce
carrots stalks
cucumber
radishes
ripe olives
croutons
4 potatoes, for baking

Ahead of time, prepare the **house salad**. Wash and dry all vegetables. Peel lettuce off in layers. Cut the carrots into pencil-size shapes. Cut the cucumber into rounds then quarter to make pie-slices. Slice radishes. Toss all together, then add the ripe olives and the croutons when serving. Place salad in the refrigerator to chill.

Bake **potatoes** according to your favorite method. We typically use the microwave to completely bake or to at least partially bake the potatoes. Wash the potatoes and pierce with fork. Place potatoes in the microwave and cook on HIGH for 4 minutes per potato per side, turning once. (3 or 4 potatoes will cook in 24 minutes.)

Prepare a **lemon sauce**. In a measuring cup, combine broth, capers and lemon juice. Set aside.

To prepare the **halibut,** rinse fish and pat dry. If using fillets, slice into chunky pieces, about ½ inch thick. If using steaks, trim off skin. Cut along both sides of bone to separate flesh; discard skin and bones. In a shallow dish mix flour, salt and pepper. Dredge pieces of fish through the flour mixture to coat all surfaces. Heat 2 tablespoons oil in a frying pan over medium-high heat. When oil is hot, add fish to pan. Cook until fish is lightly brown on both sides, between 2-3 minutes each side. Transfer fish to a platter and keep warm.

Pour lemon sauce mixture from above into pan and stir to scrape up cooked bits of fish. Remove pan from heat and stir in margarine. Pour this sauce over fish.

Garnish with a lemon slice and a sprig of fresh herb.

APPLE CIDER ROAST BEEF

with Mashed Potatoes, Green Peas and Carrots

3 lb. rump roast, or beef tip
2 cloves garlic
1 teaspoon salt
¼ teaspoon pepper
2 cups apple cider
¼ cup vegetable oil
Gravy Ingredients:
  2 Tbsps. flour
  ½ cup cold water
  1 Tbsp. instant beef bouillon

Green peas (fresh or frozen)

Carrots

3 potatoes
½ stick margarine
¼ cup milk

Prepare the **apple cider beef.** If rump roast has a layer of fat covering it, prick the beef roast with a fork. Rub the surface with the cloves of garlic. Sprinkle with salt and pepper. Let sit for ten minutes or so. Place beef in a bowl large enough to hold and cover the beef. Mix the apple cider, the vegetable oil and pour over the beef. *Cover and refrigerate for at least 12-16 hours.*

Preheat the oven to 325° F.

Remove beef from marinade and reserve at least 1 cup of the marinade to serve as sauce. To cook, place beef, fat side up on a rack in a shallow pan. Insert meat thermometer into thickest portion of beef. Roast, uncovered, for 2 ½ hours, or until the thermometer registers 160° F. When done, remove beef to cutting board.

Make the **green peas and carrots** by the steaming method. Combine the two vegetables and place in a steamer and cook for about 3 minutes.

Prepare **mashed potatoes.** Wash and peel potatoes and cut into halves then quarters. Heat a pot of water and add the potato pieces. Salt the water to your taste. Cook for approximately 20 minutes; drain. Into hot potatoes place ½ stick of butter or margarine, ¼ cup of milk and whip to desired smoothness.

To make the **beef gravy**, heat the reserved marinade over medium heat until hot. In a covered container (we use an empty jar for such purposes) mix together the water, flour and instant bouillon; stir this mixture gradually into the beef marinade. While stirring, bring the mixture to a boil. Cook for 1 minute.

APPETIZERS

When there's too little time

- Spear toothpicks with browned sausage rounds and cubes of cheddar cheese. Make a dipping sauce of ½ cup mild taco sauce and ¼ cup picante sauce.
- Saturate a block of cream cheese with soy sauce and roll in sesame seeds.
- Top a cracker with cream cheese and a slice of sweet pickle.
- Wedge a partially-split cherry tomato with a slice of mushroom.
- In a double boiler, melt a roll of Jalapeno cheese with a can of chili and beans; serve as a dip.
- Top Triscuits with melted butter and lemon-pepper seasoning; bake at 350° F until hot.
- Pop corn
- Use Cheddar cheese and hot pepper jelly as a cracker spread.

Late Night Snacks

These take a bit more preparation

- Celery avocado: fill short lengths of celery with a mixture of whipped avocado, juice from 1 lemon and a tablespoon of diced onions.
- Beef and or chicken nachos. See page 588.
- Stuffed cherry tomatoes. See page 579.
- Deviled eggs. See page 207.
- Sausage balls. See page 358.
- Pizza See page 558.
- Cheese and Broccoli Soup See page 109.

October

The best of the Shrimp Menus!

Cooler Weather at last! But we're still grilling outside for a final time-- once with pork chops and once with red meat. The *Grilled Pork Chop* with cole slaw has a Chinese flavor that is unique. We'll close the month with a grilled steak and *Spicy Potatoes*.

It is also time to get out the terra cotta garlic roaster baking dish or to purchase one for the best of the Italian and garlic menus.

The month of October has the best of the shrimp menus. You know by now how *Cajun Shrimp* tastes, and you can probably imagine the taste of *Curried Shrimp*. But the real treat for the month is a tasty, delightful and unusual *Seafood Pasta* that is courtesy of Texas A & M University.

Included in October are menus from some of our favorite vacation trips. From New Orleans, a change of pace *Club Sandwich* and a universal *Cajun Shrimp*. Then there are the Italian dishes such as *Pasta Della Casa* with the roasted garlic. The chicken menus remain consistently good. You've come to know by now that chicken is versatile, tasty and always moist. And so it continues into October with menus found from Texas to Colorado. A *Chicken Broccoli Casserole* leads off the month with rice and herbed tomatoes that we've all come to love. Then there's a *Tart Chicken Breast* that combines pineapple cubes with green bell pepper and canned tomatoes sautéed over butter. We have an oven *BBQ chicken* and an unforgettable *Sour Cream Bleu Chicken.*

October is the month of new things. A new method of cooking fish: in a *Lunch Sack*. One of the easiest and best of the pork chop menus: *Winter Baked Pork Chops*. The best of the cold shrimp menus, including a *Pickled Shrimp and Pepper* masterpiece. All in all, October has five different ways to prepare shrimp and each result is perfect.

October Menus

Chicken

Chicken-Broccoli Casserole with Rice and Herbed Tomatoes
Oven Barbecued Chicken with Ranch Style Beans and Potato Salad
Tart Chicken Breast with Mashed Potatoes and Green Peas
Swiss Cordon Bleu Chicken with Mashed Potatoes and Green Peas
Chicken With Snow Peas with Carrots, Pasta and Fresh Bread

Quick & Easy

Easy Spaghetti Meat Sauce with Italian Salad, Bread and Red Wine
Cabbage Meat Loaf with Linguine
Mexican Hash with Spaghetti and Guacamole Salad
Club Sandwiches with Tomato Soup
Chicken and Potato Hash with Tossed Salad

Shrimp

Cajun Shrimp with Salad, Baked Potatoes and Fresh Bread
Shrimp and Spinach Alfredo with Tossed Salad and Italian Bread Sticks
Cold Seafood Pasta with Green Salad
Curried Shrimp with Rice and Green Salad
Pickled Shrimp and Peppers with Tossed Salad and Fresh Bread

Pork

Winter Baked Pork Chops with Spinach
Cheese-Stuffed Pasta Shells with House Salad and Fresh Bread Rolls
Grilled Pork Chops with Buttered Cauliflower, Cole Slaw and Dinner Rolls
Fruit Glazed Baked Ham with Potato Salad and Green Beans
Tangy Pork Patties with Mashed Potatoes and Spinach
Cornbread Sausage with Spinach

Pasta / Soup

Pasta Della Casa with Roasted Garlic and Fresh Bread
Chicken and Vegetable Soup with Rice and Tossed Salad
Vegetable Lasagna with Green Salad and Fresh Bread
Country Ham & Potato Soup with Caesar Salad and Dinner Rolls
Mozzarella Spinach Salad with Fresh Bread, Bacon and Risotto

Fish

Sack Lunch Fish with Herbed Rice and Green Wedge Salad
Chunky Tuna Salad with Baked Potatoes and Fresh Bread
Bread Crusted Baked Cod with Snow Peas and Rice
Steamed Sole Fillet with Rice and Broiled Peppers
Broiled Swordfish Steaks with Baked Potatoes and Green Wedge Salad

Red Meats

Barbecued Potatoes with Grilled Steak and Tomato Slices
Mushroom Beef in Burgundy with Mashed Potatoes and Broccoli
Steak with Spicy Potatoes with Fresh Fruit Salad
Pepper Roast and Gravy with Mashed Potatoes and Carrots

OCTOBER

Sunday	Monday	Tuesday	Wednesday	Thursday	Friday	Saturday
Chicken Broccoli Casserole Rice, Herbed Tomatoes	**Easy Spaghetti Meat Sauce** Italian Salad, Italian Bread, Red Wine	**Cajun Shrimp** Baked Potatoes, Fresh Bread	**Winter Baked Pork Chops** Spinach	**Pasta Della Casa** Roasted Garlic	**Sack Lunch Fish** Herbed Rice, Green Wedge Salad	*Plan ahead* **Barbecued Potatoes** Grilled Steak, Sliced Tomatoes
Tart Chicken Breast Mashed Potatoes Green Peas	**Cabbage Meat Loaf** Linguine	**Shrimp & Spinach Alfredo** Tossed Salad, Italian Bread	**Cheese Stuffed Pasta Shells** House salad Fresh Rolls	**Chicken & Vegetable Soup** Rice, Tossed Salad	**Chunky Tuna Salad** Baked Potato, Fresh Bread	**Mushroom Beef in Burgundy** Mashed Potatoes, Broccoli
Plan ahead **Oven Barbecued Chicken** Ranch Style Beans, Potato Salad	**Mexican Hash** Spaghetti, Guacamole Salad	*Plan ahead* **Cold Seafood Pasta** Green Salad	**Grilled Pork Chops** Buttered Cauliflower Cole Slaw	**Vegetable Lasagna** Green Salad, Fresh Bread	**Bread Crusted Baked Cod** Snow Peas, Rice,	*Plan ahead* **Fruit Glazed Baked Ham** Green Beans, Potato Salad
Swiss Cordon Bleu Chicken Mashed Potatoes, Green Peas	**Club Sandwich** Tomato Soup	**Curried Shrimp** Rice, Green Salad	**Tangy Pork Patties** Mashed Potatoes, Spinach	**Mozzarella Spinach Salad** Bacon and Risotto	**Steamed Sole Fillet** Rice, Broiled Peppers	*Plan ahead* **Pepper Roast and Gravy** Mashed Potatoes, Carrots
Chicken Snow Peas Carrots, Pasta, Fresh Bread	**Chicken & Potato Hash** Tossed Salad	*Plan ahead* **Pickled Shrimp & Peppers** Tossed Salad, Fresh Bread	**Corn-bread Sausage** Spinach	**Country Ham & Potato Soup** Caesar Salad, Dinner Rolls	*Plan ahead* **Broiled Swordfish Steaks** Baked Potatoes, Green Wedge Salad	*Plan ahead* **Steak & Spiced Potatoes** Molded Fruit Salad

First week OCTOBER

Sunday	*Monday*	*Tuesday*	*Wednesday*	*Thursday*	*Friday*	*Saturday*
Chicken Broccoli Casserole	**Easy Spaghetti Meat Sauce**	**Cajun Shrimp**	**Winter Baked Pork Chops**	**Pasta Della Casa**	**Sack Lunch Fish**	*Plan ahead* **Barbecued Potatoes**
Rice, Herbed Tomatoes	Italian Salad, Italian Bread, Red Wine	Baked Potatoes, Fresh Bread	Spinach	Roasted Garlic, Fresh Bread	Herbed Rice, Green Wedge Salad	Grilled Steak, Tomato Slices

Fresh Vegetables \ Fruits		**Herbs \ Spices**	**Basics**
broccoli - 1 lb. tomatoes - 15 white onions - 3 iceberg lettuce - 2 red leaf lettuce - 1 cucumbers - 2 carrot bundle red cabbage head lemons - 7 celery bundle	garlic pod - 1 elephant garlic pods - 2 red onion - 1 potatoes - 8 green bell pepper - 1 fresh basil - 1 Tbsp. radishes - bunch mushroom - 1 spinach bunch	red pepper sauce bay leaf Italian seasoning ground rosemary paprika oregano rosemary dry mustard	sugar Worcestershire sauce peanut oil olive oil salad oil white wine vinegar red wine vinegar white vinegar Converted Rice Marsala wine vinegar

Entrée Food	*Dairy*	*Miscellaneous*	*Cans \ Jars*
skinless, boneless chicken breasts - 2 ground beef - 1 lb. raw shrimp, shell on - 1 lb. butterfly pork chops - 2 sole fillets - 2 sirloin steaks - 3	milk - ⅓ cup butter - 2 sticks margarine - 2 sticks sharp Cheddar cheese - ¾ C Romano cheese 2 oz. **Wine** Valpolicella red wine bottle	bread crumbs - 2 T sea shell pasta ½ lb croutons - pkg. Italian bread loaf fresh bread pkg. fresh pasta - ½ lb. French buns - 6 herbed rice pkg brown lunch paper bags - 2 almond nuts - 1 oz. terra cotta garlic baker	cream of chicken soup - 1 whole tomatoes - 1 tomato sauce - 1 tomato paste - 1 ripe olives - 4 oz salad pepper - 4 oz vlasic® Pepperoncini chicken bouillon cubes - 2

CHICKEN - BROCCOLI CASSEROLE

with Rice and Herbed Tomatoes

2 boneless, skinless chicken breasts
1 lb. fresh broccoli
1 can cream of chicken soup
¼ cup milk
¾ cup grated sharp Cheddar cheese
2 Tbsps. fine, dry bread crumbs
1 Tbsp. melted butter

Converted Rice

Herbed Tomatoes:
2 tomatoes
1 clove garlic
Marsala wine vinegar

Preheat oven to 450° F.

Pound chicken slightly to tenderize. Boil **chicken** in water until done, about 15 minutes. Set aside to cool.

Undercook **broccoli** (5 minutes) and drain well. Butter a 9 x 13 inch baking dish. Place fresh broccoli pieces on bottom. Cut chicken into bite-size pieces and spread over broccoli.

In a small bowl, combine soup and milk; pour over chicken. Sprinkle with cheese. In cup, combine bread crumbs and butter; sprinkle over cheese.

Bake for about 15 minutes.

Make **rice** while chicken cooks, following package directions.

For the **herbed tomatoes** slice the tomatoes into ¼ inch slices. Sprinkle minced garlic on top as well as fresh ground black pepper. Pour some Marsala wine vinegar over the slices.

EASY SPAGHETTI MEAT SAUCE

with Italian Salad, Italian Bread and Red Wine

1 lb. ground beef
1 onion, chopped
1 clove garlic, crushed
1 teaspoon salt
1 teaspoon sugar
1 bay leaf
1 cup water
1 (15 oz.) can whole tomatoes
1 (8 oz.) can tomato sauce
1 (6 oz.) can tomato paste
2 teaspoons Italian seasoning
½ lb. sea shell pasta
Red wine, Valpolicella

Italian Salad Ingredients:
- **red leaf lettuce**
- **iceberg lettuce**
- **cucumber**
- **tomato, in wedges**
- **red cabbage, julienned**
- **ripe olives**
- **carrot, shredded**
- **salad pepper**
- **croutons (optional)**

Romano cheese
Italian bread

Prepare **meat sauce**. Cook and stir ground beef, with chopped onion and minced garlic in medium-size pan until meat loses its redness. Stir in the remaining ingredients (except for pasta): salt, sugar, bay leaf, water, whole tomatoes crushed with liquid, tomato sauce, tomato paste and Italian seasoning. Heat to boiling; reduce heat. Cover and simmer, stirring occasionally, 1 hour.

Make the **Italian salad** next. Tear lettuces into bite-size pieces. Slice cucumber. Cut tomato into wedges in desired thickness. Cut red cabbage into julienne strips. Add a few ripe olives. Shred the carrot on top. Toss well. Add a salad pepper to top and spread croutons around.

When meat is cooked, prepare the **sea shell pasta** according to package directions. Pour sauce over the pasta. Sprinkle with Romano cheese.

Serve with **Italian bread**, spread with garlic sauce. A **red wine** such as a Valpolicella makes the meal.

CAJUN SHRIMP

with Baked Potatoes, Mushroom Cheese Salad and Fresh Bread

1 stick butter, melted
or 1 stick margarine, melted
¼ cup Worcestershire sauce
2 Tbsps. ground black pepper
½ teaspoon ground rosemary
1 teaspoon Tabasco ® sauce
2 cloves garlic, crushed
2 lemons: 1 juiced, 1 sliced
1 lb. raw shrimp in shell

Mushroom Cheese Salad:
iceberg lettuce
mushroom, sliced
Cheddar cheese, cubed
red onion, julienned

4 potatoes, for baking
Fresh bread

Preheat oven to 400° F.

If **bread** requires baking, do it now, following package directions.

Bake **potatoes** according to your favorite method. We typically use the microwave to completely bake or to at least partially bake the potatoes. Wash the potatoes and pierce with fork. Place potatoes in the microwave and cook on HIGH for 4 minutes per potato per side, turning once. (3 or 4 potatoes will cook in 24 minutes.)

In a medium bowl mix melted butter, Worcestershire sauce, ground black pepper, rosemary, Tabasco® sauce and crushed garlic. Squeeze the juice from one lemon and mix well. Place ½ of the mixture in a small baking dish. Lay in the **shrimp** and cover with sliced lemons, then add the remaining sauce. Bake for 5 to 10 minutes or until done, stirring occasionally.

While the shrimp bakes, make the **mushroom cheese salad**. Cut lettuce into round shapes. Arrange mushroom slices and cheese cubes as you like.

Serve with baked potatoes, crusty bread and lots of napkins.

WINTER BAKED PORK CHOPS

with Spinach

2 butterfly pork chops
Peanut oil
2 chicken bouillon cubes
1 ½ cups water*
¾ cup Converted Rice*
1 teaspoon salt*

½ onion, chopped
¼ green bell pepper, chopped
1 tomato, peeled and sliced
Pepper
Paprika

Spinach
½ cup vinegar

** The amount of rice, water and salt should match the number of servings. Consult the package directions and adjust amounts.*

Preheat oven to 350°F.

In a skillet, heat peanut oil and brown **pork chops.** Place browned chops in a shallow baking dish. Dissolve bouillon cubes in measured water; pour over chops. Add measured rice and salt. Chop onion and green pepper; mix and add to chops. Blanch tomato in hot water until skin loosens; peel and slice. Place sliced tomato over top of pork chops in the manner of toppled dominoes. Sprinkle with black pepper and paprika. Cover and bake in 350° F oven for 1 hour.

When the pork is just about ready, prepare the **spinach.** We wash fresh spinach in a basin of water mixed with ½ cup of vinegar. Thoroughly rinse the spinach after washing. We then steam the fresh spinach using a small steamer basket over boiling water, or you can just as well place the spinach in a pot with a minimum of water and let the spinach steam for a few minutes.

This should remind you of the other One-dish meal. Ginger Nut Pork Chops, on page 102.

PASTA DELLA CASA

with Roasted Garlic with Fresh Bread

2 large elephant garlic pods
or 1 regular pod per person
Terra cotta garlic baker
½ lb. fresh pasta, any type
1 Tbsp. olive oil
6 French buns

Fresh Tomato Sauce:
8 fresh, ripe tomatoes, skinned and seeded
1 Tbsp. fresh basil leaves
Salt and pepper

This menu calls for **roasted garlic pods**. To make the roasted garlic, use a terra cotta garlic baker. Purchase several whole garlic pods, known as elephant garlic pods the size of a large lemon or small apple.. *If the large variety is unavailable substitute with the normal size, allow one per person and cut down on the baking time.* Remove some of the wrapping skin around the pod, cut some of the heads off so the garlic is exposed. Place the pods in the baking dish, drizzle them with extra-virgin olive and salt and pepper. Place the terra cotta bowl into a cold oven, then heat to 350° F and cook for 45 minutes. Remove cover and bake for an additional 45 minutes or until garlic is tender. The garlic should be spreadable when it is cooked perfectly.

While the garlic roasts, prepare the **fresh tomato sauce**. Clean the tomatoes and seed them; in a saucepan, crush the ripe tomatoes. Add minced garlic. Cook for about 15 minutes until the sauce begins to thicken. Add fresh basil leaves, salt and pepper. Continue to cook for another 5 minutes.

Cook **pasta** according to package directions. Drain, rinse with cold water and drain well again. Add pasta to the other ingredients and mix well. Add pepper to taste.

Heat French buns before serving.

SACK LUNCH FISH

with Herbed Rice and Green Wedge Salad

Sole or orange roughy fish
½ stick butter
¼ cup salad oil
1 Tbsp. grated onions
4 lemons, juiced
½ teaspoon pepper, grated
1 clove garlic, crushed
Almonds slivers, walnuts or pecans

Herbed Rice

Green Wedge Salad Ingredients:
½ head, iceberg lettuce
½ cucumber, in thick slices
2 radishes, in thin slices
2 celery stalks, julienned

2 brown lunch paper bags

A version of fish en papillotte.

Preheat the oven to 400° F.

Prepare the **rice** according to package directions.

Prepare the **fish** for baking. Brown fish in ½ stick butter on both sides in a skillet. Spray the insides of the lunch sack with a vegetable spray and lay each portion of fish inside the lunch bag.

In a small bowl, mix together salad oil, grated onion, the juice from 4 lemons, freshly-ground pepper and garlic. Stir well and spoon over the fish. Top each portion of fish with almond slivers, walnuts or pecans. Seal the open end of the lunch sack. We fold the end a couple of times then secure them with staples.

Bake the fish in the bag for ten minutes and serve in their sealed bags.

While fish cooks, prepare the **green wedge salad.** Cut the iceberg lettuce into wide wedges. Remove center portion and chop, spreading on salad plate. Cut the cucumber and place in the remaining curved portion of lettuce wedge. Slice the radishes and place on cucumbers. Julienne the celery and place on top of and around the wedge.

2 hours - Plan ahead

BARBECUED POTATOES

with Grilled Steak and Tomato Slices

Vinaigrette Dressing Ingredients:

- **2 cloves garlic, peeled and minced**
- **¼ teaspoon dried oregano**
- **¼ teaspoon dried rosemary**
- **¼ teaspoon dry mustard**
- **½ teaspoon sugar**
- **½ teaspoon salt**
- **¼ teaspoon freshly ground pepper**
- **1 cup olive oil**
- **¼ cup white wine vinegar**
- **2 Tbsps. water**
- **1 lemon, squeezed**
- **1 tsp. Worcestershire sauce**
- **3 sirloin steaks**
- **4 potatoes, for baking**
- **3 tomatoes, sliced**
- **2 cloves garlic, minced**
- **Red wine vinegar**
- **Salt**
- **Ground pepper**

Make **vinaigrette dressing.** Mince the garlic and place in a small bowl. Add oregano, rosemary, mustard, sugar, salt, pepper, olive oil, vinegar, water, lemon juice and Worcestershire sauce. Beat until it thickens. Store in the refrigerator for at least 1 ½ hours before using.

Preheat the oven to 450° F.

Bake the **potatoes** in their skin for about 30 minutes in 450° F oven, or cook in microwave for about 4 minutes each side turning once. (3 or 4 potatoes will cook in 24 minutes.) Remove potatoes and cut lengthwise in half, then each half lengthwise into quarters. Place the pieces in a glass baking dish and cover with the vinaigrette dressing. Let stand for 1 hour, turning once.

Prepare the **steak** for grilling. Rub garlic on both sides. Sprinkle black pepper on both sides. Prepare cooking grill with coals. Place steak on grill to cook or in oven to broil. Time will vary depending on how well done you like them.

Remove potatoes from dressing, place on grill alongside the steaks. Salt and pepper potatoes to taste. Grill until golden brown, about 10 minutes total time. Remove steaks when done.

While the steak and potatoes broil, cut **tomatoes** into thick slices. Top with garlic and drizzle them with red wine vinegar. Add salt and pepper to taste.

Second week OCTOBER

Sunday	*Monday*	*Tuesday*	*Wednesday*	*Thursday*	*Friday*	*Saturday*
Tart Chicken Breast Mashed Potatoes, Green Peas	**Cabbage Meat Loaf** Linguine	**Shrimp & Spinach Alfredo** Tossed Salad, Italian Bread Sticks	**Cheese Stuffed Pasta Shells** House salad, Fresh Rolls	**Chicken and Vegetable Soup** Rice, Tossed Salad	**Chunky Tuna Salad** Baked Potato, Fresh Bread	**Mushroom Beef in Burgundy** Mashed Potatoes, Broccoli

Fresh Vegetables \ Fruits		*Herbs \ Spices*	*Basics*
white onion - 4 green bell pepper - 1 potatoes - 10 cabbage head - 1 lemons - 4 red leaf lettuce - 1 apple - 1 iceberg lettuce - 2 red onions - 2	garlic pod celery bundle carrot bundle zucchini - 2 tomatoes - 4 corn ears - 3 cucumber - 1 radishes - bunch fresh mushrooms - 3 broccoli - 2 stalks	garlic salt arrowroot dry mustard nutmeg cumin oregano bay leaf	ketchup cornstarch white vinegar flour sea salt olive oil sugar mayonnaise Worcestershire sauce balsamic vinegar Converted Rice

Entrée Food	*Dairy*	*Miscellaneous*	*Cans \ Jars*
boneless, w/ skin chicken breasts - 2 ground beef - 1 lb. raw shrimp - 1 lb. sweet Italian bulk sausage - ½ lb. skinless, boneless chicken breasts -2 beef kabob - 1 ½ lb. **Frozen** green peas - pkg chopped spinach - pkg	margarine - 1 stick butter - 2 sticks milk - 1 ½ cup Parmesan cheese ¾ C egg -1 Ricotta cheese - 8 oz. Mozzarella cheese 8 oz Cheese assortment 3 **Wine** red Chianti bottle dry white- ¼ C burgundy - 1 C	linguine - ½ lb Alfredo sauce mix - pkg. spinach pasta ¾ lb. Italian bread sticks - 1 pkg. jumbo pasta shells - 1 lb. spaghetti sauce - 15 oz. fresh bread rolls 4 croutons (pkg.) fresh bread pkg.	whole tomatoes - 1 cubed pineapple - 1 mushroom stems and pieces - 4 oz tomato sauce - 2 ripe olives - 4 oz green chilies - 1 chicken broth - 3 white tuna (6 oz.) - 2 tomato paste - 1 condensed beef bouillon - 1 capers - 4 oz.

TART CHICKEN BREAST

with Mashed Potatoes and Green Peas

2 whole chicken breasts, boneless with skin
Flour
¼ cup butter, melted
1 medium onion, chopped
1 clove garlic, minced
1 green bell pepper, chopped
1 (14 oz.) can tomatoes, with liquid
1 can cubed pineapple, with 3 Tbsps. of liquid

3 Tbsps. ketchup
2 Tbsps. vinegar
1 Tbsp. cornstarch

3 potatoes
½ stick butter
¼ cup milk
1 (10 oz.) pkg. green peas, frozen

Pound the **chicken** to achieve even thickness. Cut chicken breasts into 1-inch pieces. Season with salt and pepper; coat with flour and set aside.

Meanwhile, prepare **potatoes** and **green peas.**

Prepare **sauce** in saucepan, over medium heat. Melt 2 tablespoons of butter and cook onions, garlic and green peppers for 5 minutes, stirring often.

Add tomatoes, pineapple, juice, ketchup and vinegar. Stir and simmer over low heat.

Meanwhile, in large skillet, over medium-high heat, melt remaining 2 tablespoons of butter. Sauté chicken until golden brown and cooked through (about 5-7 minutes). Drain and place on serving platter.

To sauce, add dissolved cornstarch in 2 tablespoons water; cook stirring frequently, over high-heat until sauce thickens. Pour over chicken pieces.

CABBAGE MEAT LOAF

with Linguine

6 cabbage leaves
1 lb. ground beef
½ cup uncooked Converted rice
½ cup onion, chopped
1 (4 oz.) can mushroom stems and pieces
Sea salt and pepper
Dash garlic salt
2 (8 oz.) cans tomato sauce
1 teaspoon sugar
½ teaspoon lemon juice
½ lb. linguine pasta
1 Tbsp. arrowroot
1 Tbsp. water

Preheat oven 350° F.

To prepare **cabbage**, carefully remove outer layer of leaves from cabbage head. Cut and remove core with a knife. Place cabbage in cold water. Let stand until the leaves loosen, about 12 minutes. Being careful, remove the outer layer of leaves. It may be necessary to let cabbage sit in water again. Prepare a large pot with water and cook the leaves in boiling water. This should also take about 10 minutes. Remove leaves from water and allow to drain on paper towels.

To prepare the **meat loaf,** mix together in a large mixing bowl the ground beef, rice, onion, mushrooms (with liquid), sea salt, pepper, garlic salt and tomato sauce. Shape this mixture into a loaf form that will fit in the baking dish.

Line the inside of the dish with a couple of layers of cabbage leaves. Place meat loaf in the cabbage leaves. Mix remaining tomato sauce, sugar, lemon juice and pour over cabbage.

Cover and cook for 45 minutes.

Before the cabbage meat loaf is cooked, prepare the **linguine** according to package directions. Drain and rinse with water to halt cooking process. Make linguine sauce. Mix arrowroot and 1 tablespoon water in saucepan. Stir in liquid from cabbage. Heat to boiling, stirring constantly. Boil and stir 1 minute. When serving, pour sauce over the linguine.

SHRIMP AND SPINACH ALFREDO

with Tossed Salad and Italian Bread Sticks

¾ pound spinach pasta
2 Tbsps. butter
1 pkg. Alfredo sauce mix
1 cup milk
1 lb. uncooked shrimp
1 Tbsp. olive oil
2 cloves garlic
½ cup grated Parmesan cheese

Tossed Salad Ingredients:
½ lb. red leaf lettuce
1 clove garlic, minced
½ teaspoon dry mustard
Salt and pepper, to taste
¼ cup olive oil
Italian bread sticks
1 red apple

This is a "busy" meal. It takes lots of action and attention. You will have three things going at the same time. Have all ingredients rėady when you start.

Prepare **tossed salad** beforehand. Tear red leaf lettuce into bite-size pieces. Mince garlic and add to lettuce. Add the dry mustard . Season with salt and pepper. Gradually, add the olive oil and mix well. Refrigerate.

For the main course, put 2 quarts of water on to boil for cooking pasta. Continue with the menu while the water heats. When it begins to boil, add 2 tablespoons of olive oil and the pasta. Cook until *al dente,* according to package directions..

Prepare the **Alfredo sauce**. Melt butter in a skillet and add the package of Alfredo mix. Gradually add the milk. Bring mixture to a boil and allow to simmer five minutes or until the sauce begins to thicken.

While the Alfredo sauce cooks, prepare the **shrimp.** Pour olive oil in a frying pan. Add minced garlic and sauté for a minute. Add cleaned shrimp and sauté until shrimp is opaque in center; set aside and keep warm.

When pasta is cooked add to Alfredo sauce and arrange on plates. Top with cooked shrimp and Parmesan cheese

Heat **bread sticks** and serve with tossed salad. Cut **red apples** into wedges as garnish.

CHEESE STUFFED PASTA SHELLS

House Salad, Fresh Bread Rolls, Chianti Wine

6 ounces jumbo pasta shells*
½ lb. sweet Italian sausage bulk
1 (15 oz.) jar spaghetti sauce
½ (10 oz.) package frozen, chopped spinach, thawed, squeezed dry
1 egg, beaten
8 oz. Ricotta cheese
8 oz. Mozzarella cheese,
1 teaspoon minced onion
1 clove garlic, minced
Dash nutmeg
¼ cup grated Parmesan cheese

House Salad Ingredients:
iceberg lettuce
carrots
celery
red onion
ripe olives
croutons

Fresh bread rolls

Red wine, Chianti

** This menu calls for jumbo pasta shells. If they are unavailable, try the normal size, and instead of stuffing the shells, pour the meat sauce over them.*

Preheat oven to 350° F.

Cook the **pasta shells** until tender; drain, rinse with cold water and set aside. Brown **sausage**; drain fat and add spaghetti sauce. Cover and simmer 15 minutes.

Combine spinach, egg, cheeses, onion, garlic and nutmeg. Pour ½ cup spaghetti sauce mixture in the bottom of a 2 quart baking dish. Stuff each pasta shell with about 2 rounded teaspoons of the spinach and cheese mixture. (The meat sauce should cover the shells.) Arrange shells in a single layer in the baking dish, pour remaining spaghetti sauce over the shells. Top with Parmesan cheese.

Bake at 350° F for 30-40 minutes.

To prepare the **house** salad, wash and dry all vegetables. Tear the lettuce into bite-size pieces. Slice the carrots. Julienne the celery. Chop onion. Toss all together; add the ripe olives and the croutons.

Serve with **fresh bread rolls** and a **Chianti wine.**

CHICKEN AND VEGETABLE SOUP

with Rice and Tossed Salad

2 chicken breasts
3 cans chicken broth
½ cup onions, chopped
2 zucchini, chopped
3 tomatoes, peeled and chopped
4 green chilies, peeled and chopped
1 ½ cups uncooked corn kernels
1 teaspoon cumin
1 teaspoon oregano
Pepper and salt to taste

Converted Rice
Cheese assortment

Tossed Salad Ingredients:
- **iceberg lettuce**
- **red leaf lettuce**
- **cucumber**
- **radishes**
- **tomato**
- **ripe olives**
- **croutons**

Prepare the **tossed salad** beforehand. Wash and dry all vegetables. Tear the lettuces into bite-size pieces. Slice the cucumber and radishes. Cut the tomatoes into wedges. Toss all together. Store salad in refrigerator until ready to serve. When serving, add the ripe olives and the croutons.

Begin by preparing the soup liquid. In a large saucepan, add chicken broth and all the ingredients but the chicken. Heat to a boil and let simmer for about 25 minutes.

When you have the soup liquid going, prepare the **chicken**. Pound the chicken slightly. Boil chicken breasts in water until done, about 20 minutes; cool and shred.

Meanwhile, prepare **rice** according to package directions.

For a more complete meal, you can cut up an **assortment of cheeses.**

When the chicken broth has been cooking for 25 minutes, add chicken and serve immediately.

CHUNKY TUNA SALAD

with Baked Potato and Fresh Bread

1 quart water
¼ cup dry white wine
2 (6 ⅛ oz.) cans white tuna
1 Tbsp. olive oil
½ cup diced red onions
3 celery stalks, roughly chopped
½ cup mayonnaise
2 Tbsps. Worcestershire sauce
2 Tbsps. balsamic vinegar
2 Tbsps. lemon juice
1 clove garlic, crushed
¾ teaspoon ground pepper
2 Tbsps. drained capers (optional)

Lettuce leaves

4 potatoes, for baking

Fresh bread

If having **fresh bread,** bake it now before proceeding.

Bake **potatoes** according to your favorite method. We typically use the microwave to completely bake or to at least partially bake the potatoes. Wash the potatoes and pierce with fork. Place potatoes in the microwave and cook on HIGH for 4 minutes per potato per side, turning once. (3 or 4 potatoes will cook in 24 minutes.)

Prepare the **tuna salad**. Drain canned tuna and separate into chunks.

Heat a small frying pan to medium heat. Add olive oil, stir in the onions and chopped celery and cook until vegetables become clear. Set aside to cool.

In a bowl, mix onions, celery, mayonnaise, Worcestershire sauce, vinegar, lemon juice, garlic and pepper; stir in tuna. You can add capers to the mixing bowl or serve them atop the salad for those who may find the tartness a bit much.

Layer two whole lettuce leaves on each plate. Spoon on the tuna salad and add the baked potato.

MUSHROOM BEEF IN BURGUNDY

with Mashed Potatoes and Broccoli

Butter or margarine
2 cloves garlic, minced
1 ½ lb. kabob meat, cut into 1 inch cubes
1 onion, sliced into rings
3 fresh mushrooms
1 Tbsp. all-purpose flour
1 Tbsp. tomato paste
1 cup burgundy
1 can condensed beef bouillon, undiluted
Dash pepper
1 small bay leaf

3 potatoes
½ stick margarine
¼ cup milk

½ lb. broccoli

Preheat oven to 350° F.

To prepare the **beef**, slowly heat a 2 quart covered pot. Add 1 tablespoon of butter or margarine and sauté garlic. Over medium heat brown beef cubes. Remove beef cubes and set aside.

To the same pot, add 1 tablespoon of butter and the onion circles. Cook onions over low heat, covered, until browned slightly. Add mushrooms; cook, stirring, for a minute or two. Remove pot from heat; add in the flour and tomato paste and stir until well blended. Add the burgundy wine and beef bouillon. Bring this wine mixture to a boil and return beef cubes back to pot. Season with pepper and bay leaf.

Bake, covered, in 350° F oven, about 1 hour.

When beef is done, remove from oven.

Prepare **mashed potatoes**. Heat a pot of water and add potato pieces. Salt the water to your taste. Cook for approximately 20 minutes; drain. Into hot potatoes place ½ stick of butter or margarine, ¼ cup of milk and whip to the desired smoothness.

At the same time steam the fresh **broccoli.**

GRAVY TIPS

Gravy is best when we make it from the natural fats that come from fried meats.

Below are some general rules or guidelines for making the best gravy in the world.

After meat is done and removed from pan, skim off fat from the pan and measure out 2 tablespoons. If not enough fat has accumulated then you can fill the amount necessary with chicken or beef stock. We use the chicken and beef bouillon cubes or, at times, the instant variety of bouillon.

Pour measured fat back into the skillet or pan and stir in 2 level tablespoons of flour and stir until smooth.

Finally, add 1 cup of liquid, be it sour cream, milk or water and stir until well mixed. Season with salt and pepper to taste.

For variety, you can add chopped mushrooms for beef or giblets for chicken.

Gravy can also be made in large pots or slow cookers by removing a cup of the broth in which meat has cooked and mix with ⅛ cup of water and a couple of tablespoon of flour. This mixture should be mixed well then heated until smooth.

Third week OCTOBER

Sunday	*Monday*	*Tuesday*	*Wednesday*	*Thursday*	*Friday*	*Saturday*
Plan ahead **Oven Barbecued Chicken** Ranch Style Beans® Potato Salad	**Mexican Hash** Spaghetti, Guacamole Salad	*Plan ahead* **Cold Seafood Pasta** Green Salad	**Grilled Pork Chops** Buttered Cauliflower Cole Slaw	**Vegetable Lasagna** Green Salad, Fresh Bread	**Bread Crusted Baked Cod** Rice, Snow Peas	*Plan ahead* **Fruit Glazed Baked Ham** Green Beans, Potato Salad

Fresh Vegetables \ Fruits		*Herbs \ Spices*	*Basics*
red potatoes -12 celery bundle green onions - 12 white onions - 5 lemons - 5 avocado - 1 green chili pepper 1 tomatoes - 3 red bell peppers - 2 yellow bell pepper 1 green bell pepper - 1 iceberg lettuce - 1	garlic pod - 1 parsley bunch broccoli bunch cherry tomatoes - 8 cauliflower - ¼ lb. cucumbers - 1 cabbage head zucchini - 1 fresh mushrooms - 2 snow peas - ½ lb. green beans - 1 lb. orange - 3	paprika chili powder Tabasco® sauce ground cumin lemon pepper whole cloves Adolph's® tenderizer ground cloves dry mustard celery seeds herb seasoning garlic powder fennel seeds basil leaves	mayonnaise sugar mustard Worcestershire sauce peanut oil soy sauce white vinegar olive oil flour Italian dressing

Entrée Food	**Dairy**	**Miscellaneous**	**Cans \ Jars**
chicken broilers -2 ground beef -1 lb. cooked shrimp ¼ lb pork chops - 4 cod fillets - 2 ham half 8-10 lb. **Frozen** green peas pkg. spinach pkg.	eggs - 4 bacon - 1 slice margarine - 1 stick Parmesan cheese ½ C butter - 4 T Ricotta cheese - 7 oz. Mozzarella cheese ½ C **Wine** sherry ¼ cup	flour tortillas -12 pasta - 8 oz. dinner rolls - 12 spaghetti - 1 lb. lasagna - ½ lb. fresh bread - 2 pkg herbed rice pkg oven cooking bag (19" x 23 ½") bread slice - 1	whole tomatoes - 1 olives - 4 oz. jellied cranberry 8 oz crushed pineapple 1 can Ranch Style Beans® - 23 oz pimientos - 4 oz.

OVEN BARBECUED CHICKEN

with Ranch Style Beans® and Potato Salad

Potato Salad Ingredients:

6 medium-size red potatoes
½ cup chopped white onions
2-3 tsp. peanut oil
1 cup chopped celery
Salt and pepper
1 Tbsp. mustard
¼ cup mayonnaise
2 eggs, hard boiled
Paprika

Barbecue Sauce Ingredients:

1 stick margarine
¼ cup lemon juice
1 Tbsp. Worcestershire sauce
1 teaspoon salt
¼ teaspoon black pepper
¼ cup sherry wine

2 chicken broilers, halved
1 (23 oz.) can Ranch Style Beans®

Prepare **potato salad.** Boil potatoes for 30 minutes. Set aside to cool, then peel and cube to desired size. Sauté onions in 2 to 3 teaspoons of peanut oil. Mix onions, celery, salt, pepper and potatoes. Add mustard and mayonnaise; mix again. For topping, slice hard-boiled eggs and sprinkle with paprika. The potato salad will be better if prepared and stored in refrigerator for a day.

When ready for the meal, prepare **barbecue sauce** by combining margarine, lemon juice, Worcestershire sauce, salt and pepper in a small saucepan. Heat slowly, stirring occasionally, until margarine is melted. Add sherry.

Salt and pepper chicken to taste. Place **chicken** in shallow baking dish. Coat with barbecue sauce. Broil in oven for 20 minutes, turning once and re-coating. Five minutes before chicken is done, heat **Ranch Style Beans®**.

MEXICAN HASH

with Spaghetti and Guacamole Salad

GUACAMOLE SALAD

1 ripe avocado, skinned, cut up
¼ cup chopped white onions
1 green chili pepper, finely chopped
1 teaspoon lemon juice
½ teaspoon salt
¼ teaspoon pepper, coarsely ground
¼ teaspoon orange juice
1 Tbsp. mayonnaise
½ tomato, finely chopped
1 small clove garlic, chopped

Before starting the hash, prepare the **guacamole salad.** Beat avocado, onions, chili peppers, lemon juice, salt, pepper, orange juice and mayonnaise until creamy. Stir in tomato bits and garlic. Cover and refrigerate *at least 1 hour.*

THE HASH

1 small onion, chopped
3 Tbsps. peanut oil
1 lb. ground beef
1 red bell pepper, chopped
1 (14 oz.) can whole tomatoes
1 Tbsp. chili powder
½ teaspoon ground cumin
1 teaspoon salt
½ teaspoon pepper
1 cup water
1 cup uncooked spaghetti

12 flour tortillas

Begin the preparation of the **Mexican hash**. In a large skillet, cook onions in oil until yellow. Add meat and cook until light brown. Add red bell peppers, tomatoes with liquid, chili powder, ground cumin, salt, pepper and 1 cup water; simmer for 45 minutes.

Prepare the **spaghetti pasta** according to package directions; drain.

We usually serve flour tortillas with the hash and guacamole salad. You can warm the tortillas by wrapping them in a damp cloth and micro waving for about 30 seconds, or until they are hot.

2 hours - Plan ahead

COLD SEAFOOD PASTA

with Green Salad

Salad Dressing:

½ cup mayonnaise
¼ cup Italian dressing
2 Tbsps. grated Parmesan cheese

Green Salad Ingredients:

lettuce, cucumber
celery, julienned
parsley

Pasta:

8 oz. pasta
1 pkg. frozen peas
1 ½ cups broccoli florets
½ cup red bell pepper
½ cup yellow bell pepper
½ cup cooked shrimp
½ cup halved cherry tomatoes
¼ cup green onions, chopped

Make the **salad dressing**. Mix together the mayonnaise and the Italian Dressing. Add the Parmesan cheese. Mix well and place in refrigerator until ready to serve.

Prepare the **pasta**. Cook the pasta according to package directions. Drain and flood with cold water to halt cooking process. Add the peas, broccoli.

Cut the bell peppers into chunks. Add to bowl. Add the **shrimp**, cherry tomatoes and onions. Store all **pasta** ingredients in refrigerator *at least 2 hours* before serving.

When ready to eat, make the **green salad.** Wash, dry and tear the lettuce into bite-size pieces. Slice cucumber thinly, julienne the celery stalk into 2-inch lengths, the size of match sticks. Add parsley as garnish.

GRILLED PORK CHOPS

with Cole Slaw, Buttered Cauliflower and Dinner Rolls

4 pork chops
Dash lemon pepper seasoning
Adolph's® meat tenderizer
2 teaspoons soy sauce
1 teaspoon ground cloves
2 Tbsps. butter

2 Tbsps. butter
¼ lb. cauliflower
Cole Slaw (Instructions Below)

Dinner rolls

Prepare the grill before proceeding.

Begin by preparing the **cole slaw** according to the instructions below.

For the grilled **pork chops**, in a bowl, combine lemon-pepper seasoning, meat tenderizer, soy sauce and cloves and 2 tablespoons butter. Brush this mixture over the pork chops before you place on grill. Use mixture also when you turn the chops after about 6 - 8 minutes.

While the chops grill, prepare the buttered cauliflower. In a saucepan melt the butter and add the cauliflower in pieces and sauté.

Serve with dinner rolls warmed in the microwave.

JULIENNED COLE SLAW

1 teaspoon salt
¼ teaspoon pepper
½ teaspoon dry mustard
Scant teaspoon celery seeds
1 Tbsp. sugar
¼ cup chopped green bell pepper
1 Tbsp. chopped pimento

1 teaspoon grated onion
3 Tbsps. olive oil
¼ cup white vinegar
3 cups finely-chopped cabbage

¼ cup chopped olives

Place ingredients in a large bowl in the order listed. Mix well. Cover and chill through. Garnish with sliced stuffed olives just before serving.

VEGETABLE LASAGNA

with Green Salad and Fresh Bread

½ lb. lasagna, uncooked
2 medium tomatoes, cut up
¼ cup finely-chopped onion
½ teaspoon herb seasoning
Dash pepper
Dash garlic powder
Dash fennel seeds
1 teaspoon basil leaves
1 (10 oz.) package frozen spinach, thawed and well-drained
1 medium zucchini (optional)
2 fresh mushrooms
7 oz. ricotta cheese
2 Tbsps. chopped fresh parsley
½ cup grated Mozzarella cheese
2 Tbsps. Parmesan cheese
Green Salad Ingredients:
- **lettuce, green leaf**
- **cucumber**
- **celery, julienned**
- **parsley**

Fresh bread

Preheat the oven to 350° F.

If baking **fresh bread** do it now, before proceeding. Follow package directions.

Prepare **lasagna** according to package directions. Cook until *al dente* according to package directions.

Using a food blender or a wire whisk beat crushed tomatoes until smooth. Pour the tomatoes into a large saucepan, then add onion and seasonings. Heat to a simmer and cook for about 15 minutes.

Using a glass baking dish, make several layers. Pour ¼ cup of the tomato mixture in a 13 x 9 baking dish. Cover with a layer of lasagna, then with a layer of spinach, zucchini (optional), mushrooms, ricotta cheese, parsley, mozzarella and Parmesan cheese. Repeat this layering until ingredients are exhausted. Use your imagination: there are no fast rules for lasagna.

Cover lasagna dish with aluminum foil and bake in 350° F oven for about 40-45 minutes.

While lasagna bakes, prepare the **green salad.** Wash, dry and tear the lettuces into bite-size pieces. Slice cucumber thinly, julienne the celery stalk into 2- inch lengths. Add parsley as a garnish.

When lasagna is finished, remove from oven, let stand 5 minutes before cutting.

BREAD CRUSTED BAKED COD

with Snow Peas and Rice

1 slice bread
2 lemons
1 clove garlic, minced
2 Tbsps. chopped fresh parsley
1 Tbsp. minced green onion or shallots

Salt and pepper, to taste
2 Tbsps. olive oil
2 cod fillets

Herbed rice

½ lb. snow peas

Preheat the oven to 450° F.

Make **herbed rice** following package directions.

To make **bread crusting** mixture, cut crust from bread and discard. Tear bread into small pieces and place in a bowl.

Remove skin from lemon and grate the peel. Add about 1 tablespoon of the lemon peel, the minced garlic, parsley and green onions to the bread crumbs. Mix well. Season with salt and pepper. Mix the olive oil and the bread mixture; stir to mix thoroughly.

Next, rinse **fish** and pat dry. Spray a wide, shallow baking dish with vegetable spray and arrange pieces. Do not overlay the fish. Squeeze juice from the peeled lemon over the fish then top with the bread mixture.

Bake fish in a 450° F oven until fish flakes, about 8-10 minutes. The fish should flake easily when prodded with a fork.

While fish bakes, prepare the **snow peas** by blanching them in hot water then holding them under cold water to stop the cooking process.

Garnish fish with lemon wedges.

FRUIT GLAZED BAKED HAM

with Potato Salad and Green Beans

1 (8-10 lb.) ham half, bone-in
1 Tbsp. flour
1 oven cooking bag (19" x 23 ½ ")
6 whole cloves
Green beans (Facing Page ==>)
Potato Salad (Facing Page ==>)
1 (8 oz.) can jellied cranberry
1 (8 oz.) can crushed pineapple
½ cup orange juice
Tabasco® red pepper sauce
¼ teaspoon garlic powder
½ teaspoon salt

This menu uses a Reynolds® cooking method for the ham. We've added a fruit glazing.

The day before, make **potato salad**, facing page, and let it marinate in refrigerator.

On the morning of the ham feast, preheat oven to 350° F.

Bake the **ham**. Shake flour in Reynolds oven bag; place in large roasting pan at least 2 inches deep. Remove skin; trim fat from **ham**, leaving a thin layer. Lightly score surface of ham; stud with cloves. We normally use only six cloves. You may want more or less. Place ham in bag. Close bag with nylon tie; make 6 half-inch slits in top. Insert meat thermometer through slit in bag.

Bake 2 hours or until meat thermometer registers 140° F.

An hour after the ham begins, prepare the fruit glazing. Place cranberry, pineapple, orange juice, red pepper sauce, garlic powder and salt in a large saucepan. Heat to a simmer and cook for 15 minutes. Set aside to cool.

When ham is fully cooked, remove it from the bag and place on a baking sheet. Spoon the fruit mixture over the ham and bake, uncovered, for 30 minutes.

While glazed ham bakes, prepare the **green beans**. Follow directions on facing page.

POTATO SALAD

6 medium size red potatoes
½ cup chopped white onions
1 cup chopped celery
1 tsp. salt
1 tsp. pepper

Dash of sugar
1 Tbsp. mustard
¼ cup mayonnaise
2 eggs, hard boiled
Paprika

Boil **potatoes** for 30 minutes. Set aside to cool, then peel and cube to desired size.

Sauté onions in 2 to 3 teaspoons of bacon grease (or oil).

Mix onions, celery, salt, pepper, sugar and potatoes.

Add mustard and mayonnaise then mix again.

For topping, slice hard-boiled eggs and sprinkle with paprika.

GREEN BEANS

1 lb. green beans

Salt, to taste
1 slice bacon

Prepare **green beans** by the boiling method. Cut ends off beans and cut in half or leave long. Barely cover them with water and add one slice of bacon; sprinkle with salt. Cook until they are tender: 20 minutes for *al dente.*

Fourth week OCTOBER

Sunday	*Monday*	*Tuesday*	*Wednesday*	*Thursday*	*Friday*	*Saturday*
Swiss Cordon Bleu Chicken Green Peas, Mashed Potatoes	**Club Sandwich** Tomato Soup	**Curried Shrimp** Rice Green Salad	**Tangy Pork Patties** Mashed Potatoes, Spinach	**Mozzarella Spinach Salad** Bacon and Risotto, Fresh Bread	**Steamed Sole Fillet** Rice, Broiled Peppers	*Plan ahead* **Pepper Roast and Gravy** Mashed Potatoes, Carrots

Fresh Vegetables \ Fruits		*Herbs \ Spices*	*Basics*
potatoes - 9 tomato - 2 iceberg lettuce - 2 green leaf lettuce - 1 red onion - 1 cucumber - 1 celery bundle parsley bunch	garlic pod orange - 1 fresh spinach 2 pkg. lemons - 4 red bell pepper - 1 yellow bell pepper - 1 carrot bundle	oregano paprika curry dill weed garlic powder whole cloves	mayonnaise flour ketchup Worcestershire sauce extra-virgin olive oil olive oil red wine vinegar soy sauce vinegar, white Converted Rice

Entrée Food	*Dairy*	*Miscellaneous*	*Cans \ Jars*
skinless, boneless chicken breasts - 2 Canadian bacon - 4 slices chicken or turkey slices - 4 ¼ lb cooked shrimp pork tenderloin patties - 4 sole fillets - 2 top round roast - 3 lbs	butter - 1 stick margarine 1 ½ sticks Swiss cheese 8 slices eggs - 3 bacon - 18 slices milk - 2 ½ cups sour cream - ½ cup Mozzarella cheese - 6 oz **Wine** white wine ½ C sherry wine ¼ C red wine - bottle	bread crumbs - 1 C Stove Top® Chicken stuffing brown sugar - 2 T Risotto - 1 pkg. fresh bread loaf white bread loaf **Frozen** green peas - 1 pkg.	chicken broth - 1 tomato soup - 1 tomato paste - 1

SWISS CORDON BLEU CHICKEN

with Mashed Potatoes and Green Peas

4 Tbsps. butter
2 boneless, skinless chicken breasts
1 Tbsp. fresh, minced parsley
4 slices Canadian bacon
4 slices Swiss cheese
1 egg, beaten
1 cup plain bread crumbs
Salt and pepper to taste

½ cup white wine
1 can chicken broth
Dash oregano
3 potatoes
½ stick margarine
¼ cup milk
1 pkg. green peas and or
Stove Top® Chicken stuffing

Begin the preparation of the **mashed potatoes** first. Wash and peel potatoes and cut into halves then quarter into smaller pieces. Heat a pot of water and add the potato pieces. Salt the water to your taste. Cook for approximately 20 minutes; drain. Into hot potatoes place ½ stick of margarine, ¼ cup of milk and whip to the desired smoothness

While the potatoes boil, prepare the **chicken**. Pound chicken to achieve an even thickness. Spread chicken with butter and sprinkle with parsley. Place slice of Canadian bacon and a slice of Swiss cheese on each breast, folding to fit. Roll the chicken with bacon and cheese inside and secure with toothpicks.

Dip chicken in beaten egg and roll in bread crumbs and salt and pepper to taste. In skillet over medium heat, heat the wine and chicken broth. Add dash of oregano. Carefully lower chicken into mixture and cook for about 12 minutes, turning once.

While chicken cooks, prepare the **green peas** by steaming them and or prepare the packaged Stove Top® stuffing, following package directions.

CLUB SANDWICHES

with Tomato Soup

Ingredients are for one sandwich.

White bread, toasted
Mayonnaise or salad dressing
Lettuce
1 slice cooked chicken or turkey
Swiss cheese
Red onion (optional)
2 slices tomato
1 hard-cooked egg
3 slices of bacon, crispy fried
Tomato soup

Make each **sandwich** with toasted bread slices. You can have a triple decker or a regular two-slice sandwich. The instructions are for three slices.

Coat each slice with mayonnaise on one side. Tear lettuce leaf and place on first slice. A slice of chicken or turkey goes over the lettuce. Place a slice of Swiss cheese on the turkey. Red onion slices are optional. Top second slice with lettuce leaf, 2 tomato slices, 2 slices of egg, 3 slices of bacon. Sprinkle with salt and pepper. Cover with third slice of toast bread. Toothpicks will hold the triple decker together. To serve, cut diagonally.

Serve with potato chips, or for a full meal, canned **tomato soup**.

Egg slices will do for garnish. Prepare the hard-cooked egg using the ten-ten method. Ten minutes in boiling water then remove from heat and let egg sit in water for another ten minutes. When egg is cool, peel and slice.

CURRIED SHRIMP

with Rice and Green Salad

¼ cup melted butter
¼ cup flour
½ teaspoon salt
Dash of paprika
½ teaspoon curry
1 ½ cups milk
3 Tbsps. ketchup
¼ cup sherry wine
¼ lb. cooked shrimp

Converted Rice

Green Salad Ingredients:
iceberg lettuce
green leaf lettuce
cucumber
celery, julienned
parsley

Make the **green salad** first. Wash, dry and tear the lettuces into bite-size pieces. Slice cucumber thinly, cut the celery stalk into 2-inch lengths, the size of match sticks. Add parsley as a garnish. Place the salad in a large bowl and refrigerate until mealtime.

Prepare the **rice** before proceeding. Follow package directions.

While the rice cooks prepare the **sauce.** Blend butter, flour, salt, paprika and curry powder; gradually stir in milk. Cook sauce until thick and smooth, stirring constantly.

Add ketchup, sherry, and the cleaned shrimp, to the sauce and heat thoroughly.

TANGY PORK PATTIES

with Mashed Potatoes and Spinach

2-4 pork tenderloin patties
size and number to suit
2 Tbsps. orange juice
½ cup sour cream
1 Tbsp. orange rind
¼ teaspoon Worcestershire sauce
2 Tbsps. olive oil

3 potatoes
½ stick margarine
¼ cup milk

Fresh spinach
½ cup vinegar

Make **sauce** by combining orange juice, sour cream, orange rind, and Worcestershire sauce.

Brown **pork tenderloins** in olive oil in medium-hot skillet until browned on both sides. Add sauce from above. Cover and simmer 30 minutes.

Meanwhile, prepare **mashed potatoes**. Wash and peel potatoes and cut into halves then quarter into smaller pieces. Heat a pot of water and add potato pieces. Salt the water to your taste. Cook for approximately 20 minutes; drain. Into hot potatoes, place ½ stick of margarine, ¼ cup of milk and whip to the desired smoothness.

While potatoes cook, prepare the **spinach**. Wash fresh spinach in a basin of water mixed with ½ cup of vinegar. Thoroughly rinse the spinach after washing. Steam the fresh spinach using a small steamer basket over boiling water, or place the spinach in a pot with a minimum of water and let the spinach steam for a few minutes.

MOZZARELLA SPINACH SALAD

with Bacon and Risotto

6 oz. Mozzarella cheese
6 slices bacon
Risotto
1 spinach bunch
½ cup vinegar
2 Tbsps. brown sugar, packed
½ cup red wine vinegar
½ cup extra-virgin olive oil
Fresh ground pepper
Fresh bread
Red wine

If you are having **fresh bread** make it now, following package directions.

While the bread cooks, prepare the ingredients for the **Mozzarella salad**. Cut the Mozzarella cheese into small cubes the size of sugar squares. Cook the bacon in the microwave; for six slices of bacon cook on HIGH for 4 minutes. Remove bacon slices and allow to cool before crushing them into small pieces.

Cook the **risotto** according to package directions.

As the risotto cooks, prepare the **spinach**. Wash fresh spinach in a basin of water mixed with ½ cup of vinegar. Thoroughly rinse the spinach after washing. Steam the fresh spinach using a small steamer basket over boiling water, or place the spinach in a pot with a minimum of water and let the spinach steam for a few minutes.

Time the making of the Mozzarella salad to coincide with the bread and the risotto. In a small skillet, mix together the brown sugar, red wine vinegar, olive oil and fresh ground pepper; heat to blend. Add risotto and stir to mix well. Add in the steamed spinach, the cubes of cheese and the bits of bacon.

Serve with a **red wine**.

STEAMED SOLE FILLET

with Rice and Broiled Peppers

2 sole fillets, number to please

4 lemons
Dash dill weed

2 Tbsps. extra-virgin olive oil
1 red bell pepper
1 yellow bell pepper
1 clove garlic, minced
Converted Rice

Prepare **rice** following package directions.

This menu calls for *steamed* **sole fillet**. Steaming can be accomplished with a boiler pan and water, the traditional steaming, or one can use the *en papillotte* method which involves the use of aluminum foil or parchment paper. The *Sack Lunch Fish* menu earlier this month uses the *en papillotte* method. Compare this menu to that earlier one to decide which method you like better.

Arrange the **fish** over boiling water on a steaming rack. You may have to cut the fish in portions unless you have a specific fish boiler. Lay slices of lemon over the top of the fish. Sprinkle a bare amount of dill weed. Cook over steaming water for 8 - 10 minutes until the fish flakes easily when prodded with a fork.

While the fish and rice cook, prepare the **broiled peppers**. Heat the broiler in the oven. Cut the peppers into halves and paint with a small amount of extra-virgin olive oil. Broil the peppers about 4 - 5 inches away from heat source until they start to brown, remove to cool. Mince the garlic and sprinkle over the peppers. Add lemon juice to the vegetables. Mix well and spoon this mixture over the fish to give it some moisture.

Serve with a garnish of lemon wedges.

PEPPER ROAST AND GRAVY

with Mashed Potatoes and Carrots

3 lbs. top round roast
¼ cup coarsely cracked pepper
¼ teaspoon whole cloves
1 Tbsp. tomato paste
½ teaspoon paprika
¼ teaspoon garlic powder
½ cup soy sauce
½ cup vinegar

3 potatoes
½ stick margarine
¼ cup milk

Gravy Ingredients:
1 cup water
¾ Tbsp. flour
3 carrots, sliced

This menu calls for a marinated **roast**. Rub roast with pepper and insert cloves uniformly over surface; press in firmly. Place in baking dish. In a small mixing bowl, combine tomato paste, paprika and garlic powder. Stir in the soy sauce and the vinegar. Pour mixture over roast and marinate *overnight* in refrigerator.

Remove roast from refrigerator and while still in marinade, let stand in open air while you proceed.

Preheat the oven to 325° F.

Remove roast from marinade and wrap in aluminum foil. Save the marinade for later use in a gravy. Cook foil-wrapped beef in shallow pan for about 1 ½ hours.

Before roast is done, prepare the **mashed potatoes**. Wash and peel potatoes and cut into halves then quarter into smaller pieces. Heat a pot of water and add potatoes pieces. Salt the water to your taste. Cook for approximately 20 minutes; drain. Into hot potatoes, place ½ stick of margarine, ¼ cup of milk and whip to the desired smoothness.

When roast is done, open foil and drain off pan drippings. Raise oven to 350° F. Brown roast, uncovered, at 350° F until brown. Meanwhile, strain and defat pan drippings. To 1 cup drippings, add 1 cup water and bring to boil. Add 1 ½ cups reserved marinade. Thicken with flour mixed with 2 tablespoon of additional water.

Serve with mashed potatoes and raw **carrot slices**.

Fifth week OCTOBER

Sunday	*Monday*	*Tuesday*	*Wednesday*	*Thursday*	*Friday*	*Saturday*
Chicken with Snow Peas Carrots Pasta, Fresh Bread	**Chicken & Potato Hash** Tossed Salad	*Plan ahead* **Pickled Shrimp & Peppers** Tossed Salad, Fresh Bread	**Cornbread Sausage** Spinach	**Country Ham & Potato Soup** Caesar Salad Dinner Rolls	*Plan ahead* **Broiled Swordfish Steaks** Baked Potatoes, Green Wedge Salad	*Plan ahead* **Steak with Spicy Potatoes** Fresh Fruit Salad

Fresh Vegetables \ Fruits		*Herbs \ Spices*	*Basics*
carrot bundle snow peas - 1 cup fresh basil - bunch green bell pepper - 2 red bell pepper -1 iceberg lettuce- 2 green leaf lettuce - 1 romaine lettuce head cucumbers - 2 tomatoes - 2 radishes - bunch	garlic pod - 1 white onion - 2 apples - 2 fresh spinach - pkg. cabbage - 1 cup fresh basil - 1 C celery bundle potatoes - 6 red potatoes - 4 lemons - 10 strawberries - 10 grapes - bunch	pickling spice celery salt whole cloves garlic powder dry mustard chili powder ground cumin dried oregano leaves red pepper flakes hot pepper sauce	peanut oil white vinegar sugar (white, brown) flour olive oil Worcestershire sauce Dijon mustard vegetable oil Marsala cooking wine vegetable cooking spray baking powder - Calumet® 1 T

Entrée Food	*Dairy*	*Miscellaneous*	*Cans \ Jars*
skinless, boneless chicken breasts -4 cooked shrimp - ½ lb pork sausage links - ½ lb. cooked ham - ¼ lb. swordfish steak - 1 top sirloin steak - 1	Parmesan cheese 2 oz. butter - 9 T eggs - 3 milk - 1 C margarine - 1 T **Wine** red wine - bottle	macaroni pasta 1 lb fresh bread loaf croutons - pkg. French bread - 1 yellow cornmeal 1 C dinner rolls - 12 Jell-O® lime gelatin pkg.	whole tomatoes - 1 chicken broth - 1 ripe olives - 4 oz. Campbell's® condensed cream of potato soup - 1 whole pimentos 1 oz.

CHICKEN WITH SNOW PEAS

with Carrots, Pasta and Fresh Bread

2 boneless, skinless chicken breasts
1 cup carrots, julienned
1 cup snow peas
½ teaspoon fresh basil leaves
¼ cup Marsala red cooking wine
2 oz. grated Parmesan cheese

3 cups pasta (macaroni)

Fresh bread

If you are having the **fresh bread** and need to cook it in oven, do it now, before beginning the meal.

Pound the **chicken breasts** slightly. Cook chicken breasts in boiling water for about 15 minutes. Set aside. When cool, chop into bite-sized chunks.

Prepare **pasta** according to package directions. Drain, flood with cold water; drain again.

In large skillet, heat olive oil; add chicken chunks, carrot strips, snow peas and fresh basil. Cook and stir over medium heat until all ingredients are hot. Add Marsala wine and cook for another 2 minutes.

Add hot, cooked **macaroni** to the mixture and top with Parmesan cheese.

CHICKEN AND POTATO HASH

with Tossed Salad

2 boneless, skinless cooked chicken breasts (1 ½ cups)
2 Potatoes
1 green bell pepper, chopped
1 small onion, chopped
3 Tbsps. peanut oil
1 (14 oz.) can whole tomatoes
1 can chicken broth
1 teaspoon salt
½ teaspoon pepper

Tossed Salad Ingredients:
iceberg lettuce
green leaf lettuce
cucumber
radishes
tomato
ripe olives
croutons

Red wine

To prepare the **tossed salad**, wash and dry all vegetables. Tear the lettuces into bite-size pieces. Slice the cucumber and radishes. Cut the tomatoes into wedges. Toss all together, then add the ripe olives and the croutons.

Cook the chicken in boiling water for about 15 minutes. Remove from water and allow to cool.

Meanwhile to make the **chicken hash**, coarsely chop the skinned potatoes into ½ inch shapes. Put potatoes, chopped bell peppers and chopped onion in a large skillet. Brown in peanut oil. Add tomatoes with liquid, chicken broth, salt and pepper; simmer for 20 minutes.

Chop the cooled chicken into bite-size pieces and add to potatoes. Cook for another 10 minutes.

Serve with tossed green salad, French bread and a red wine.

PICKLED SHRIMP AND PEPPERS

with Tossed Salad and Fresh Bread

½ lb. cooked shrimp
¾ cup white vinegar
5 oz. sugar
2 lemons, juiced
½ Tbsp. pickling spices
1 teaspoon salt
½ teaspoon celery salt
2 dashes liquid hot pepper sauce
2 whole cloves
1 small onion, thinly sliced
½ green pepper, cut into 1" squares
½ small red pepper, cut into 1" squares

Pimientos, cut into chunks

French bread

Tossed Salad Ingredients:
- **iceberg lettuce**
- **green leaf lettuce**
- **cucumber**
- **radishes**
- **tomato**
- **ripe olives**
- **croutons**

The pickled shrimp in this menu originated at Texas A & M University. It was presented as part of a display during the opening of the underground annex to the Texas State Capitol. If you're ever in Austin be sure to visit the capitol and the underground annex. You'll be impressed.

For the **pickled shrimp:** in a saucepan, combine vinegar, sugar, lemon juice, pickling spices, salt, celery salt, liquid hot pepper sauce (Tabasco®) and cloves. Heat until sugar dissolves, stirring constantly. Chill. Add pimientos when serving.

Arrange layers of onions, peppers and shrimp in a glass serving bowl. Pour vinegar mixture over shrimp, cover and chill *overnight.*

When you are ready to prepare the meal, bake the **bread** first, following package directions.

To prepare the **tossed salad,** wash and dry all vegetables. Tear the lettuces into bite-size pieces. Slice the cucumber and radishes. Cut tomato into wedges. Toss all together, then add the ripe olives and the croutons.

CORNBREAD SAUSAGE

with Spinach

2 apples, cut into eighths
½ lb. pork sausage links
4 Tbsps. butter or margarine
½ cup brown sugar
1 bunch spinach, fresh
or 1 pkg. frozen, chopped spinach
½ cup vinegar

1 cup all purpose flour
¾ cup yellow cornmeal
3 Tbsps. brown sugar
1 Tbsp. baking powder
1 teaspoon salt
1 egg, beaten
4 Tbsps. butter
1 cup milk

Cut **apples** into eights.

To prepare the **sausage**, cook sausage links over medium heat until they are uniformly browned. Remove and set aside. Retain about 2 tablespoons of drippings, discarding the remainder. Add four tablespoons of butter or margarine and brown sugar to the skillet. Cook, stirring constantly until the sugar is melted. Add the apples and sauté over medium heat for about 10 minutes, stirring occasionally.

Lightly grease a baking dish with vegetable spray or peanut oil. Arrange sausages on the bottom, side by side. Wedge the apples between the sausage and place remaining apples across the top. Pour juice from skillet over the apples and sausage.

Preheat the oven to 400 °F.

While oven heats, prepare the **cornbread**. Mix together the flour, cornmeal, brown sugar, baking powder and salt in a mixing bowl. Add beaten egg, butter and milk. Mix thoroughly. Pour the cornbread mixture over the apples and sausage.

Bake for about 20-25 minutes or until the cornbread is done.

Just before the sausage casserole is finished cooking, prepare the **spinach.** Wash fresh spinach in a basin of water mixed with ½ cup of vinegar. Thoroughly rinse the spinach after washing. Steam the fresh spinach using a small steamer basket over boiling water, or place the spinach in a pot with a minimum of water and let the spinach steam for a few minutes. If using fresh spinach, be sure to clean the spinach thoroughly.

COUNTRY HAM AND POTATO SOUP

with Caesar Salad and Dinner Rolls

1 Tbsp. margarine or butter
1 cup shredded cabbage
¼ lb. fully cooked ham, cut into strips (about 1 cup)
1 (10 ¾ oz.) can Campbell's® condensed cream of potato soup
1 soup can water

Dinner rolls

Caesar Salad Ingredients:
Baked croutons
2 hard-cooked eggs
¼ cup olive oil
1 tsp. Worcestershire sauce
½ teaspoon salt
1 clove garlic
Garlic powder (optional)
¼ teaspoon dry mustard
Ground pepper
1 bunch romaine lettuce
2 lemons

The baked croutons can be store-bought or you can make them fresh. To make fresh **baked croutons,** remove crust from bread; cut bread into cubes. You will need 2 cups of these cubes, or about 4 slices of bread. If you like, you can melt butter and sprinkle garlic powder on these cubes. Bake in 400° F oven until crispy brown; set aside.

Prepare 2 **hard-cooked eggs** for garnish. Use the 10-10 method, 10 minutes in boiling water then 10 in hot water. Remove the eggs from water, run under cold water to stop the cooking process and refrigerate until needed.

Prepare the **Caesar salad.** Mix the olive oil, Worcestershire sauce, salt, garlic, mustard and pepper in a bowl; toss with the romaine lettuce until all leaves are coated. Squeeze the lemons over the salad and toss.

Before serving, sprinkle the croutons and toss. Serve eggs in slices.

Prepare **ham and potato Soup.** In 2-quart saucepan over medium-high heat, in hot margarine, cook cabbage and ham 5 minutes or until cabbage is tender, stirring occasionally. Stir in remaining ingredients on left side above and heat to boiling. Reduce heat to low; heat through. Serve with dinner rolls.

BROILED SWORDFISH STEAKS

with Baked Potatoes and Green Wedge Salad

1 swordfish steak (1 inch thick)
1 Tbsp. Dijon-style mustard
4 lemons, juiced
¼ cup olive oil
¼ cup vegetable oil
1 garlic clove, crushed
1 cup shredded fresh basil

Green Wedge Salad:
½ head iceberg lettuce
½ cucumber, sliced
2 radishes, sliced
2 celery stalks, julienned

4 potatoes, for baking

Rinse and dry the **swordfish steaks** with paper towels; place in shallow dish in a single layer. In a small bowl, whisk together the mustard, the juice from 4 lemons, olive and vegetable oils. Whisk in the garlic and basil. Pour this marinade over the swordfish, turning to coat both sides.

Marinate in refrigerator for 1 hour, turning once.

Bake **potatoes** according to your favorite method. We typically use the microwave to completely bake or to at least partially bake the potatoes. Wash the potatoes and pierce with fork. Place potatoes in the microwave and cook on HIGH for 4 minutes per potato per side, turning once. (3 or 4 potatoes will cook in 24 minutes.)

Preheat the oven broiler for a few minutes. Place the swordfish steaks on a broiler pan and broil about 7 inches from the heat source for about 5 minutes per side, turning once, until cooked through.

While the fish cooks, prepare the **green wedge salad**. Cut the iceberg lettuce in half and then into wide wedges. Remove center portion and chop, spreading on salad plate. Cut the cucumber and place in the remaining curved portion of lettuce wedge. Slice the radishes and place on cucumber. Julienne the celery and place on top of and around the wedge.

2 hours - Plan ahead

STEAK WITH SPICED RED POTATOES

with Molded Fruit Salad

1 top sirloin steak
Vegetable cooking spray
4 red potatoes, halved
3 Tbsps. chili powder
2 teaspoons ground cumin
1 ½ teaspoons garlic powder
¾ teaspoon dried oregano leaves
½ teaspoon red pepper flakes
2 Tbsps. olive oil

Molded Fruit Salad:
1 box Jell-O® lime gelatin
10 strawberries, halved
30 grapes

Make the **molded fruit salad** before proceeding. Following instructions on the Jell-O® box to prepare the gelatin. Let it chill for about an hour then remove and stir in the fruits. Place back in the refrigerator to chill solid.

Cook the **potatoes** in the microwave. Cut into halves and place in baking dish. Cover with plastic wrap paper and vent one corner. Microwave on HIGH for 5 minutes or until the potatoes are just about done. You do not want them fully cooked for they will complete cooking with the steak.

Prepare the **spicy sauce.** Combine chili powder, ground cumin, garlic powder, oregano leaves and red pepper flakes. Mix well and stir in 2 tablespoons of olive oil.

For the **steak**, preheat the oven broiler. Brush steak with the seasoned oil and place on baking rack that has been sprayed with vegetable oil. Cook about 3 to 4 inches from heat. When it is time to turn the steak, place new potatoes around the steak. Brush the potatoes with seasoned oil. Brush the new side of steak with any remaining oil. Cook until the steak is done the way you like it.

Fish Substitution Chart

FLAVOR	Soft Fish	Pliable	Firm
FULL	Herring Sardine Butterfish	Salmon Carp	Tuna Swordfish
PARTIAL	Pink Salmon Catfish	Sea Bass Perch	Shark
MILD	Orange Roughy Sole Flounder	Snapper Cod Halibut	

Cooking Methods

Orange roughy : use the pan poaching technique.

Sole or Flounder: oven baked with a covering.

Salmon: pan fried with small amount of olive oil.

Tuna, Shark or Swordfish: grilled

Snapper or Cod: oven baked with wine sauce.

Halibut: Pan fried with vegetables.

November

Turkey and Spice and Everything Nice

November is the month of traditions.

We offer two menus for Thanksgiving meals. The first is a *Chicken and Sage Dressing* meal that leads off the month. This meal roasts a whole chicken. You will make sage dressing from scratch, and be thrilled with the result. Traditional mashed potatoes go with this first Thanksgiving meal.

Our second offering for Turkey Day is the more common turkey meal, but this meal will introduce you to cooking turkey in a bag, specifically doubled grocery bags. The result will amaze you. Try this meal with fresh turkey for best results. As a side dish, the traditional turkey feast offers Instant Turkey Dressing Mix found in grocery stores. Green beans and mashed potatoes and relish dishes of large olives complete this setting.

The spice for November is added by some Cajun and San Francisco meals: *Chicken and Shrimp Gumbo*, *Shrimp Creole* and *Northern Italian Shrimp*. There is also a tart taste from Interior Mexico, *Beef Chile Relleno* that should be made the night before.

To complete the traditional American Month, we offer *Stuffed Green Peppers*, *American Goulash*, a *Tenderloin of Beef*, *Chicken Fried Steak* and a *Garlic Orange Beef*. True American beef eaters should be ready.

For those many cold winter days we suggest *Vegetable Soup* the way Mom used to make it as well as an *Old-fashioned Cheese Soup*.

In February, we mentioned how sweet food compliments pork and of course sour side dishes do the same. This month we offer a menu that has both sweetness and tartness to add to pork. This menu we call *King's Apple Pork,* for it is fit for a king, or a queen.

We close with a great gift suggestion. A copy of *More Than Recipes* for that special friend or for a new couple.

November Menus

Chicken

Chicken w/ Sage Dressing with Mashed Potatoes and Cranberry Sauce
St .Petersburg Chicken with Dutch Potatoes and Green Peas
Thanksgiving Meal with Mashed Potatoes, Green Beans, Cranberry Salad
Chicken Drumsticks Parmesan with Mashed Potatoes, Corn and 3-C Salad
Chicken Cordon Bleu w/ Mashed Potatoes, Green Peas, Stuffing
Chicken Pot Pie with Rice and Green Salad
Turkey Tenderloin with Rice and Mixed Vegetables, Easy Tomato Slices

Quick & Easy

Oklahoma Hash with French Bread and Italian Salad
Stuffed Green Peppers with Corn and Cucumber Salad
American Goulash with Noodles, Tossed Salad and French Bread
Beef Chile Rellenos with Tossed Avocado Salad and Black Beans
Sunshine Meat Loaf with Rice and Spinach

Shrimp

Chicken & Shrimp Gumbo with Rice and Green Salad
Shrimp Creole with Curried Rice and Cole Slaw
Northern Italian Shrimp with Risotto and Italian Salad
Boiled Shrimp with Rice and Green Salad
Shrimp and Refried Beans with Sake and Egg Rolls

Pork

King's Apple Pork with Macaroni & Cheese and Fresh Spinach
Baked Pork Chops with Spinach Salad and Macaroni & Cheese
Breaded Pork Chops with Rice, Sautéed Celery and Tart Beets

Pasta / Soup

Bow-Tie Pasta with Italian Sauce, Herbed Tomatoes and Green Salad
Angel Hair Pasta with Italian Salad and French Bread
Hypocrite Vegetables with Rice, Green Wedge Salad, Fresh Bread
Vegetable Soup with House Salad
Old-Fashioned Cheese Soup with Buttered Toast and Tossed Salad

Fish

Fish Fillets with Noodles with Frozen Vegetables and Green Wedge Salad
Butter Baked Fish with Baked Potatoes and Green Wedge Salad
Baked Cod with Baked Potato and Sweet Peas
Baked Fish Lasagna with Roasted Red Peppers and Green Wedge Salad
Pan-Fried Sole with Penne Pasta and Snow Peas

Red Meats

Mustard Steaks w/ Baked Vegetables, House Salad, Herbed Tomatoes
Sesame Beef Floats with Rice and Sesame Biscuits
Tenderloin of Roast Beef with Mashed Potatoes and Green Beans
Garlic Orange Beef with Hot Noodles and Tossed Salad
Chicken-Fried Steaks with Mashed Potatoes and Green Peas

NOVEMBER

Sunday	Monday	Tuesday	Wednesday	Thursday	Friday	Saturday
Plan ahead **Chicken w/ Sage Dressing** Mashed Potatoes, Gravy	**Oklahoma Red River Hash** French Bread, Italian Salad	**Chicken & Shrimp Gumbo** Rice, Green Salad	**Bow-Tie Pasta** Italian Sauce, Green Salad, Herbed Tomatoes	**King's Apple Pork** Macaroni & Cheese, Spinach	**Fish Fillets w/ Noodles** Frozen Vegetables, Green Wedge Salad	**Mustard Steaks** Baked Vegetables, House Salad
Plan ahead **St. Petersburg Chicken** Dutch Potatoes, Green Peas	**Stuffed Green Peppers** Corn, Cucumber Salad	*Plan ahead* **Shrimp Creole** Curried Rice, Cole Slaw	**Baked Pork Chops** Macaroni & Cheese, Spinach Salad	**Angel Hair Pasta** Italian Salad, French Bread	**Butter Baked Fish** Baked Potatoes, Green Wedge Salad	**Sesame Beef Floats** Rice, Sesame Biscuits
Chicken Drum-sticks Parmesan Mashed Potatoes, Corn, 3-C Salad	**American Goulash** Noodles, Tossed Salad, French Bread	**Northern Italian Shrimp** Risotto, Italian Salad	**Breaded Baked Pork Chops** Rice, Sautéed Celery, Tart Beets	**Vegetable Soup** House Salad	**Baked Cod** Baked Potato, Sweet Peas	**Tenderloin of Beef** Mashed Potatoes, Green Beans
Chicken Cordon Bleu Mashed Potatoes, Green Peas, Stuffing Mix	*Plan ahead* **Beef Chiles Rellenos** Black Beans, Tossed Avocado Salad	**Boiled Shrimp** Rice, Green Salad	**Old-Fashioned Cheese Soup** Buttered Toast, Tossed Salad	*Plan ahead* **Thanks-giving Meal** Mashed Potatoes, Green Beans, Cranberry Salad	**Baked Fish Lasagna** Roasted Red Peppers, Green Wedge Salad	**Garlic Orange Beef** Hot Noodles, Tossed Salad
Chicken Pot Pie Rice, Green Salad	**Sunshine Meat Loaf** Rice, Spinach	**Shrimp & Refried Rice** Sake, Egg Rolls	**Turkey Tenderloin** Rice, Mixed Vegetables, Easy Tomato Slices	**Hypocrite Vegetables** Rice, Green Wedge Salad. Fresh Bread	**Pan-Fried Sole** Penne Pasta, Snow Peas,	**Chicken Fried Steak** Mashed Potatoes, Green Peas

First week NOVEMBER

Sunday	*Monday*	*Tuesday*	*Wednesday*	*Thursday*	*Friday*	*Saturday*
Plan ahead **Chicken w/ Sage Dressing** Mashed Potatoes, Gravy.	**Oklahoma Red River Hash** French Bread, Italian Salad	**Chicken & Shrimp Gumbo** Rice, Green Salad	**Bow-Tie Pasta** Italian Style Green Salad, Herbed Tomatoes	**King's Apple Pork** Macaroni & Cheese, Spinach	**Fish Fillets w/ Noodles** Frozen Vegetables, Green Wedge Salad	**Mustard Steaks** Baked Vegetables, House Salad, Herbed Tomatoes, Dinner Rolls

Fresh Vegetables \ Fruits		*Herbs \ Spices*	*Basics*
white onions - 5 celery bundle parsley bunch potatoes - 3 iceberg lettuce - 2 green leaf lettuce - 1 carrot bundle red cabbage head - 1 green bell pepper - 1 red bell peppers - 1	garlic pod - 1 green onions - 13 cucumber - 2 apple - 1 spinach bunch fresh basil bunch lemon - 3 tomatoes- 3	sage thyme chili powder cayenne pepper nutmeg cinnamon paprika bay leaf parsley flakes basil leaves poultry seasoning	flour cooking oil olive oil sugar peanut oil Dijon style mustard Converted Rice Marsala wine vinegar vinegar, white baking soda - 1 t hot pepper sauce

Entrée Food	*Dairy*	*Miscellaneous*	*Cans \ Jars*
whole chicken or roaster - 1 beef tip - 1 lb. skinless, boneless chicken breast - 1 fresh shrimp - ½ lb. butterfly pork chops - 2 fish fillet - 1 or 2 boneless beef rib eye steaks - 2	eggs - 4 butter - 2 ½ sticks margarine - ½ stick milk - 1 C Parmesan cheese - 1 C American cheese ¼ lb **Wine** dry white wine ½ cup red wine - bottle	loaf of stale bread French bread - 1 rottini pasta - 1 C macaroni pasta 2 C bow-tie pasta - ½ lb egg noodles - 2 C seafood file ½ tsp. **Frozen** mixed vegetables pkg	whole tomatoes - 2 tomato paste - 1 ripe olives - 4 oz. salad pepper vlasic® Pepperoncini - 4 oz Italian spaghetti sauce - 1 C chicken flavored instant bouillon 1 T croutons - pkg

3 hours - Plan ahead

CHICKEN WITH SAGE DRESSING

with Mashed Potatoes and Gravy

1 whole chicken or roaster
Salt and pepper, to taste
Dash poultry seasoning
1 loaf stale bread, in crumbs
¾ cup chopped onions
1 cup chopped celery
¼ cup chopped fresh parsley
1 teaspoon dried sage
¼ teaspoon dried thyme
Salt and pepper, to taste
2 eggs
1 Tbsp. butter

3 potatoes
½ stick margarine
¼ cup milk

Gravy Ingredients:
1 cup drained liquid
3 oz. milk
2 Tbsps. flour

Preheat the oven to 350° F. Wash chicken or roaster and remove giblets. Season inside with salt and pepper and a dash of poultry seasoning. Bind the legs and wings and place in roaster pan. Add 2 or 3 cups of hot water. Roast in the oven for about 1 hour, basting occasionally.

While the chicken roasts, prepare the sage dressing. Mix together the bread crumbs, onions, celery, fresh parsley, dried sage and dried thyme. Sprinkle with salt and pepper to taste. Mix thoroughly and set aside.

When an hour has passed, remove chicken and drain the liquid, reserving about 1 cup for the gravy. Take whatever juices remain, add water to increase to about 1 cup and pour this liquid into the sage dressing. Add beaten eggs and mix well with the sage dressing. Form a cake of the sage dressing and place next to the chicken. Brush both the chicken breast and the sage dressing with butter. Cook dressing and chicken in oven for another hour or until done.

Prepare **mashed potatoes.** Cook for approximately 20 minutes; drain. Into hot potatoes place ½ stick of margarine, ¼ cup of milk and whip to desired smoothness.

To make the gravy, add the 2 cups of reserved liquid and pour into pan. Add the milk and flour and stir until the gravy is thick. Season with salt and pepper to taste.

OKLAHOMA RED RIVER HASH

with French Bread and Italian Salad

1 small onion, chopped
4 celery stalks, in wide slices
3 Tbsps. peanut oil
1 lb. beef tip (cut in sugar cube size)
1 (14 oz.) can whole tomatoes
1 teaspoon chili powder
1 teaspoon salt
½ teaspoon pepper
1 (6 oz.) can tomato paste
1 cup uncooked rotini pasta*

* *also known as wagon wheels*

Italian Salad Ingredients:
iceberg lettuce
tomato in wedges
red cabbage, julienned
ripe olives
carrot, shredded
salad pepper
croutons (optional)
1 bottle red wine
1 loaf fresh French bread

If you're having fresh **French bread**, bake it now, following package directions.

Prepare the **Oklahoma hash.** In a large skillet, cook onions and celery in oil until yellow. Add beef tip meat, cut into small cubes and cook until meat is light brown. Add tomatoes with liquid, chili powder, salt, pepper and tomato paste and simmer for 45 minutes. Add water as needed.

While the meat cooks, prepare the **wagon wheel pasta** according to package directions.

Now prepare the **Italian salad.** Tear lettuce into bite-size pieces. Cut tomato into wedges in desired thickness. Cut red cabbage into julienne strips. Add a few ripe olives. Shred the carrot on top. Toss well. Add a salad pepper to top and spread croutons around.

Serve with French **bread** and a red wine.

CHICKEN AND SHRIMP GUMBO

with Rice and Green Salad

1 whole, skinless, boneless chicken breast
½ cup flour
½ cup olive oil
½ onion, chopped
2 stalks of celery, chopped
½ green bell pepper, chopped
2 green onions, chopped
2 cloves garlic, crushed
1 can whole tomatoes, drained
Salt, pepper, cayenne pepper

½ lb. fresh shrimp, shelled and cleaned
½ teaspoon file*
Converted Rice
Green Salad Ingredients:
iceberg lettuce
green leaf lettuce
cucumber
celery, julienned
parsley

* File *can be found in the supermarket near the fish counter or where the herbs and spices are located.* File is powered young leaves of sassafras used to thicken soups or stews.

The gumbo portion of this meal is courtesy of Sammie Seale of Austin.

Make the **green salad.** Wash, dry and tear the lettuces into bite-size pieces. Slice cucumbers thinly, julienne the celery stalk into 2-inch lengths, the size of match sticks. Add parsley as a garnish. Place the salad in a large bowl and refrigerate until mealtime.

Measure 2 quarts of water. Boil **chicken** in this water until tender, about 15 minutes; set aside.

Cook **rice** according to package directions before proceeding.

Meanwhile, in heavy skillet, make a roux by adding the flour to hot oil, stirring constantly over medium heat until flour turns reddish brown. Remove roux from heat and add onion, celery, bell pepper, green onions, garlic and tomatoes.

Bring the chicken broth to boiling and add the vegetables and roux. Cook on medium heat until the vegetables are tender, about 2 minutes. Add chicken, salt, pepper and cayenne; simmer 10 minutes. Add the shrimp and simmer 7 more minutes; remove from heat and add file and serve over rice.

BOW-TIE PASTA

with Italian Sauce, Green Salad and Herbed Tomatoes

1 cup Italian spaghetti sauce
9 green onions
4 Tbsps. olive oil
1 garlic clove, crushed
½ lb. bow-tie pasta, cooked *al dente*
Freshly ground black pepper, to taste
½ cup freshly grated Parmesan or Romano cheese

Green Salad Ingredients:
iceberg lettuce
cucumber
celery, julienned
parsley

Herbed Tomatoes:
2 tomatoes
2 Tbsps. Marsala wine vinegar
2 green onions, chopped
Salt and pepper to taste

Make the **herbed tomatoes** beforehand. Cut tomatoes into thick slices. Place them on salad plate in the manner of toppled dominoes. Chop the green onions and sprinkle about. Pour the red wine vinegar over the tomatoes and sprinkle with salt and pepper to taste. Refrigerate until serving.

Make the **green salad** next. Wash, dry and tear the lettuce into bite-size pieces. Slice cucumbers thinly, julienne the celery stalk into 2-inch lengths, the size of match sticks. Add parsley as a garnish. Place the salad in a large bowl and refrigerate until mealtime.

Prepare the **bow-tie pasta** according to package directions; cook until *al dente.* Drain the pasta but leave a tablespoon of water for moisture. Heat the spaghetti sauce over medium heat in a skillet. Cut the green onions into 1-inch pieces. Heat another small frying pan and add the olive oil and garlic. Cook for just a moment and then put the onions and oil on the cooked pasta.

Add the hot Italian spaghetti sauce and the pepper to taste.

Toss and top with the **Parmesan** or **Romano cheese.**

Overnight - Plan ahead

HOLIDAY FRUITCAKE COOKIES

A Blanche Barnes Recipe

½ cup butter
1 cup brown sugar
2 eggs
3 ⅓ cups flour, divided
1 teaspoon baking soda
½ nutmeg
½ teaspoon cinnamon
½ teaspoon vanilla

2 lbs. candied fruit
2 cups golden raisins
3 cups, pecans, shelled
1 lb. chopped dates
1 cup apple sauce

2 teaspoons whisky

This recipe was one of many scavenged from mother's store of old dessert recipes.

The **candied fruits** can be found in most supermarkets among the ingredients for fruit cake.

In a large mixing bowl, using a blender, cream together the butter and sugar; gradually add the eggs. Stir in the soda and seasonings: the nutmeg, cinnamon, vanilla; blend well. Sift in 2 1/3 cups of flour, stir well and set aside.

In another large mixing bowl, mix the candied fruit, golden raisins, chopped pecans and chopped dates. Add the apple sauce and stir to mix completely.

In the larger of the two mixing bowls, combine the fruit mixture with the flour ingredients. Mix thoroughly. *If you desire to spike the cookies, add a couple of teaspoons of whisky or rum.* Add a dusting of the remaining 1 cup of flour; cover with plastic wrap and refrigerate until chilled, several hours.

When ready to bake, preheat the oven to 325° F.

Form the fruitcake mixture into 1 teaspoon balls and place on greased cookie sheet. Cook for 10-12 minutes until the cookies begin to brown.

Ingredients are not on grocery list for this week.

KING'S APPLE PORK

with Macaroni and Cheese and Fresh Spinach

2 butterfly pork chops
Salt and pepper, to taste
2 Tbsps. peanut oil
1 onion, chopped coarsely
1 apple, chopped
½ cup dry white wine
Dash thyme

Macaroni & Cheese Ingredients:
2 cups uncooked macaroni
2 Tbsps. butter, melted
¼ lb. American cheese
¼ cup milk
Salt and pepper, to taste
Spinach, fresh
½ cup vinegar

Preheat the oven to 350° F.

To cook the **pork chops**, season both sides with salt and pepper. Brown pork chops in peanut oil in heavy skillet over medium heat. Remove from skillet and place in shallow baking dish. In the same skillet, use the drippings from the chops and add additional oil. Brown the onion and apple. Spread these over the pork chops. Add wine and thyme. Bake, covered for approximately 45 minutes.

While pork cooks, prepare the **macaroni and cheese**. In a large pot boil the pasta. Add salt and some olive oil. Drain the pasta when cooked. Melt 2 tablespoons of butter; have ready. Cut thin slices of cheese to spread over macaroni. In a deep baking dish, layer cooked macaroni, cheese slices, portions of the milk and ½ of the butter. Make at least two layers. Sprinkle with salt and pepper.

Cover and bake the macaroni and cheese with the pork chops, timing the cheese to cook for about 10-15 minutes.

As the food cooks in the oven, prepare the **fresh spinach**. We wash fresh spinach in a basin of water mixed with ½ cup of vinegar. Thoroughly rinse the spinach after washing. We then steam the fresh spinach using a small steamer basket over boiling water, or you can place the spinach in a pot with a minimum of water and let the spinach steam for a few minutes.

FISH FILLETS WITH NOODLES

with Frozen Vegetables and Green Wedge Salad

Water
1 small onion, sliced
1 lemon, juiced
1 Tbsp. chicken-flavor instant bouillon
4 drops, hot pepper sauce
1 bay leaf
1 fish fillet
Frozen mixed vegetables
Egg Noodles Ingredients:
- **2 cups egg noodles, uncooked**
- **1 teaspoon butter or margarine**
- **1 Tbsp. grated Parmesan cheese**
- **½ teaspoon, parsley flakes**

Dash pepper
Paprika

Green Wedge Salad:
- **½ head lettuce**
- **½ cucumber, sliced**
- **2 radishes, in thin slices**
- **2 celery stalks, julienned**

Prepare the **green wedge salad** first. Cut the iceberg lettuce into wide wedges. Remove center portion and chop, spreading on salad plate. Cut the cucumber and place in the remaining curved portion of lettuce wedge. Slice the radishes and place on cucumbers. Julienne the celery and place on top of and around the wedge.

For the **fish**, in medium skillet, add water to ½ inch depth. Add onion, lemon juice, chicken bouillon, hot pepper sauce and bay leaf; bring to boil. Add fish; return to boil and reduce heat to simmer, covered, until fish is done, in 4 to 6 minutes.

Meanwhile, prepare **frozen vegetables** following package directions.

At the same time prepare **egg noodles**; drain, wash and drain again. Add butter, Parmesan cheese, parsley flakes and pepper; toss to coat. Arrange on serving plate.

With slotted spatula, remove fish from cooking liquid. Place fish on top of buttered noodles. Top with Parmesan cheese and paprika.

MUSTARD STEAKS

with Baked Vegetables and House Salad

2 boneless beef rib eye steaks, or top sirloin

Mustard Marinade:
- **2 cloves garlic, crushed**
- **2 teaspoons water**
- **2 Tbsps. Dijon-style mustard**
- **1 teaspoon dried basil leaves**
- **½ teaspoon pepper**
- **½ teaspoon dried thyme leaves**

Baked Vegetables Ingredients:
- **1 red bell pepper, halved**
- **1 green bell pepper, halved**
- **2 Tbsps. lemon juice**
- **2 Tbsps. fresh basil leaves**

House Salad Ingredients:
- **iceberg, green leaf lettuce**
- **carrot**
- **cucumber**
- **ripe olives, croutons**

The steaks in this menu (*courtesy of the beef industry*) can be grilled if the weather is moderate or they can be broiled in the oven.

Prepare the outdoor grill if you will be cooking outside. If cooking inside, set oven rack 4 inches from top broiler.

To prepare the **house salad,** wash and dry all vegetables. Peel lettuce off in layers. Cut the carrot into pencil-size shapes. Cut the cucumber into rounds then quarter to make pie slices. Toss all together, then add the ripe olives and the croutons.

Prepare the **mustard marinade**. In a microwave-proof bowl, combine 2 crushed garlic cloves and 2 teaspoons water. Cook in microwave for 2 minutes on HIGH. Stir in mustard, basil leaves, pepper and thyme. Coat both sides of steak with this marinade.

Place **steaks** on grill or in oven. Cook between 14-20 minutes depending on how well done you like them. Cut into the steaks to test.

While steaks cook, grill the **bell peppers** until the skin begins to blister. Remove peppers from grill and let cool, then cut into chunks and add to bowl of lemon juice and basil leaves.

Second week NOVEMBER

Sunday	*Monday*	*Tuesday*	*Wednesday*	*Thursday*	*Friday*	*Saturday*
Plan ahead **St. Petersburg Chicken** Dutch Potatoes, Green Peas	**Stuffed Green Peppers** Corn, Cucumber Salad	*Plan ahead* **Shrimp Creole** Curried Rice, Cole Slaw	**Baked Pork Chops** Macaroni & Cheese, Spinach Salad	**Angel Hair Pasta** Italian Salad French Bread	**Butter Baked Fish** Baked Potatoes, Green Wedge Salad	**Sesame Beef Floats** Rice, Sesame Biscuits

Fresh Vegetables \ Fruits		*Herbs \ Spices*	*Basics*
lemons - 3 tomatoes - 3 white onions - 5 potatoes - 6 parsley bunch green bell peppers - 4 fresh corn - 4 cucumbers - 3 green onions - 3	garlic pod red cabbage head spinach bunch yellow onion - 1 broccoli - ½ lb iceberg lettuce - 2 green leaf lettuce - 1 carrot bundle radishes - bunch celery bundle	basil oregano dried dill weed chili powder red pepper sauce curry powder dry mustard celery seeds sesame seed chives	vegetable oil peanut oil sea salt sugar cornstarch olive oil Dijon-style mustard extra-virgin olive oil white vinegar ketchup quick rising flour tarragon vinegar Converted Rice

Entrée Food	*Dairy*	*Miscellaneous*	*Cans \ Jars*
skinless boneless chicken breasts - 2 ground chuck ¾ lb large shrimp 12-16 butterfly pork chops - 2 fish fillets - 2 lean beef tips - 1 ½ lb. **Frozen** peas - pkg mixed vegetables	butter - 2 sticks margarine - 2 T egg - 1 sour cream - 1 C American cheese ¼ lb milk - 2 C whipping cream ¼ C Swiss cheese - ¼ lb. Romano cheese - 4 T **Wine**	bread crumbs - 1 C brown sugar - ¼ C macaroni - 2 C angel hair pasta ½ lb French bread loaf shortening ¼ C Rex ® Crab Boil almonds - 2 T croutons - pkg	V-8 juice (5.5 oz) - 4 pimiento - 1 T olives - 4 oz. ripe olives - 4 oz. chicken bouillon cubes - 2 cubes salad pepper vlasic® Pepperoncini beef bouillon - 1 Franco American beef gravy - 1

2 hours - Plan ahead

ST. PETERSBURG CHICKEN

with Dutch Potatoes and Green Peas

2 boneless, skinless breasts of chicken
½ cup butter or margarine
1 Tbsp. lemon juice
1 Tbsp. snipped chives
½ teaspoon salt to taste

1 egg, beaten
1 cup bread crumbs
1 teaspoon basil
Vegetable oil for deep frying

2 tomatoes, quartered

Dutch Potato Ingredients:
1 onion, chopped
1 Tbsp. peanut oil
2 large potatoes
2 Tbsps. parsley
salt
pepper
Frozen peas

Pound **chicken breasts** to achieve an even thickness.

On each breast, place a 2-tablespoon block of butter. Squeeze the juice of a lemon over the butter. Sprinkle a few chives over the butter as well. Salt to taste.

Roll the chicken breast around the butter mold and secure with toothpicks.

In a small bowl, beat one egg. Mix the basil with the bread crumbs. Dip the rolled chicken in beaten egg and roll in bread crumbs. Place the chicken in the refrigerator from ½ to 1 ½ hours.

When you are ready to eat, prepare **Dutch potatoes**. Cook chopped onion in peanut oil until clear. Add cubed potatoes. Add water to barely cover potatoes. Boil until the potatoes are about done, say 12 minutes. Add parsley, salt and pepper then cook for another five minutes. Drain.

Before the potatoes are done, prepare the **frozen peas** following package directions.

Cut the tomatoes into quarters and have ready. When potatoes are about done, fry chicken in deep oil for 8-10 minutes or until crust is golden brown. Two minutes before the chicken is done, place the quartered tomatoes in the oil for them to fry for a moment.

STUFFED GREEN PEPPERS

with Corn and Cucumber Salad

2 large green bell peppers
¾ lb. ground chuck
¾ cup uncooked, Converted Rice
1 teaspoon sea salt
½ teaspoon pepper
4 (5.5 oz) cans V-8 juice
1 teaspoon sugar
1 Tbsp. cornstarch

4 ears fresh corn
Sour Cream Cucumber Salad:
3 green onions, chopped
1 cup sour cream
2 Tbsps. tarragon vinegar
1 Tbsp. dried dill weed
2 Tbsps. olive oil
dash of salt
black pepper, ground
dash sugar
1-2 cucumbers

Make the **sour cream cucumber salad** first. Chop the green onions into small pieces. Mix sour cream, tarragon vinegar, chopped green onions and the dried dill. Blend in the olive oil. Season with salt pepper and add a dash of sugar. Adjust seasonings to your taste. Place the salad in a large bowl and refrigerate until mealtime.

Peel the cucumbers and cut into thick slices. Arrange cucumber on a salad plate and drizzle the sour cream dressing over it. If using fresh dill, garnish with sprigs.

Prepare the **stuffed peppers**: remove tops from the green peppers; mix meat, rice, sea salt and pepper together. Fill peppers to brim with rice mixture. Remaining meat will be placed in liquid.

Place peppers in a heavy saucepan. Pour V-8 juice over and around peppers and add sugar. Pour remainder of rice mixture into pot.

Cover and cook slowly for about 1 hour.

Thirty minutes before the stuffed peppers are done, prepare the **fresh corn**. You can cook the corn in the microwave by cooking on HIGH for 3 minutes then turning for another three minutes, or you can cook the corn in a pot of boiling water for 10 minutes.

1 hour - Plan ahead

SHRIMP CREOLE

with Curried Rice and Cole Slaw

4 Tbsps. olive oil
1 Tbsp. Dijon-style mustard
½ teaspoon chili powder
Dash basil
Dash oregano
¼ teaspoon pepper, coarsely ground
1 clove garlic, crushed
¼ teaspoon Rex® crab boil
¼ teaspoon red pepper sauce
12 - 16 large shrimp, in shells

Curried Rice Ingredients:
Converted Rice
1 Tbsp. onion, minced
2 Tbsps. butter
½ tsp. curry powder
¼ tsp. salt
¼ tsp. pepper
2 Tbsps. almonds
Cole Slaw
(Facing Page==>)

The plan ahead on this menu has to do with the cole slaw which should be made an hour before.

Cook **rice** before proceeding. Follow package directions.

Preheat oven to 375°F.

Make the spicy **Shrimp Creole**. In small frying pan, heat 4 tablespoons of olive oil. Add Dijon mustard, chili powder, basil, oregano, pepper, garlic, crab boil and the red pepper sauce. Stir mixture until fully blended.

Rinse **shrimp** in their shells and place in an open baking dish. Pour sauce over shrimp and stir to coat all shrimp evenly. Bake, uncovered, for about 6 minutes, stirring twice during the baking process.

When white rice is done, prepare the **curry rice**. Cook onions in margarine or butter until onion is tender. Stir in the curry powder, salt and pepper. Stir this mixture into the hot rice. Mix well and sprinkle in almonds, if desired.

COLE SLAW

in Olive Oil

1 teaspoon salt
¼ teaspoon pepper
½ teaspoon dry mustard
Scant teaspoon celery seeds
1 Tbsp. sugar
¼ cup chopped green bell pepper
1 Tbsp. chopped pimiento
1 teaspoon grated onion
3 Tbsps. extra-virgin olive oil
¼ cup white vinegar
3 cups cabbage, julienned

¼ cup chopped olives

In a bowl measure salt, pepper, dry mustard and celery seeds.

Add 1 tablespoon sugar.

Chop ¼ cup of green bell pepper and add. Do the same for 1 tablespoon of pimento. Grate a teaspoon of onion and add to bowl.

While mixing the ingredients, pour 3 tablespoons of **olive oil**, then the white vinegar. Stir well.

Cover and chill for thirty minutes.

A half hour before serving, add the julienned cabbage and stir to coat; refrigerate for about thirty minutes.

Garnish with sliced, stuffed olives just before serving.

BAKED PORK CHOPS

with Spinach Salad and Macaroni and Cheese

2 butterfly pork chops
Salt
2 chicken bouillon cubes
Water
1 onion, sliced thin
1 lemon, sliced thin
¼ cup ketchup
¼ cup brown sugar

Spinach Salad Ingredients:
1 tsp. Dijon mustard
3 Tbsps. tarragon vinegar
pepper to taste
2 Tbsps. olive oil
1 bunch spinach leaves

Macaroni and Cheese Ingredients:
2 cups uncooked macaroni
2 Tbsps. butter, melted
¼ lb. American cheese
¼ cup of milk

Preheat the oven to 350° F.

Season both sides of **pork chops** with salt. Place pork chops in ungreased, covered baking dish. Blend 2 chicken bouillon cubes in a ½ cup of water. We use the microwave to dissolve the cubes. Pour broth over pork chops. Top each chop with an onion slice, lemon slice, 1 tablespoon of ketchup and 1 tablespoon brown sugar. We reverse the order for the toppings on the second chop.

Cover and bake in oven for 30 minutes. Uncover and bake another 30 minutes.

While the chops bake, prepare the **spinach salad**. In a bowl, mix together the Dijon mustard, tarragon vinegar and pepper. While beating this mixture, slowly add the olive oil. Set aside. In a large salad bowl, tear the spinach leaves into bite-size pieces. When placing the spinach on the individual salad plates, pour the mustard sauce over the spinach.

For the **macaroni and cheese:** in a large pot, boil the pasta. Add salt and some olive oil. Drain the cooked pasta. Melt 2 tablespoons of butter; have ready. Cut thin slices of cheese to spread over macaroni.

In a deep baking dish, layer cooked macaroni, cheese slices, portions of the milk, ½ of the butter. Make at least two layers. Sprinkle with salt and pepper. Bake, covered, until the cheese is melted, about 10-15 minutes.

ANGEL HAIR PASTA

with Italian Salad and French Bread

2 cloves garlic, crushed
2 Tbsps. olive oil
½ yellow onion, peeled and chopped
½ lb. broccoli, florets only
¼ cup whipping cream
Fresh ground pepper, to taste
Salt to taste
½ lb. angel hair pasta
¼ lb. Swiss cheese, grated
4 Tbsps. Romano cheese, grated
2 Tbsps. parsley

Packaged French bread

Italian Salad Ingredients:
- **iceberg lettuce**
- **green leaf lettuce**
- **tomato, in wedges**
- **red cabbage**
- **ripe olives**
- **carrot, shredded**
- **salad pepper**
- **croutons (optional)**

If baking the **fresh bread**, preheat the oven to about 400° F. Follow package directions.

While oven heats, make the **Italian salad**. Wash, dry and tear the lettuces into bite-size pieces. Slice tomato into wedges in desired thickness. Cut red cabbage into julienne strips. Add a few ripe olives. Shred the carrot on top. Toss well. Place the salad in a large bowl and refrigerate until mealtime. Add a salad pepper to top and spread croutons around before serving.

Next prepare the **vegetables**. Sauté garlic in olive oil until it just begins to brown. Add the yellow onion and the broccoli florets and sauté until the broccoli is barely tender, about three minutes. Add the cream, pepper and salt to taste.

Meanwhile, cook the **angel hair pasta** following package directions until the pasta is *al dente.* Drain the pasta, and toss with Swiss and Romano cheeses. Add the cream and the vegetables, toss and serve. Garnish top with more cheese and some parsley.

BUTTER BAKED FISH

with Baked Potatoes and Green Wedge Salad

2 fish fillets
½ teaspoon salt
Dash of pepper
2 Tbsps. butter or margarine
1 Tbsp. lemon juice
1 teaspoon grated onion
Paprika

Green Wedge Salad Ingredients:
- **½ head iceberg lettuce**
- **½ cucumber in thick slices**
- **2 radishes, in thin slices**
- **2 celery stalks, julienned**

4 potatoes, for baking

Preheat the oven to 350° F.

Prepare the **green wedge salad** before proceeding: cut the iceberg lettuce into wide wedges. Remove center portion and chop, spreading on salad plate. Cut the cucumber and place in the remaining curved portion of lettuce wedge. Slice the radishes and place on cucumbers. Julienne the celery and place on top of and around the wedge.

Bake **potatoes** according to your favorite method. We typically use the microwave to completely bake or to at least partially bake the potatoes. Wash the potatoes and pierce with fork. Place potatoes in the microwave and cook on HIGH for 4 minutes per potato per side, turning once. (3 or 4 potatoes will cook in 24 minutes.)

Cut **fish** into serving pieces. Sprinkle both sides with salt and pepper. Mix margarine, lemon juice and onion. Dip fish pieces into margarine mixture; arrange in ungreased baking dish. Pour remaining liquid over fish.

Bake, uncovered, at 350° F until fish flakes when prodded with a fork, about 10 minutes. Top with paprika.

SESAME BEEF FLOATS

with Rice and Sesame Biscuits

1 ½ lbs. lean beef tips, cut into 1-inch cubes
2 Tbsps. peanut oil
1 can beef bouillon
1 small onion, chopped
2 Tbsps. chopped green pepper
1 (10 oz.) pkg. frozen mixed vegetables
1 cup Franco American beef gravy
¼ cup water

Sesame Biscuits Ingredients:
1 ¾ cup self-rising flour
¼ cup shortening
¼ cup sesame seed
1 cup milk

Converted Rice

For the **beef cubes**, cut beef into 1-inch cubes. In a saucepan, with peanut oil, cook the beef until it is brown on all sides. Toss the beef cubes into a pot. Add the can of bouillon. Heat to boiling, then reduce to a simmer. Cook the beef tips for 30 minutes.

Preheat the oven to 450° F.

In large pan, cook and stir onion and green pepper in oil, until tender. Stir in **beef**, frozen vegetables, gravy and water; heat until hot, about 5 minutes. Pour into ungreased oblong baking dish.

Prepare the **rice** according to package directions.

Prepare **sesame biscuits**. Cut shortening into flour beating into a mixture that resembles fine crumbs. Stir in milk just until soft dough forms (dough will be sticky). Shape dough into small, tablespoon-size balls. Coat the ball with sesame seeds, coating all sides.

Lower sesame biscuits into hot beef mixture. Cook, uncovered, in oven until biscuits are light brown.

Third week NOVEMBER

Sunday	*Monday*	*Tuesday*	*Wednesday*	*Thursday*	*Friday*	*Saturday*
Chicken Drum-sticks Parmesan Mashed Potato, Corn, 3-C Salad	**American Goulash** Noodles, Tossed Salad French Bread	**Northern Italian Shrimp** Risotto, Italian Salad	**Breaded Baked Pork Chops** Rice, Sautéed Celery, Tart Beets	**Vegetable Soup** House Salad	**Baked Cod** Baked Potato, Sweet Peas	**Tenderloin of Beef** Mashed Potatoes, Green Beans

Fresh Vegetables \ Fruits		*Herbs \ Spices*	*Basics*
tomatoes -2 corn - 3 green bell peppers 2 potatoes - 13 carrot bundle celery bundle - 2 cucumbers - 2 white onions - 2	garlic pod red cabbage head green beans - ¾ lb. green onions - 4 mushrooms - 3 iceberg lettuce - 2 green leaf lettuce - 1 radishes - bunch	chili powder dried thyme celery salt onion powder ground sage dry tarragon leaves garlic salt	Dijon mustard Worcestershire sauce peanut oil cornstarch sugar sea salt white wine vinegar red wine vinegar olive oil Converted Rice

Entrée Food	*Dairy*	*Miscellaneous*	*Cans \ Jars*
chicken drumsticks 6-12 ground beef - 1 lb. medium shrimp with shell - ½ lb. butterfly pork chops - 2 beef cubes - 1 lb. cod fillets - 2 beef tenderloin whole - 1 ½ lb. **Wine** Chardonnay wine bottle	Parmesan cheese 1 ¼ C butter - 2 sticks margarine - 1 stick milk - 1 ½ C whipping cream ¼ pint bacon - 1 slice **Frozen** green peas cut okra sweet peas	Italian bread crumbs - ½ C wide egg noodles 1 pkg French bread loaf croutons (pkg.) Risotto w/ mushrooms - pkg. yellow cornmeal - 2 T whole wheat flour 2 T crackers - 1 stack	tomato sauce - 2 ripe olives - 4 oz salad pepper vlasic Pepperoncini® 4 oz pickled beets - 8 oz pineapple chunks 8 oz sliced pimentos 2 oz whole tomatoes - 2 instant chicken bouillon 1 ½ T beef bouillon cubes 3

CHICKEN DRUMSTICKS PARMESAN

with Mashed Potatoes, Corn and 3-C Salad

6-12 chicken drumsticks
½ cup Italian bread crumbs
¼ cup grated Parmesan cheese
¼ cup melted butter or margarine
1 Tbsp. Dijon mustard
1 ½ teaspoons Worcestershire sauce

Corn, fresh (2 ears)
¼ green bell pepper, minced

3 potatoes
½ stick margarine
¼ cup milk
3 - C Salad Ingredients:
carrots
celery
cucumber
red wine vinegar
Tomato for garnish

Prepare the **3-C salad** by slicing the carrots, celery and cucumber; place in a serving dish. A red wine vinegar will do the trick for the topping. Let this salad marinate for about ten minutes before serving.

Prepare **mashed potatoes**. Wash and peel potatoes and cut into halves then quarter into smaller pieces. Heat a pot of water and add in the potatoes pieces. Salt the water to your taste. Cook for approximately 20 minutes; drain. Into hot potatoes place ½ stick of margarine, ¼ cup of milk and whip to desired smoothness.

Meanwhile, for the **chicken**, remove skin from drumsticks. On wax paper, combine Italian bread crumbs and Parmesan cheese. In small bowl, combine butter, mustard and Worcestershire sauce. Brush drumsticks with mixture, then roll in crumbs. Save the remaining butter mixture and crumbs.

Place drumsticks in microwave-safe shallow baking dish. Cover with plastic wrap. Microwave at medium-high (70 percent), 10 minutes per pound.

Halfway through cooking time, rotate drumsticks and spoon on remaining butter mixture; sprinkle with remaining bread crumbs. Recover and complete cooking. Remove and let stand, uncovered, before serving.

While the chicken cooks, prepare the **corn** in boiling water, cooking for ten minutes. Remove kernels and mix corn with chopped green peppers.

Cut the **tomato** into wedges as garnish.

AMERICAN GOULASH

with Noodles, Tossed Salad and French Bread

1 lb. ground beef
3 Tbsps. peanut oil
½ cup green bell pepper, chopped
¼ cup onion, chopped
1 teaspoon salt
1 ½ Tbsps. chili powder
1 (8 oz.) can tomato sauce
1 cup water
1 (2 ¼ oz.) can ripe olives, sliced
Dash dried thyme

½ lb. wide egg noodles
Fresh French bread
Tossed Salad Ingredients:
- **iceberg lettuce**
- **green leaf lettuce**
- **cucumber**
- **radishes**
- **tomato**
- **ripe olives**
- **croutons**

The goulash portion of this menu is courtesy of Barbara Boyd of Austin, Texas.

If you're having **fresh French bread**, bake it now, following package directions.

To prepare the tossed salad, wash and dry all vegetables. Tear the lettuces into bite-size pieces. Slice the cucumber and radishes. Cut the tomatoes into wedges. Toss all together, then add the ripe olives and the croutons.

For the **goulash**, cook and stir ground meat in peanut oil until meat is light brown. Add green pepper and onion and sauté until limp. Add all other ingredients: salt, chili powder, tomato sauce, water, ripe olives and dried thyme and simmer 30 minutes. Add more water as needed. Adjust seasoning.

Cook **noodles** according to package directions. Pour into finished goulash sauce.

NORTHERN ITALIAN SHRIMP

with Risotto and Italian Salad

½ lb. medium-size raw shrimp with shells

1 package Risotto* with mushrooms
1 Tbsp. butter or margarine
¼ cup grated Parmesan cheese

Chardonnay wine

Italian Salad Ingredients:
iceberg lettuce
green leaf lettuce
red cabbage, julienned
ripe olives
carrot, shredded
salad pepper
croutons (optional)

** Risotto is a traditional northern Italian rice. You may find it in the rice section. It comes in a variety of spiced flavors. Choose one that strikes you.*

If you are unable to find the packaged risotto, make your own by adding minced onions, basil leaves, thyme and rosemary spices to Converted rice.

Make the **Italian salad** beforehand. Tear lettuces into bite-size pieces. Cut red cabbage into julienne strips. Add a few ripe olives. Shred the carrot on top. Toss well. Place salad in refrigerator until serving. When serving, add a salad pepper to top and spread croutons around.

Cook **risotto** according to package directions.

Peel and devein **shrimp**; rinse and set aside until risotto has five minutes to cook. Stir shrimp into risotto, simmer 30 seconds. Remove pan from heat and let the shrimp cook for about 5 minutes. Sprinkle the Parmesan cheese over the rice and shrimp.

Serve the meal with a glass of Chardonnay wine.

BREADED BAKED PORK CHOPS

with Rice, Sautéed Celery and Tart Beets

2 butterfly pork chops
1 cup milk
Sautéed Celery Salad:
- **5 stalks of celery, cut diagonally**
- **1 Tbsp. instant chicken bouillon**
- **½ teaspoon salt**
- **Dash celery salt**
- **2 Tbsps. sliced pimentos**

Tart Beets Ingredients:
- **1 (8 oz.) jar pickled beets**
- **1 Tbsp. cornstarch**
- **1 (8 oz.) can pineapple chunks**

Cornmeal Mix:
- **2 Tbsps. yellow cornmeal**
- **2 Tbsps. whole wheat flour**
- **1 teaspoon salt**
- **½ teaspoon onion powder**
- **½ teaspoon ground sage**
- **½ teaspoon sugar**
- **½ teaspoon thyme**
- **½ teaspoon sea salt**

Converted Rice

Preheat oven to 350° F.

Prepare the **cornmeal mix**. Combine all ingredients on right side onto a sheet of wax pepper. Pour milk into a mixing bowl. Dip the **pork chops** in the milk then into the coating mix. When all chops are coated, place in a shallow baking dish. Cover and bake chops in oven for one hour.

While pork chops cook, prepare **rice** according to package directions.

To prepare the **sautéed celery**, cook and stir celery slices in skillet with 1 tablespoon peanut oil. Add the instant bouillon, salt, celery salt and cook over medium heat, turning often until the celery is tender, about 8 minutes. Toss in the pimentos to heat before serving.

For the **tart beets:** empty the liquid from the pickled beet jar into a large saucepan. Turn on the heat and add 1 tablespoon of cornstarch and heat. Cook, stirring frequently until the sauce begins to thicken. Stir in the pickled beets and add the drained pineapple chunks; heat thoroughly.

VEGETABLE SOUP

with House Salad

1 lb. beef cubes
2 Tbsps. peanut oil
2 (9 oz.) cans whole tomatoes
1 (6 oz.) can tomato sauce
32 oz. water
3 beef bouillon cubes
1 cup each of following vegetables:
fresh corn, carrots, green peas,
cut okra, celery
3 potatoes, skinned and cubed
1 small onion, chopped
Salt, pepper to taste

House Salad Ingredients:
iceberg lettuce
green leaf lettuce
cucumber
carrots
radishes
ripe olives
croutons

Crackers

For the **soup**: brown beef cubes in peanut oil in skillet. Pour into Dutch oven. Pour whole tomatoes, tomato sauce, water and bouillon cubes over meat and cook for 30 minutes. Add remaining vegetables: corn, carrots, green peas, okra, celery, potatoes. and onion. Cook for another 30 minutes, covered.

Season according to taste.

While the soup cooks, prepare the **house salad**. Wash and dry all vegetables. Tear lettuces into bite-size pieces. Cut the cucumber and radishes into rounds then quarter to make pie-slices. Cut the carrots into pencil-size shapes. Toss all together, then add the ripe olives and the croutons.

Serve the soup and salad with crackers on the side.

BAKED COD

with Baked Potatoes and Sweet Peas

2 Tbsps. white wine vinegar *
1 Tbsp. Dijon mustard *
2 Tbsps. olive oil *
½ teaspoon dry tarragon leaves *
Dash pepper *

¼ cup mustard-tarragon sauce
2 cod fillets
4 potatoes, for baking
Sweet peas, frozen

* Mustard-tarragon scratch ingredients

This menu calls for a mustard-tarragon marinade which you can purchase or prepare from scratch.

If you want to make your own mustard tarragon marinade, in a flat baking dish, mix together vinegar, mustard, olive oil, tarragon and pepper. Stir to blend completely.

Rinse fish and pat dry. Add the **fish** to the marinade and turn to coat completely. Cover and place fish in refrigerator for about 30 minutes.

Preheat the oven to 450° F.

Prepare **baked potatoes** according to your favorite method. We typically use the microwave to completely bake or to at least partially bake the potatoes. Wash the potatoes and pierce with fork. Place potatoes in the microwave and cook on HIGH for 4 minutes per potato per side, turning once. (3 or 4 potatoes will cook in 24 minutes.)

When oven is heated, uncover fish and bake at 450° F until fish flakes in thickest part when prodded with fork and flesh is opaque, about 8-10 minutes.

At the same time that you cook the fish, prepare the **sweet peas** following package directions.

TENDERLOIN OF BEEF

with Mashed Potatoes and Green Beans

1 ½ lbs. whole, peeled beef tenderloin
3 cloves, garlic
Worcestershire sauce
Garlic salt, to taste
Cracked pepper
¾ lb. green beans
1 slice bacon
Salt and pepper, to taste

Carrots, for garnish

Sauce Ingredients:
3 green onions, chopped
3 fresh mushrooms, sliced
½ stick butter
½ Tbsp. instant chicken bouillon
1 Tbsp. Dijon mustard
¼ pint whipping cream
3 potatoes
½ stick margarine
¼ cup milk

First, rub the entire surface of the **tenderloin** with peeled garlic cloves. Add Worcestershire sauce, garlic salt and cracked pepper. Let stand for about 1-2 hours at room temperature.

Preheat oven to 350° F.

Place tenderloin on flat baking sheet. Cook uncovered, for 45 minutes.

After an hour, check beef for desired doneness. Meat should be slightly pink in center. Remove from oven and let sit for 20 minutes; it will continue to cook while resting.

While beef sits, prepare the **green beans** for cooking. Cut off ends of green beans in a pot of water. Add a slice of bacon; season with salt and pepper. Cook for approximately 20 minutes.

At the same time, prepare **mashed potatoes**. Wash and peel potatoes and cut into halves then quarter into smaller pieces. Heat a pot of water and add in the potato pieces. Salt the water to your taste. Cook for approximately 20 minutes; drain. Into hot potatoes place ½ stick of butter or margarine, ¼ cup of milk and whip to the desired smoothness.

While potatoes cook, prepare the **sauce**. The sauce makes the meal! Sauté onions and mushrooms in butter; add chicken bouillon and cook until liquid from mushrooms has been reduced. Mix mustard with cream and add to mushrooms and onions. Simmer over low heat until slightly thickened.

Fourth week NOVEMBER

Sunday	*Monday*	*Tuesday*	*Wednesday*	*Thursday*	*Friday*	*Saturday*
Chicken Cordon Bleu Mashed Potatoes, Green Peas, Stuffing Mix	*Plan ahead* **Beef Chiles Rellenos** Black Beans, Tossed Avocado Salad	**Boiled Shrimp** Rice, Green Salad	**Old-Fashioned Cheese Soup** Buttered Toast, Tossed Salad	*Plan ahead* **Thanks-giving Meal** Mashed Potatoes, Green Beans, Cranberry Salad	**Baked Fish Lasagna** Roasted Red Pepper, Green Wedge Salad	**Garlic Orange Beef** Hot Noodles Tossed Salad

Fresh Vegetables \ Fruits		*Herbs \ Spices*	*Basics*
potatoes - 6 iceberg lettuce - 2 red leaf lettuce - 1 avocado - 1 lemons - 2 white onions - 6 cucumber - 2 celery bundle - 2 parsley bunch carrots - bundle	garlic pod - 1 green beans - 1 lb. fresh cranberries - 9 oz almonds - 2 oz. oranges - 3 red bell peppers - 1 green leaf lettuce -1 tomatoes - 3 radishes-bunch	parsley flakes cinnamon ground cloves cayenne pepper paprika ground coriander marjoram red pepper Tabasco® sauce	sea salt sugar vinegar, white Marsala red wine vinegar flour, cornstarch peanut oil olive oil Converted Rice baking soda

Entrée Food	*Dairy*	*Miscellaneous*	*Cans \ Jars*
skinless, boneless chicken breasts - 2 ham - 4 slices lean ground beef 1 lb medium shrimp 2 lb fresh turkey or roaster fish fillets 1-2 beef sirloin steak 1 ½ lb **Frozen** green peas - pkg	butter - 1 ½ stick margarine - 1 stick Swiss cheese 4 slices eggs - 5 bacon - 1 slice Monterey Jack 2 C low fat milk - 3 ¼ C American process cheese - ¾ lb. whipping cream 4 oz **Wine** dry white wine- ¼ C brandy - 2 oz. imported beer - 6	bread crumbs - 1 C Stove Top® chicken stuffing - 2 boxes seedless raisins ¼ C black beans - 1 C shrimp boil mix Zatarain® croutons - pkg. vegetable spray lasagna ½ lb. molasses - 2 T extra wide noodles ¼ lb bread slices - 8	tomato puree - 1 whole green chilies 4 oz. - 3 picante sauce - 1 chicken broth - 2 ripe olives - 4 oz beefy mushroom soup - 1 tomato paste - 1 French dressing - 4 oz. chili sauce - 2 T

CHICKEN CORDON BLEU

with Mashed Potatoes, Green Peas, Stove Top® Stuffing

2 boneless-skinless chicken breasts
4 Tbsps. butter
1 teaspoon parsley flakes
4 slices high quality ham
4 slices Swiss cheese
1 egg, beaten
1 cup plain bread crumbs

3 potatoes
½ stick margarine
¼ cup milk

Green peas and or
Stove Top®
chicken stuffing
Salt and pepper to taste

Pound **chicken** to an even thickness. Spread chicken with butter and sprinkle with parsley.

Place slice of ham and slice of cheese on each breast, folding to fit. Roll the chicken around the ham and cheese and secure with toothpicks.
Dip chicken in beaten egg and roll in bread crumbs.

Make **mashed potatoes**. Wash and peel potatoes and cut into halves then quarter into smaller pieces. Heat a pot of water and add in the potatoes pieces. Salt the water to your taste. Cook for approximately 20 minutes; drain. Into hot potatoes, place ½ stick of margarine, ¼ cup of milk and whip to desired smoothness.

Steam the **green peas** and or prepare the packaged **Stove Top® stuffing** following package directions. Season either with salt and pepper to taste.

In skillet over medium heat, in hot oil, cook chicken 10 minutes, turning occasionally.

BEEF CHILES RELLENOS

with Black Beans, Tossed Avocado Salad and Import Beer

1 lb. lean ground beef
2 Tbsps. olive oil
2 cloves garlic, finely minced
½ cup tomato puree
2 teaspoons cinnamon
Dash ground cloves
1 teaspoon sea salt
1 Tbsp. sugar
2 Tbsps. vinegar
¼ cup seedless raisins
2 cups grated Monterey Jack cheese, divided

3 (4 oz.) cans whole green chilies
4 eggs
2 cups milk
Salt, pepper and Tabasco® sauce to taste
1 jar picante sauce

1 cup black beans
1 slice bacon
Imported beer

Prepare the **beef mixture** for the chiles rellenos. Sauté meat in olive oil in large saucepan over medium heat until meat turns brown. Add garlic, tomato puree, cinnamon, ground cloves, sea salt, sugar, vinegar and raisins. Cover and simmer for 20 -25 minutes. Add in 1 cup grated Monterey Jack cheese and stir. Cool.

Remove the seeds from the **chiles** and spoon 2 tablespoons of the meat mixture on each chile. Roll the chile onto itself and place seam side down on well-buttered baking dish. Any extra stuffing meat can be spread across the top of the chiles. Place lid on baking dish and allow the chiles to *marinate overnight* in refrigerator.

Also the night before, soak the black beans in water.

When ready for the meal, preheat the oven to 375° F. Cook the **black beans** with a slice of bacon in salted water for 1 hour on stove top.

Make the **chiles rellenos**. Beat the eggs, adding milk, salt, pepper and red hot sauce. Pour this mixture over the chiles and sprinkle with remaining cup of cheese. Bake for 40-45 minutes or until puffed, brown and firm.

While the chiles rellenos cook, prepare the **tossed avocado salad** as instructed on the Facing page ====>.

With about thirty minutes before chiles rellenos are done, prepare the **rice** according to package directions. Serve chiles rellenos, with a little picante sauce on each serving, along with beans and rice.

TOSSED AVOCADO SALAD

Lettuce
Avocado
½ cup French dressing
2 Tbsps. chili sauce
Dash Tabasco® sauce

While chiles rellenos cook, prepare **avocado salad**.

Tear lettuce into bite-size pieces.

Cut avocado lengthwise into halves; cut halves into slices.

Make dressing by mixing ½ cup French dressing with 2 tablespoons chili sauce. To make avocado spicier, add a dash or two of red pepper sauce.

Pour sauce over the avocados and mix well.

Refrigerate until served.

BOILED SHRIMP

with Rice and Green Salad

1-2 lbs. medium size shrimp, unshelled
1 Tbsp. shrimp boil mix
2 Tbsps. vinegar
2 cloves garlic, crushed
1 lemon, sliced
1 small onion, in rings

Green Salad Ingredients:
- **iceberg lettuce**
- **cucumber**
- **celery, julienned**
- **parsley**

Converted Rice

This menu calls for a commercial brand of crab or shrimp boil. We prefer Zatarain's® Brand, a New Orleans style boil. *Look for the boil at the seafood counter.*

Cook **rice** before proceeding, according to package directions.

Make the **green salad** next. Wash, dry and tear the lettuce into bite-size pieces. Slice cucumber thinly, cut the celery stick into 2-inch lengths, the size of match sticks. Add parsley as a garnish. Place the salad in a large bowl and refrigerate until mealtime.

When rice and salad are made and ready, prepare **shrimp boil**. Follow directions on bottle. Fill pot with water sufficient to cover shrimp. Add 1 tablespoon of boil for each 5 pounds of shrimp. Add vinegar, lemon slice and onion rings. Bring water to a heavy, full boil and carefully place in shrimp. Cook until done, about 2 minutes. Remove shrimp with a slotted spoon.

Serve immediately.

OLD-FASHIONED CHEESE SOUP

with Buttered Toast and Tossed Salad

¼ cup butter
2 carrots, grated
2 celery stalks, chopped
½ small onion, minced
1 cup low fat milk, divided
3 Tbsps. cornstarch
2 dashes baking soda
¾ lb. American process cheese
¼ cup flour
1 teaspoon salt
Ground pepper to taste
2 cups chicken broth
Cayenne pepper, to taste
1 Tbsp. fresh parsley

Tossed Salad Ingredients:
iceberg lettuce
red leaf lettuce
cucumber
radishes
tomato
ripe olives
croutons

Toast

To prepare the **tossed salad,** wash and dry all vegetables. Tear the lettuces into bite-size pieces. Slice the cucumber and radishes. Cut tomato into wedges. Toss all together, then add the ripe olives and the croutons.

To make the **cheese soup,** put butter in a large saucepan and when melted, place in the carrots, celery and onion. Sauté over medium heat until done, about five minutes.

In a measuring cup, measure ½ cup of milk and blend in the cornstarch and baking soda. Blend into the cheese. Repeat with another ½ cup of milk with cornstarch and flour. Blend in the cheese. Stir until it melts. Gradually add the salt, pepper and chicken stock.

When soup is heated, add cayenne pepper to taste and the parsley to garnish.

Serve with buttered toast.

3 hours - Plan ahead

THANKSGIVING MEAL

Turkey or Roaster, Dressing, Mashed Potatoes, and Green Beans

1 turkey, ***fresh if available***
or 1 roaster hen
½ stick butter, melted
2-4 onions
Salt and pepper to taste
6 stalks of celery (w/leaves)
Vegetable spray

Stove Top Chicken Dressing
Cranberry/Orange Salad
(Facing Page ===>)
1 lb. green beans
3 potatoes
½ stick margarine
¼ cup milk

An office stapler and 2 grocery bags

If using frozen turkey, follow directions as provided and ignore all instructions below for the turkey or roaster; these instructions call for the use of a fresh, unfrozen turkey or hen.

Wash both inside and outside of the fresh **turkey** or **roaster.** Cut onions into wedges. Toss into cavity of bird. Cut large pieces of celery and toss into cavity along with the celery leaves. Brush melted butter over turkey. Lightly salt and pepper the bird.

Double the brown grocery bags. Spray inside with vegetable spray. Lay in the turkey, breast up. Roll up the opening and with a stapler, completely seal the bird. Place sack in roaster pan.

Set the oven temperature to that specified on the packaged bird.
Consult the baking chart on Facing page ===>.

Before the turkey is done prepare the green beans and the mashed potatoes.

Prepare **green beans** by the boiling method. Cut ends off beans and cut in half or leave long. Barely cover them with water and add one slice of bacon; add beans and sprinkle with salt. Cook until they are tender: 20 minutes for *al dente.*

Prepare **mashed potatoes**. Wash and peel potatoes and cut into halves then quarter then into smaller pieces. Heat a pot of water and toss in the potato pieces. Salt the water to your taste. Cook for approximately 20 minutes; drain. Into hot potatoes, place ½ stick of margarine, ¼ cup of milk and whip to desired smoothness.

Carefully, remove turkey from pan and sack. Let turkey sit 15 minutes before carving.

ORANGE CRANBERRY SALAD

9 oz. fresh cranberries
3 ½ oz. processed sugar
Dash of ground coriander
Sliced almonds
2 medium-size oranges
2 oz. brandy
Whipping cream

Wash the cranberries and drain. In a large saucepan, mix together the cranberries, the processed sugar and a pinch of coriander. Simmer on medium-low heat until the cranberries begin to burst and the sugar dissolves.

Remove from heat. Place pan in a basin of iced-water to cool.

In a baking dish spread the almonds. Roast them under the oven broiler until they begin to change color.

Peel the orange and slice across the ribs to give a wagon wheel effect. Place sliced oranges in a bowl and pour brandy over them. Let the oranges marinate until you are ready to assemble.

To assemble the salad, place the orange rings around a serving platter, leaving space in middle. Into the middle space pour the cool cranberries. Spray on the whipping cream and add the roasted sliced almonds.

TIME-TEMPERATURE CHART FOR BAKED TURKEY

Weight	Approximate minutes per pound	Meat thermometer reading when done
8 - 10 lbs.	16-18	200° F
12-15 lbs.	14-16	200° F
16-18 lbs.	12-14	200° F

BAKED FISH LASAGNA

with Roasted Red Peppers and Green Wedge Salad

4 slices of lasagna noodles
1 or 2 fish fillets
¼ cup dry white wine
2 Tbsps. lemon juice
½ teaspoon marjoram
1 Tbsp. margarine

1 red bell pepper (roasted)

Green Wedge Salad:
½ head iceberg lettuce
½ cucumber, sliced
2 radishes, in thin slices
2 celery stalks, julienned

Herbed Tomatoes Ingredients:
2 tomatoes, sliced
1 clove garlic, minced
Black pepper
Marsala red wine

Note: Orange roughy, cod or sole fillet are good candidates.

Prepare **green wedge salad:** cut the iceberg lettuce into wide wedges. Remove center portion and chop, spreading on salad plate. Cut cucumber and place in remaining curved portion of lettuce wedge. Slice radishes and place on cucumbers. Julienne celery and place on top of and around the wedge. Place in refrigerator until serving.

Preheat oven to 400° F.

For **herbed tomatoes** slice tomatoes into ¼ inch slices. Sprinkle minced garlic on top as well as fresh ground black pepper. Pour some Marsala wine vinegar over slices.

Cook **lasagna** according to package directions. Drain and run under cold water to halt cooking process.

Lightly grease a baking dish with margarine. Place one layer of lasagna in bottom of baking dish. Lay each **fish fillet** lengthwise along the strip of lasagna. Mix the wine and lemon juice together and pour over fish; sprinkle with marjoram and black pepper. Top with more strips of lasagna. Bake uncovered until tender, about 10-12 minutes.

While fish bakes, prepare **red peppers**. Cut red bell pepper into large pieces. Coat with virgin olive oil.

After fish is finished, place bell peppers under broiler and broil for 1 minute until brown.

GARLIC ORANGE BEEF

with Hot Noodles and Tossed Salad

3 Tbsps. peanut oil, divided
1 ½ lb. beef sirloin steak, thinly sliced
1 medium onion, chopped
1 clove garlic, minced
1 teaspoon orange peel
1 (10 ¾ oz.) can beefy mushroom soup
¼ cup water
¼ cup tomato paste
¼ cup orange juice
2 Tbsps. molasses
Pepper to taste

½ lb. extra-wide noodles

Tossed Salad Ingredients:
iceberg lettuce
green leaf lettuce
cucumber
tomato
radishes
ripe olives
croutons

In 10- inch skillet, over high heat, place 2 tablespoons of peanut oil.

Add and cook **beef** until color just changes, stirring often; transfer beef to bowl.

Reduce heat to medium. Add remaining tablespoon of oil and cook onion, garlic and orange peel for 5 minutes, stirring often.

Stir in soup, water, tomato paste, orange juice, molasses and pepper. Heat to boiling, then reduce heat to low. Simmer for 5 minutes. Add **beef** to mixture and cook 15 minutes more, stirring occasionally

While beef cooks, prepare **tossed salad**. Wash and dry all vegetables. Tear lettuces into bite-size pieces. Slice cucumber. Cut the tomato into wedges. Slice radishes. Toss all together, then add the ripe olives and the croutons.

Meanwhile, prepare **extra-wide noodles** according to package directions.

Serve beef over noodles.

Fifth week NOVEMBER

Sunday	Monday	Tuesday	Wednesday	Thursday	Friday	Saturday
Chicken Pot Pie Rice, Green Salad	**Sunshine Meat Loaf** Rice, Spinach	**Shrimp & Refired Rice** Sake, Egg Rolls	**Turkey Tenderloin** Rice, Mixed Vegetables, Easy Tomato Slices	**Hypocrite Vegetables** Rice, Green Wedge Salad. Fresh Bread	**Pan-Fried Sole** Penne Pasta, Snow Peas	**Chicken Fried Steak** Mashed Potatoes, Green Peas

Fresh Vegetables \ Fruits		*Herbs \ Spices*	*Basics*
onions - 2 iceberg lettuce - 2 green leaf lettuce - 1 celery bundle carrots bunch tomato - 4 spinach bunch pkg. parsley bunch	garlic pod - 1 green onions - 6 cucumbers - 3 yellow squash - 1 green bell pepper - 1 lemon - 1 snow peas - ½ lb. potatoes - 3	celery seeds dry mustard white pepper garlic powder paprika	flour sea salt cornstarch vegetable oil red wine vinegar white vinegar olive oil shortening Converted Rice soy sauce

Entrée Food	*Dairy*	*Miscellaneous*	*Cans \ Jars*
boneless chicken breast - 1 ground beef - 1 lb. raw shrimp w/ shells - ½ lb. turkey tenderloin 1 lb sole fillet - 2 round steak 1-2 lbs **Frozen** mixed vegetables 2 green peas - 2 chicken egg rolls 1	butter - 4 T margarine - 1 stick milk - 2 cup eggs - 5 pasteurized process cheese spread ¾ lb. Parmesan cheese 4 oz. **Wine** Sake - 4 C Cabernet Sauvignon wine - bottle	bread crumbs - 2 C French bread pkg Penne pasta - ½ lb. crackers - 1 stack pecans - ¼ cup	chicken broth - 2 whole tomatoes - 3 beef gravy - 10 oz.

CHICKEN POT PIE

with Rice and Green Salad

1 boneless chicken breast
¼ cup margarine or butter
¼ cup all-purpose flour
¼ cup chopped onion
½ teaspoon salt
¼ teaspoon black pepper
1 ¾ cups chicken broth
5 oz. milk
1 (10 oz.) pkg. frozen mixed vegetables

9 x 9 x 2" baking dish

Pastry Ingredients:
5 oz. shortening
2 cups all-purpose flour
2 teaspoons celery seed
1 teaspoon salt
4 - 5 Tbsps. water

Converted Rice

Green Salad Ingredients:
iceberg lettuce
green leaf lettuce
cucumber
celery, julienned

Prepare the **chicken**. Boil chicken in water for about 15 minutes. In a skillet, heat margarine over low heat until melted. Blend in flour, onion, salt and pepper. Cook over low heat, stirring constantly, until mixture is smooth and bubbly; remove from heat. Stir in broth and milk. Heat to boiling, stirring constantly. Boil and stir 1 minute. Stir in cooked chicken and frozen vegetables; reserve.

Prepare the **pastry.** Mix shortening into flour; add celery seeds and salt. Sprinkle in water, 1 tablespoon at time, tossing with wire or fork until all flour is moistened and pastry is easy to handle. (It may be necessary to add 1 or 2 tablespoons of water). Gather pastry into balls. Dampen drain board and lay out a sheet of wax paper. Place dough on wax paper. Lay another sheet of paper on top and roll two-thirds of pastry into a large square. Ease pastry into square pan, 9 x 9 x 2 inches, pressing dough onto sides. Pour in the chicken filling. Roll remaining dough to size of pan and place over chicken filling. Roll edges under; flute. Pierce the center of the pie to allow steam to escape.

Cook, uncovered, in 425° F oven, until crust is browned, 30 to 35 minutes.

Prepare rice according to package directions.

While the chicken cooks, make the **green salad.** Wash, dry and tear the lettuces into bite-size pieces. Slice cucumber thinly, cut the celery stick into 2 inch lengths, the size of match sticks.

SUNSHINE MEAT LOAF

with Rice and Spinach

1 (8 oz.) can tomatoes, drained and chopped
½ cup shredded carrots
½ cup chopped celery
1 lb. ground beef
1 cup soft bread crumbs
1 egg
1 teaspoon salt
¼ tsp. dry mustard
Dash pepper
1 (10 ¼ oz.) can beef gravy

1 tomato, sliced

Converted Rice

Spinach
½ cup white vinegar

Preheat the oven to 350° F.

Prepare the vegetables as indicated for the **sunshine meat loaf**. In small bowl combine tomatoes, carrots, celery and set aside. In large bowl, mix thoroughly beef, bread crumbs, egg, salt, mustard, pepper and ⅛ cup gravy. On wax paper, shape half of beef into a rectangle. Spread vegetable mixture on top. Top with remainder of beef. Shape into a loaf form and place in shallow baking pan. Top with slices of tomato.
Bake uncovered at 350° F for 1 hour. Let cool while rice cooks.

Prepare **rice** according to package directions.

While rice cooks, prepare the **spinach**. When using fresh spinach, we always wash the leaves in a basin of cold water with ½ cup of vinegar. Rinse well. Place spinach in a steamer basket or in a pot with minimum water and turn up the heat for a couple of minutes.

Before serving, warm the remaining beef gravy and pour over meat loaf.

SHRIMP AND REFRIED RICE

with Sake and Egg Rolls

2 cups chicken broth
¼ teaspoon soy sauce
¼ teaspoon white pepper
¼ teaspoon garlic powder
¼ teaspoon sea salt
1 cup white Converted Rice
¼ cup frozen green peas
½ teaspoon white onion, chopped
1 pkg. frozen chicken egg rolls
2 eggs, beaten
½ lb. raw shrimp
½ cup cornstarch
¼ cup vegetable oil
4 green onions, chopped
Sake

Preheat the oven to 400° F for the **egg rolls**.

Combine chicken broth, soy sauce, white pepper, garlic powder, and sea salt. Stir to blend. Add uncooked rice, peas and onion. Cook according to package directions for rice. Cover and set aside.

When oven is heated insert the egg rolls and cook to the time specified on the package.

Beat the eggs and set aside.

Prepare the **shrimp**. Peel, devein and clean shrimp. Add cornstarch to shrimp, mixing well to cover all parts of shrimp. Set aside.

Set clean wok over very hot fire. Pour 1 cup vegetable oil; add shrimp and stir fry 30-45 seconds. Remove shrimp from wok. Set aside. Pour off vegetable oil; flood the shrimp briefly with warm water to rinse off the oils.

Pour ¼ cup vegetable oil into wok. Pour lightly-beaten eggs in a circle into hot oil with a spatula; stir them up like scrambled eggs. Lower heat to medium; add shrimp and stir to mix. Add prepared rice. Immediately begin to shake wok, tossing and stirring mixture 30-40 times. (Cooking rice twice is an important step.)

Add green onions just before serving.

Serve a cup of warm sake before or during the meal.

TURKEY TENDERLOIN

with Rice, Mixed Vegetables and Easy Tomato Slices

1 lb. turkey tenderloin, cut into 1-inch cubes

2 Tbsps. margarine or butter

1 clove garlic, minced

3 cups frozen mixed vegetables

¾ lb. pasteurized process cheese spread, cubed
¼ cup pecans, chopped
Easy Tomato Slices:
2 whole ripe tomatoes
2 green onions, chopped
2 Tbsps. red wine vinegar
Salt and pepper to taste
Converted Rice

The turkey portion of this menu is based on a Kraft recipe.

Prepare **rice** now, following package directions.

While rice cooks, prepare **turkey.** Cut turkey into cubes. In a saucepan melt butter. Add minced garlic and cook for five minutes. Add turkey and cook over low heat for about 7 minutes, stirring occasionally.

Stir in the **frozen mixed vegetables**. Cook 6 to 8 minutes or until vegetables are heated, stirring occasionally.

As the turkey cooks, make the **easy tomato slices**: cut tomatoes into thick slices. Place them on salad plate in the manner of toppled dominoes. Chop the green onions and sprinkle about. Pour the red wine vinegar over the tomatoes and sprinkle with salt and pepper to taste.

When turkey is done, add cheese spread; stir until cheese melts. Serve over rice.
Top with pecans that have been coarsely chopped.

HYPOCRITE VEGETABLES

with Rice, Green Wedge Salad, French Bread and Red Wine

Converted Rice
½ onion, chopped
1 cucumber
1 yellow squash
2 carrots
½ green bell pepper
2 celery stalks
1 (14.5 oz.) can whole tomatoes

Green Wedge Salad:
½ head iceberg lettuce
½ cucumber, sliced
2 radishes, sliced
2 celery stalks, julienned

Cabernet Sauvignon wine
Fresh bread

Preheat the oven to 400° F. Place **bread** in the oven and proceed.

Next, prepare the **green wedge salad**. Cut the iceberg lettuce into wide wedges. Remove center portion and chop, spreading on salad plate. Cut the cucumber and place in the remaining curved portion of lettuce wedge. Slice the radishes and place on cucumbers. Julienne the celery and place on top of and around the wedge.

Prepare the **rice** according to package directions before proceeding.

Begin the **hypocrite vegetables.** Place chopped onion in a small saucepan and barely cover with water. Simmer 2-3 minutes; remove onion to a large skillet. To the large skillet, add cucumbers, yellow squash, carrots, green pepper and celery. Add ½ inch of water to skillet; heat until the water begins to steam. Remove pan from heat and keep covered for about 3 minutes. Into the smaller skillet, add the whole tomatoes with liquid and allow to heat over medium-high heat.

Serve the vegetables over a mound of rice and top with the tomatoes.

A **Cabernet Sauvignon wine** goes well with this meal. Don't forget the fresh bread!

PAN-FRIED SOLE

with Penne Pasta and Snow Peas

2 sole fish fillets
Salt and pepper
¼ cup dry bread crumbs
½ teaspoon paprika
1 lemon
1 Tbsp. olive oil

½ lb. snow peas

½ lb. Penne pasta*

Parmesan cheese

* *Penne is pasta in the shape of quills, or old-fashioned fountain pen tips.*

Prepare the **snow peas**. Trim stem ends. Remove any visible string. Set aside.

Cook the **pasta** according to package directions. Rinse under cold water and set aside. When you are about to serve, place the pasta and snow peas in boiling water for about 30 seconds then run both under cold water. This will perk the snow peas up and make them very green.

Rinse the **fish** and pat dry. Lightly season the fish with salt and pepper. Check that the fish will fit the frying pan; it may be necessary to cut the fish to fit. Combine the crumbs and paprika in a shallow dish. Dip the fillets into the crumb mixture and turn to thoroughly coat.

Heat the non-stick pan over medium-high heat. Add the olive oil and heat for a moment. Lay in the fish and cook until the edges turn opaque and the bottom is browned. Flip fish and cook until the fish flakes in the middle when gently prodded with a fork, about 2 minutes.

Transfer the fish to serving plates and cover to keep warm.

If you want sauce for the fish, squeeze the juice from half the lemon into the fish pan; scrape the cooked fish bits in the pan and boil until thickened. Cut the remaining half lemon into thin wedges to use as garnish.

CHICKEN-FRIED STEAK

with Mashed Potatoes and Green Peas

1 - 2 lb. round steak, ½ inch thick
2 beaten eggs
2 Tbsps. milk
1 cup fine cracker crumbs
½ cup olive oil
Salt and pepper to taste

Frozen green peas

3 potatoes
½ stick margarine
¼ cup milk
Green Salad Ingredients:
- **iceberg lettuce**
- **green leaf lettuce**
- **cucumber**
- **celery, julienned**
- **parsley**

Pound **steak** thoroughly with sharp-edged meat-tenderizer. Dip into egg mixed with milk, then into bread crumbs. Heat skillet until hot. Brown steak on both sides in olive oil. Season with salt and pepper. Cover and cook over low heat about 30-45 minutes.

While steak cooks, prepare **mashed potatoes**. Wash and peel potatoes and cut into halves then quarter into smaller pieces. Heat a pot of water and add in the potato pieces. Salt the water to your taste. Cook for approximately 20 minutes; drain. Into hot potatoes, place ½ stick of butter or margarine, ¼ cup of milk and whip to the desired smoothness.

Make the **green salad** next. Wash, dry and tear the lettuces into bite-size pieces. Slice cucumber thinly, cut the celery stalk into 2-inch lengths, the size of match sticks. Add parsley as a garnish. Place the salad in a large bowl and refrigerate until mealtime.

At this time, prepare the **frozen green peas** following package directions.

A Perfect Winter Night

The perfect winter night always arrives with ice in the air, and for some fortunate people, with snow on the ground. Our ideal winter night involves family and friends by the fireplace, excitedly talking over a movie previously seen and sipping soup and munching on snack food. And sipping wassail.

Make the wassail during the day and place it in a slow cooker to simmer. The aromas will set the mood for festivities.

Have one in your crowd select a movie that all have seen and enjoyed, but keep the movie a secret until the old movie house drapes separate. Once the movie begins let the comments roll. We have tried this with Father of the Bride, Roxanne and once with Dr. Zhivago. Let your taste dictate.

Broccoli-Cheese Soup see page 1-109

Wassail

4 cups apple juice
1 bottle of ale
(or another 2 cups of apple juice
2 stick cinnamon sticks
1 teaspoon allspice
1 teaspoon ground ginger
1 whole clove
1 teaspoon nutmeg
½ cup sugar

1 apple, in wedges

Combine all ingredients except apple in a slow cooker. Set heat to high and when mixture heats, stir until the sugar fully dissolves.

When ready to serve the wassail, preheat the oven to 375° F. Pour a small amount of juice over apple wedges; place in oven and cook for about 30 minutes.

Fingertip Sausage Slices and Chicken Nuggets

2 - 4 skinless, boneless chicken breasts
1 stick butter or margarine.
8 - 12 low-fat sausage links
Crackers or bread

Pound the chicken breasts slightly. Butter and place under the oven's broiler element for about 6 minutes each side. Remove and cool; cut into nugget size. Cut the sausage links into

The Best Chicken Menus

We close the year out with December, the month of holidays, good cheers and exceptional foods. But it is also a month of quick foods, eaten on the run.

December is the month for our best chicken menus, a boast you can dismiss knowing the number of exceptional chicken menus in the past eleven months, but we had to have a best month for chicken so we made it December by stacking the deck. The chicken menus range from the simple to prepare *Chicken Dijon*, first discovered on a Christmas trip to Colorado, to an elegant *Christmas Chicken*. We've included our children's favorite: *Chicken Broccoli Rice*, a consistently pleasing casserole.

December is also the month of soups and we have four of the best. *Chicken Minestrone* with a Poor Boy sandwich can be made in a jiff and tastes exquisite. A *Mexican Squash Soup* that can be made as spicy or as mild as your taste demands, served with quick tacos. The *Seafood Ravioli Soup* is a healthy soup with shrimp and halibut fish that gets its tang from Italian stewed tomatoes. And lastly, the *Tortilla Soup* that also can be moderated for heat, depending on the weather. We hope you've come to enjoy the many soups in these books and that soups have become part of your diet. Kathy and I are firm believers that there can be no better appetizer than a good soup. This in spite of all of the salads found in *More Than Recipes*.

In December, there is fish, frozen of course, and pasta that is fast and tasty, and there is pork, the best example of which is the *Holiday Pork Chops*, the best pork to end the year.

December, we cheat, just a bit, and have a favorite beef menu that we rename *December Beef Redux*.

December is the time of giving, and we hope you have enjoyed *More Than Recipes* enough to consider giving it as a Christmas or anniversary or wedding present. An order form can be found in the back of volume 2. Finally, if you can find the time, write us a note. Tell us what you think about *More Than Recipes*, what you would change, what would stay the same.

Wherever you live, we hope to see you there soon. Kathy and Leonard

December Menus

Chicken

Chicken Broccoli Rice with Tossed Salad

Sauterne Chicken Breasts with Mashed Potatoes and Snow Peas

Chicken Dijon with Rice and Confetti Corn and House Salad

Xmas Chicken with Wild Rice and Tossed Salad

Sherry Baked Chicken with Mashed Potatoes, Green Beans

Quick & Easy

Meatballs w/ Green Peppers with French Bread and Italian Salad

Pizza Night In/Out with Pizza and Tossed Salad

Frankfurters Hash with Rice and Celery Salad

Stuffed Tomatoes with Spinach and Corn

Ground Beef Nachos with Sour Cream and Guacamole Salad

Shrimp

Shrimp in Brown Butter Sauce with Rice and French Bread

Shrimp on the Rocks with Brown Rice and Spinach Salad

Seafood Ravioli Soup with French Rolls and Green Salad

Shrimp Louis Salad with Potato Flats

Pepper-Chicken Fettuccine Toss with Celery Salad

Pork

Scalloped Potatoes and Pork Chops with Spinach, Fruits and Tossed Salad

Christmas Pork Chops with Rice and Broccoli Salad

Roasted Pork Loin with Stuffed Prunes, Rice or Noodles

Pasta/Soups

Chicken Minestrone Soup with Poor Boy Sandwiches

Mexican Squash Soup with Tacos and Guacamole Salad

Chef's Salad with Fresh Bread and Baked Croutons

Tomato Pasta Salad Night with French Bread and Green Wedge Salad

Tortilla Soup with Rice and Avocado Salad

Fish

Marinated Fish Steak w/ Baked Potatoes and Roasted Peppers

Cajun Baked Fish with Risotto, Sour Cream Cucumber Salad

Baked Orange Roughy in Wine with Herbed Rice and Green Wedge Salad

Microwave Fish with Baked Potato and Tossed Salad

Broiled Swordfish with Pasta and Red Peppers

Herb Crusted Salmon Fillet with Baked Potato and Corn

Red Meats

Veal Cordon Bleu with Noodles and Broccoli

December Beef Redux with Mashed Potatoes and Broccoli

Baked Sirloin Cubes with Broccoli and Twice-Baked Potatoes

Glazed Steaks with Dutch Potatoes and Green Peas

A Great Flank Steak with Cole Slaw and Baked Beans

Round Beef Confetti with Mashed Potatoes and Green Peas

DECEMBER

Sunday	Monday	Tuesday	Wednesday	Thursday	Friday	Saturday
Chicken Broccoli Rice Tossed Salad	**Meatballs w/ Green Peppers** French Bread, Italian Salad	**Shrimp in Brown Butter Sauce** Rice, French Bread, Caesar Salad	*Plan ahead* **Chicken Minestrone Soup** Poor Boy Sandwiches	**Chef's Salad** Fresh Bread, Baked Croutons	**Cajun Baked Fish** Risotto, Sour Cream Cucumber Salad	*Plan ahead* **December Beef Redux** Mashed Potatoes, Broccoli
Sauterne Chicken Breasts Mashed Potatoes, Snow Pea Salad	*Plan ahead* **Pizza Night In/Out** Tossed Salad	**Shrimp On The Rocks** Brown Rice, Spinach Salad	**Scalloped Potatoes & Pork Chops** Spinach, Tossed Salad, Fruits	*Plan ahead* **Mexican Squash Soup** Tacos, Guacamole Salad	**Baked Orange Roughy in Wine** Herbed Rice, Green Wedge Salad	**Glazed Steaks** Dutch Potatoes, Green Peas
Chicken Dijon Confetti Corn, House Salad	**Frank-furter Hash** Rice, Celery Salad	**Seafood Ravioli Soup** French rolls, Green Salad	**Christmas Pork Chops** Rice, Broccoli Salad	**Tomato Pasta Salad Night** French Bread, Green Wedge Salad	**Microwave Fish** Baked Potato, Tossed Salad	**Baked Sirloin Cubes** Twice Baked Potatoes, Broccoli
Xmas Chicken Wild Rice, Tossed Salad, Dinner Rolls	**Stuffed Tomatoes** Spinach, Corn	**Shrimp Louis Salad** Potato Flats	**Roasted Pork Loin** Stuffed Prunes, Rice or Noodles	**Tortilla Soup** Rice, Avocado Salad	**Broiled Swordfish** Pasta, Red Peppers	*Plan ahead* **Great Flank Steak** Cole Slaw, Baked Beans
Sherry Baked Chicken Mashed Potatoes, Green Peas	**Ground Beef Nachos** Sour Cream, Guacamole Salad	**Pepper Chicken Fettucine Toss** Celery Salad	**Veal Cordon Bleu** Noodles, Broccoli	**Marinated Fish Steak** Baked Potatoes, Roasted Peppers	**Herb Crusted Salmon Fillet** Baked Potato, Corn	**Round Beef Confetti** Mashed Potatoes, Green Peas

First week DECEMBER

Sunday	Monday	Tuesday	Wednesday	Thursday	Friday	Saturday
Chicken Broccoli Rice Tossed Salad	**Meatballs with Green Peppers** French bread Italian Salad	**Shrimp in Brown Butter Sauce** Rice, French Bread, Caesar Salad	*Plan ahead* **Chicken Mine-strone Soup** Poor Boy Sandwiches	**Chef's Salad** Fresh Bread, Baked Croutons	**Cajun Baked Fish** Risotto, Sour Cream Cucumber Salad	*Plan ahead* **December Beef Redux** Mashed Potatoes, Broccoli

Fresh Vegetables \ Fruits		*Herbs \ Spices*	*Basics*
broccoli - 1 ½ lb. carrot bundle iceberg lettuce - 2 cucumbers - 3 tomatoes - 6 radishes - bunch white onions - 2 green pepper - 1 mushrooms - 2 potatoes - 3	garlic pod - 1 red cabbage head - 1 lemons - 4 romaine lettuce bunch - 1 celery bundle green beans - ¾ lb. green onion - 9 small white (pearl) onions - 8	garlic powder chili powder dry mustard ground cumin onion powder ground red pepper dried dill weed bay leaf	Worcestershire sauce olive oil mayonnaise salad dressing sugar flour peanut oil Converted Rice tarragon vinegar

Entrée Food	*Dairy*	*Miscellaneous*	*Cans \ Jars*
skinless, boneless chicken breasts - 6 ground beef -1 lb. jumbo shrimp - 12 fish fillets - 2 beef tip - 1 ½ lb. **Wines** brandy - 2 T Cabernet - 1 C dry sherry - 1 C ruby port - ½ C	margarine - 3 sticks milk - 1 ¼ cup butter - 2 sticks mild process cheese - 3 slices eggs - 4 Parmesan cheese - 6 oz. cheese slices - 4 Swiss cheese ⅛ lb. sour cream - 1 cup	croutons -pkg. French bread 2 pkg. macaroni pasta 1 lb. fusilli pasta - 1 lb. kidney beans - 2 C wheat buns - 4 French dressing ¼ C Risotto w/ onions and herbs - 1 pkg. sesame crackers - pkg	cream of broccoli soup - 1 ripe olives - 4 oz. beef gravy - 1 salad pepper vlasic® Pepperoncini - 4 oz. stewed tomatoes - 1 chicken broth - 2 tomato paste - 1 condensed beef bouillon - 1

CHICKEN BROCCOLI RICE

with Tossed Salad

2 chicken breasts, skinless
2 Tbsps. margarine
2 cups fresh broccoli, chopped
¾ cup thinly-sliced carrots
1 can Campbell's cream of broccoli soup
1 cup milk
Dash or two of pepper

1 ¼ cups Converted Rice
Tossed Salad Ingredients:
iceberg lettuce
cucumber
radishes
tomato
ripe olives
croutons

The entrée for this meal was inspired by Campbell's soup. We've substituted long-cooking Converted Rice for the quick rice.

To prepare the **tossed salad,** wash and dry all vegetables. Tear the lettuce into bite-size pieces. Slice the cucumber and radishes. Cut the tomato into wedges. Toss all together, then add the ripe olives and the croutons.

Prepare **rice** according to package directions.

Flatten the chicken to achieve even thickness. In skillet, in hot margarine, cook **chicken** until browned on both sides, about 6 minutes each side. Add chopped **broccoli** and thinly-sliced carrots; cook until tender-crisp. Stir in soup, milk and pepper; heat to boiling. Reduce heat and cover to simmer about 10 minutes.

Stir in the cooked **rice.** Cover and let stand for 5 minutes.

MEATBALLS WITH GREEN PEPPERS

with French Bread and Italian Salad

1 lb. ground beef
½ teaspoon salt
Dash pepper
2 Tbsps. peanut oil
¼ cup chopped onion
¼ cup chopped green pepper
2 teaspoons chili powder
2 Tbsps. butter or margarine
1 (10 ¼ oz.) can Beef Gravy
1 cup cooked carrots, cut into 1-inch strips

Italian Salad Ingredients:
iceberg lettuce
tomato, in wedges
red cabbage, julienned
ripe olives
carrot, shredded
salad pepper
croutons (optional)
French bread
1 lb. macaroni pasta
3 slices mild process cheese, cut into halves

If you're having **fresh bread**, preheat oven and cook it now according to package directions.

To prepare the **Italian salad,** tear lettuce into bite-size pieces. Cut tomato into wedges in desired thickness. Cut red cabbage into julienne strips. Add a few ripe olives. Shred the carrot on top. Toss well. Refrigerate until serving, at which time you add a salad pepper to top and spread croutons around.

Combine beef, salt and pepper. Shape into 16 **meatballs**, about a heaping tablespoon per meatball. Cook meatballs in peanut oil until uniformly brown. In another skillet cook onion, green pepper and chili powder in butter until vegetables are tender. To this skillet, add the meatballs. Add gravy and carrots. Cover; simmer 20 minutes. Stir occasionally.

While meatballs and sauce cook, prepare the **macaroni pasta** following package directions. Combine meatballs and macaroni before serving. Add process cheese to top.

SHRIMP IN BROWN BUTTER SAUCE

with Rice, French Bread and Caesar Salad

1 stick butter
2 Tbsps. Worcestershire sauce
Freshly ground pepper
12 jumbo shrimp, in shells
2 lemons, juice and peel

Packaged French bread

Converted Rice

Caesar Salad Ingredients:
- **2 hard-cooked eggs**
- **¼ cup olive oil**
- **1 tsp. Worcestershire sauce**
- **½ teaspoon salt**
- **1 clove garlic**
- **¼ tsp. dry mustard**
- **Ground Pepper**
- **1 bunch romaine lettuce**
- **2 lemons**
- **¼ cup Parmesan cheese**

Preheat oven to 400° F. Prepare packaged **French bread** by baking according to package directions.

Cook **eggs** using the ten-ten method: ten minutes in boiling water and ten minutes sitting in hot water. When serving, peel and slice as a garnish to the Caesar salad described below.

Cook **rice** before proceeding. While rice cooks, prepare the **Caesar salad**. Mix the olive oil, Worcestershire sauce, salt, garlic, mustard and pepper in a bowl; toss with the romaine lettuce until all leaves are coated. Squeeze the lemons over the salad and toss. Before serving, sprinkle the Parmesan cheese and toss again.

When rice is cooked, prepare the **brown sauce**. Melt butter in skillet. Add Worcestershire sauce and pepper. When thoroughly mixed, allow sauce to cool. Rinse **shrimp**. Place shrimp in baking dish in a single layer. Grate some of the lemon and sprinkle the lemon peels over the shrimp. Pour the brown sauce over shrimp. Sprinkle with lemon juice.

Bake shrimp in 400° F oven for 5 minutes; turn shrimp and bake for another 5 minutes. Do not overcook. Place the baking dish on the table for the guests to serve themselves.

Overnight - Plan ahead

CHICKEN MINESTRONE SOUP

with Poor Boy Sandwiches

½ cup cooked kidney beans
2 skinless chicken breasts, boneless, skinless
2 cups cooked fusilli
3 cups chicken broth
½ cup sherry wine
1 teaspoon salt to taste
¼ teaspoon ground pepper
1 cup onions, sliced
1 cup carrots, julienned
1 cup celery, julienned
1 cup fresh green beans, in 2-inch pieces
1 cup chopped stewed tomatoes (in juice)
1 cup grated Parmesan cheese

Poor Boy Sandwich:
wheat buns
cheese variety
lettuce
tomato

This menu calls for **cooked kidney beans**. Prepare them the night before if you can. Place 2 cups of beans in pot with 6 cups of water. Bring to a boil, let cook for 2 minutes and remove to sit for 1 hour. Drain, refill with fresh water and cook for about 30 minutes.

Just before mealtime, flatten the chicken breasts and cook in boiling water for twenty minutes. When cool, cut into small pieces. Set aside.

Cook **pasta** according to package directions; drain, rinse under cold water and set aside.

Make the **minestrone soup**. In a large saucepan, over medium-high heat, bring broth and sherry to a boil. Season with salt and pepper. Add onions, carrots and celery; simmer 5 minutes. Stir in green beans and chicken; heat soup to boiling. Add stewed tomatoes, kidney beans and pasta; simmer 1 minute longer or until vegetables are as tender as you like. Add ½ cup grated Parmesan cheese just before serving.

If you're having the **Poor Boy sandwiches**, cut the variety of cheeses into strips. Cut the buns and insert strips of cheese. Place sandwiches in microwave to heat. Sprinkle with shredded lettuce and top with tomato.

CHEF'S SALAD

with Fresh Bread or Baked Croutons

2 whole chicken breasts
Olive oil
1 clove garlic, crushed
½ head of lettuce, torn into bite-size pieces
½ bunch romaine, torn into bite-size pieces
4 green onions, chopped
2 stalks celery, sliced
Ripe olives
½ cup mayonnaise
¼ cup French dressing
Swiss cheese, in strips
2 hard-cooked eggs, sliced
2 tomatoes, in wedges
Fresh bread

If you are having **fresh baked bread**, bake it now, following package directions.

Should you elect to have **croutons,** you can make your own by removing crust from white bread and cutting into cubes. Sprinkle the cubes with some herb seasoning and brush on a small amount of olive oil. Place the croutons under the broiler with the chicken pieces.

Prepare the hard-cooked eggs with the ten-ten method: ten minutes in boiling water; ten minutes soaking in hot water.

Flatten the **chicken breasts** to achieve an even thickness. Rub surface of chicken with garlic. Brush surface with olive oil. Pre-heat the oven broiler. Cook chicken under broiler until tender, about 4 minutes each side. Remove chicken and let cool. When cooled, slice into strips.

Make the **chef's salad**. In a large salad bowl, mix the bite-size lettuce and torn romaine lettuce, green onions, sliced celery and ripe olives. Toss in the chicken; add mayonnaise and French dressing. Spread thin strips of cheese on top.

Top with layer of cooked eggs. Cut the tomatoes into wedges to use as garnish.

CAJUN BAKED FISH

with Risotto and Sour Cream Cucumber Salad

½ cup salad dressing
½ teaspoon ground cumin
½ teaspoon onion powder
¼ teaspoon ground red pepper
¼ teaspoon garlic powder
1 cup sesame cracker crumbs
2 fish fillets

Risotto with onions and herbs

Sour Cream Cucumbers:
3 green onions, chopped
1 Tbsp. dried dill weed
2 Tbsps. tarragon vinegar
1 cup sour cream
2 Tbsps. olive oil
dash of salt
black pepper, ground
dash of sugar
1-2 cucumbers

This is a modified Kraft ® recipe for fish.

Make the **sour cream cucumbers** first. Chop the green onions into small pieces. Mix dried dill, tarragon vinegar, sour cream, and chopped green onions. Slowly add the olive oil. Season with salt, pepper and add a dash of sugar. Taste and adjust seasonings. Peel the cucumber and cut into thick slices. Arrange cucumbers on a salad plate like toppled dominoes and drizzle the sour cream dressing over them.

Preheat oven to 350° F.

Cook **risotto** according to package directions.

Meanwhile, combine salad dressing and seasonings: cumin, onion powder, red pepper and garlic powder. Wash **fish** under water and pat dry with paper towels. (*Vary the amount of salad dressing to suit the flavor of the fish. For mild fish, like orange roughy, reduce dressing to ¼ cup, for heavier fish try ½ cup.)* Brush fish with salad dressing mixture; coat with sesame cracker crumbs. Place fish in a greased baking dish and bake at 350° F until fish flakes easily when prodded with a fork, about 10 minutes.

DECEMBER BEEF REDUX

with Mashed Potatoes and Broccoli

2 Tbsps. butter
1 ½ lb. beef tip or kabob meat cut into 1 ½ inch cubes
2 Tbsps. brandy
8 small white onions, peeled
2 fresh mushrooms
1 Tbsp. tomato paste
1 Tbsp. all-purpose flour
1 cup Cabernet wine
½ cup dry sherry
½ cup ruby port
½ can condensed beef bouillon, undiluted
Dash pepper
1 small bay leaf

3 potatoes
½ stick butter
¼ cup milk
1 lb. broccoli

Preheat the oven to 350° F.

Prepare the **beef** first. Melt butter in a 2 or 3 quart covered sauce pot. Sauté the beef cubes until they are brown on every side. Add 2 tablespoons of brandy wine. Cook for two minutes. Remove beef cubes and set aside. Add more butter to the pot and sauté the onions until they become brown. Next, add the mushrooms and sauté for a minute or two. At this point, add tomato paste and flour; stir until the mixture is blended. Lastly, add the French wines: Cabernet, sherry and port. At the same time, add beef bouillon.

Toss the beef cubes, pepper and bay leaf back into the sauce pot and raise heat to boiling. At this point, the pot should be covered and placed in oven.

Bake, covered, in 350° F oven until beef is tender, about 1- 2 hours. Stir when the thought hits you. When beef is done, remove from the oven and let cool. *Place the cooled pot of beef* in the refrigerator *overnight. If you forget to do this the night before, don't worry, you can serve it when the potatoes are cooked.*

When you are ready for the meal, prepare the **mashed potatoes** following your favorite method. Steam the **broccoli**.

Second week DECEMBER

Sunday	*Monday*	*Tuesday*	*Wednesday*	*Thursday*	*Friday*	*Saturday*
Sauterne Chicken Breasts Mashed Potatoes, Snow Pea Salad	*Plan ahead* **Pizza Night In/Out** Tossed Salad	**Shrimp On The Rocks** Brown Rice, Spinach Salad	**Scalloped Potatoes & Pork Chops** Spinach, Tossed Salad, Fruits	*Plan ahead* **Mexican Squash Soup** Tacos, Guacamole Salad	**Baked Orange Roughy in Wine** Herbed Rice, Green Wedge Salad	**Glazed Steaks** Dutch Potatoes, Green Peas

Fresh Vegetables \ Fruits		*Herbs \ Spices*	*Basics*
snow peas - ¾ lb. mushrooms - 4 red bell pepper - 1 potatoes - 7 iceberg lettuce - 3 green leaf lettuce - 1 cucumbers - 2 tomatoes - 5 radishes - bunch lemons - 3 celery bundle	garlic pod ginger root - 1 oz. spinach bunch orange - 2 pears - 2 or apples - 2 avocado - 1 white onions - 4 yellow squash - 3 parsley bunch green chili pepper 1	Italian seasoning oregano rosemary sesame seeds red pepper flakes chili powder ground cumin hot pepper sauce	flour vegetable oil olive oil Dijon mustard extra-virgin olive oil mayonnaise honey peanut oil tarragon vinegar Vinaigrette dressing ½ C sugar white vinegar

Entrée Food	*Dairy*	*Miscellaneous*	*Cans \ Jars*
skinless, boneless chicken breasts -2 fresh shrimp -½ lb. butterfly pork chops - 2 ground beef - 1 lb. orange roughy 1 or 2 top loin steaks - 2 pizza toppings (see page 559) **Frozen** green peas - pkg	eggs - 4 butter - 2 sticks Mozzarella cheese - 4 slices Parmesan cheese 6 oz. margarine - ¼ lb. milk - 2 cups Monterey Jack cheese- 2 oz. Cheddar cheese - ¾ cup sour cream - 4 oz.	bread crumbs 1 cup croutons - pkg. active dry yeast pkg. brown rice - 1 C herbed rice pkg crackers - ¼ bag Taco shells - 8 taco seasoning pkg apple cider vinegar - ¾ T slivered almonds 1 oz.	ripe olives - 4 oz. tomato sauce - 3 Rotel tomatoes w/ green chilies - 2 whole tomatoes - 1 chicken broth - 1 **Wines** white wine bottle sauterne wine - 1 C

SAUTERNE CHICKEN BREASTS

with Mashed Potatoes and Snow Pea Salad

2 eggs
½ cup flour
1 ½ teaspoons salt, to taste
¼ teaspoon ground pepper
1 cup plain bread crumbs
1 teaspoon Italian seasoning
2 boneless, skinless breast of chicken
½ cup butter
4 slices Mozzarella cheese

Snow Pea Salad:
¾ lb. fresh snow peas
4 fresh mushrooms
1 red bell pepper
½ cup Vinaigrette dressing
white sweet table wine (Sauterne)
3 potatoes
½ stick margarine
¼ cup milk

Make the **snow pea salad** first. Wash and trim the stems from snow peas and, if visible, remove the string membranes. Slice the mushrooms. Core and seed the red bell pepper and julienne. Blanch the snow peas in boiling water for about one minute. They should be bright green. Drain and run cold water over them to stop the cooking process. Place snow peas in a salad bowl. Add mushrooms to snow peas. Add the julienned red bell pepper. Season to taste with salt and pepper. Add your favorite vinaigrette dressing.

Pre-heat oven to 350° F.

Prepare the **chicken coating**. In a shallow bowl, beat the eggs. On one sheet of wax paper, combine flour, salt and pepper. Combine bread crumbs, Italian seasoning on another sheet of wax paper. Cut the **chicken breasts** in half for individual servings; pound slightly to achieve an even thickness. Dredge chicken pieces in flour mixture, then in egg, then in the bread crumbs. Roll the chicken and secure with toothpicks. Place in shallow baking dish. Pour melted butter over chicken. Cover and bake 15 minutes. Add about ½ cup of white wine to the chicken and bake uncovered for another 15 minutes.

While chicken cooks, prepare **mashed potatoes**.

When chicken is done, place Mozzarella cheese on top and cook until the cheese melts.

PIZZA NIGHT OUT

with Tossed Salad

We offer three choices for this day:

- Purchase the pizza from a local pizza shop and have it delivered while you make the salad.

- Make the pizza using pizza dough already made and packaged in your local supermarket, suppling your own choice of ingredients.

- Make everything from scratch as an education for those who have often wondered how pizzas were made. *See Facing Page ==>.*

TOSSED SALAD

iceberg lettuce
cucumber
radishes
tomatoes
ripe olives
croutons

To prepare the **tossed salad**, wash and dry all vegetables. Tear the lettuces into bite-size pieces. Slice the cucumber and radishes. Cut the tomatoes into wedges. Toss all together, then add the ripe olives and the croutons.

HOME MADE PIZZA

*Dough**

½ pkg. active dry yeast (1 ½ teaspoons)
1 teaspoon sugar
5 oz. cup warm water
1 ½ cups flour
1 teaspoon salt
2 Tbsps. olive oil

Tossed Salad
(<====Facing Page)

Toppings

3 (8 oz.) cans tomato sauce
½ tsp. each of oregano, rosemary, and salt
¼ teaspoon pepper
½ cup Parmesan cheese
Choice of meat and vegetable toppings:
- **Canadian bacon**
- **Pepperoni**
- **Bell pepper**
- **Onions**
- **Olives**

* *Instead of homemade dough you can pick up a Boboli® pre-made pizza crust.*

To make the **dough**, dissolve the yeast and sugar in warm water. Set aside until mixture bubbles, 10 minutes. Meanwhile, mix flour and salt. Mix yeast mixture with flour mixture and add olive oil. Knead the flour; grease it and place in a greased bowl. Cover and let rise for about 2 hours.

When ready to make the pizza, roll out the dough. It should now be doubled in size. Roll into sheets that can be handled. Place on pizza pan and shape into a uniform thickness and size.

Preheat oven to 425° F.

Mix together tomato sauce, oregano, rosemary, salt, pepper, olive oil; spread evenly on the pasta. Arrange the toppings. Sprinkle the cheeses over the pizza. Place in oven to bake for 25 to 30 minutes or until the edges are golden brown.

SHRIMP ON THE ROCKS

with Brown Rice and Spinach Salad

¼ cup sesame seeds
1 Tbsp. olive oil
1 clove garlic, minced
Dash of fresh ginger, grated
¼ teaspoon red pepper flakes
¼ cup slivered almonds
¼ teaspoon salt
½ pound fresh shrimp, cleaned, deveined

Spinach Salad Ingredients:
2 hard-cooked eggs
1 teaspoon Dijon mustard
3 Tbsps. tarragon vinegar
pepper to taste
2 Tbsps. extra-virgin olive oil
1 bunch spinach leaves

Brown rice

Make **brown rice** according to directions before continuing. W*e use a long-cooking brown rice variety. If using a quick brown rice, prepare the spinach salad beforehand.*

While rice cooks, prepare the **spinach salad**. Cook eggs using the ten-ten method: ten minutes in boiling water; remove from heat and let eggs sit in hot water for another ten minutes.

When eggs are cool, peel and cut the eggs in half and remove yolks. In a small bowl combine the yolks, mustard, tarragon vinegar and pepper. Beat and gradually add extra-virgin olive oil.

In a large salad bowl, tear spinach leaves into bite-size pieces. Chop egg whites and add. When placing the spinach on the individual salad plates, pour the mustard sauce from above over the spinach.

For the **shrimp** entrée: toast sesame seeds over low heat in a dry skillet, stirring constantly until seeds are golden. Remove from skillet and put aside. Add olive oil to skillet. Sauté the garlic, ginger, red pepper, almonds and a taste of salt. After a moment, add the shrimp and cook until they turn a bright orange, about 2 -3 minutes. Toss in the toasted sesame seeds. Serve immediately.

SCALLOPED POTATOES AND PORK CHOPS

with Spinach and Tossed Salad and Fruits

2 butterfly pork chops
2 potatoes, peeled and in round slices
1 ½ cups milk
2 Tbsps. flour
½ teaspoon salt and pepper
½ teaspoon chopped garlic

Fruits: pears, oranges, apples

Spinach
½ cup vinegar
Tossed Salad Ingredients:
iceberg lettuce
green leaf lettuce
cucumber
radishes
tomato
ripe olives
croutons

Preheat oven to 350° F.

While oven heats, prepare the **tossed salad.** Wash and dry all vegetables. Tear the lettuces into bite-size pieces. Slice the cucumber and radishes. Cut the tomatoes into wedges. Toss all together then add the ripe olives. Refrigerate until serving; add the croutons.

Place **pork chops** in bottom of covered baking dish. Layer **potatoes** on top of pork chops. Mix milk, flour, salt, pepper and garlic together. Pour this mixture over potatoes. Cover baking dish and bake at 350° F for about 1 hour or until pork chops are done.

While scalloped potatoes bake, prepare the **fruit garnish.** Cut the pears, oranges and apples into chunks. Mix together and set in refrigerator until serving.

Just before the casserole is finished cooking, prepare the **spinach**. We wash fresh spinach in a basin of water mixed with ½ cup of vinegar. Thoroughly rinse the spinach after washing. We then steam the fresh spinach using a small steamer basket over boiling water, or you can place the spinach in a pot with a minimum of water and let the spinach steam for a few minutes.

Garnish pork chops with the fruits.

1 hour - Plan ahead

MEXICAN SQUASH SOUP

with Tacos and Guacamole Salad

1 avocado, skinned, cut up
¼ cup chopped white onions
1 green chili pepper, finely chopped
¼ teaspoon pepper, coarsely ground
1 small clove garlic, chopped
1 teaspoon lemon juice
½ teaspoon salt
¼ teaspoon orange juice
1 Tablespoon mayonnaise
½ tomato, finely chopped

1 onion, chopped
1 stick butter
3 yellow squash, chopped
2 cans Rotel Tomatoes w/ Green Chilies *
1 can whole tomatoes *
1 can chicken broth
Grated Monterey Jack cheese
Tacos (Facing page===>)
Crackers

** This soup can be made as spicy as you like by varying the mixture of plain tomatoes with the Rotel tomatoes. We tried several ratios before settling on a 2 to 1 mix.*

Make the **guacamole salad** first. You will use each of the ingredients on the left side above. Beat avocados, onions, chili pepper, pepper, garlic, lemon juice, salt, orange juice and mayonnaise until creamy. Gently stir in tomato bits. Cover and refrigerate at *least 1 hour.*

Prepare the **tacos.** Follow recipe on facing page ===>.

Prepare **squash soup.** In a large skillet, melt butter and sauté onions until they become clear, about 2 - 3 minutes. Add the chopped squash, the tomatoes and chicken broth. Cook until squash is tender, about 10 minutes.

Garnish with grated Monterey Jack Cheese.

TACOS

8 Taco shells
1 lb. ground beef
1 clove garlic, crushed
¾ cup water
½ cup chopped onions
2 Tbsps. chili powder
1 teaspoon salt
½ teaspoon ground cumin
1 (1.25 oz.) pkg. taco seasoning
1 cup shredded lettuce
¾ cup chopped tomato
½ cup chopped onion
¾ cup shredded Cheddar cheese
¼ cup dairy sour cream

For the **taco:** cook and stir meat in a 10-inch skillet until light brown; drain. You can add minced or crushed garlic if you like. We always do for ground meat. Stir in water, onion, the chili powder, salt, cumin and garlic. Heat to boiling; reduce heat. Simmer uncovered, stirring occasionally, until thickened, about 30 minutes.

Spoon about ¼ cup meat into each taco shell. Top with taco seasoning, shredded lettuce, chopped tomatoes, chopped onion, shredded cheese and a dollop of sour cream.

BAKED ORANGE ROUGHY IN WINE

with Herbed Rice and Green Wedge Salad

1 (4 - 6 oz.) box herbed rice
Butter

2 Tbsps. olive oil
1 or 2 fish fillets of orange roughy
2 Tbsps. lemon juice
¼ cup white wine

Green Wedge Salad Ingredients:
- **½ head iceberg lettuce**
- **½ cucumber, in thick slices**
- **2 radishes, in thin slices**
- **2 celery stalks, julienned**

Choice of salad dressings

This fish menu is meant to be prepared on the stove top.

To prepare the **green wedge salad**, cut the iceberg lettuce into wide wedges. Remove center portion and chop, spreading onto salad plate. Cut the cucumber and place in the remaining curved portion of lettuce wedge. Slice the radishes and place on cucumbers. Julienne the celery and place on top of and around the wedge. Place salad in refrigerator until ready to serve.

Cook **herbed rice** according to package directions.

For the **fish**: add olive oil to skillet. Rinse fish and pat dry. Add fish pieces to skillet and cook until done, about five minutes. Add lemon juice and a bit of white wine to keep the fish moist while cooking.

For a different presentation, try adding the uncooked fish to the rice when the rice still has five minutes to cook.

GLAZED STEAKS

with Dutch Potatoes and Green Peas

¼ cup Dijon-style mustard
1 Tbsp. chopped parsley
1 Tbsp. honey
¾ Tbsp. apple cider vinegar
¾ Tbsp. water
Dash hot red pepper sauce
Dash fresh ground pepper
2 top loin steaks

Dutch Potatoes Ingredients:
1 onion, chopped
1 Tbsp. peanut oil
2 large potatoes
2 Tbsps. parsley
Salt and pepper to taste

Frozen green peas

Prepare the **Dutch Potatoes**. Brown chopped onion in peanut oil. Skin and cube the potatoes and add to the chopped onion. Add enough water to barely cover potatoes. Boil until the potatoes are about done, say 15 minutes. Add parsley, salt and pepper; cook for another five minutes. Drain.

While potatoes cook, pre-heat the oven broiler. In a small bowl, combine mustard, parsley, honey, apple cider vinegar, water, pepper sauce and ground pepper. Brush both sides of beef with glaze. Place **beef** 5-6 inches under broiler. Broil until done the way you like steaks.

As the steaks broil, prepare the **frozen green peas** according to package directions.

AZTECA SOUP

Our New Favorite Soup

5 cans chicken broth
1 lb. chicken backs or chicken necks
4 tomatoes, skinned
4 Tbsps. Peanut oil
½ onion, chopped
1 clove garlic, minced
4 pasilla chiles (narrow, black)

1 whole avocado, peeled in small chunks
1 sprig epazote leaves
8 oz. panella cheese, cubed

2 cups peanut oil, for frying
12 corn tortillas, julienned

This is our favorite tortilla soup, from interior Mexico.

The ingredients for Azteca Soup are hard to find and we know of no substitutes. Try a market that specializes in herbs and cheeses.

Combine 5 cans of chicken broth into a large saucepan or soup pot. Add chicken necks and backs and allow to simmer for approximately 15 minutes.

While broth cooks, blanch fresh tomatoes in a pot of boiling water, remove skin, seeds and cut into chunks.

Heat 4 tablespoons of peanut oil and add the tomatoes. Add onion and garlic. Cook for three minutes then add chicken broth, drained of the necks and backs. Add the chiles. Simmer for ten minutes.

A this time, prepare the tortillas. Cut the tortillas into long julienned strips. Heat the peanut oil and add the tortilla sticks. Fry until they begin to brown. Remove and drain well.

When you are ready to serve, add the avocado pieces then at the last moment add the epazote leaves to the simmering soup. Pour soup into bowls and add the tortillas sticks in a heap.

Third week DECEMBER

Sunday	*Monday*	*Tuesday*	*Wednesday*	*Thursday*	*Friday*	*Saturday*
Chicken Dijon Confetti Corn, House Salad	**Frank-furter Hash** Rice, Celery Salad	**Seafood Ravioli Soup** French Rolls, Green Salad	**Christmas Pork Chops** Rice, Broccoli Salad	**Tomato Pasta Salad Night** French Bread, Green Wedge Salad	**Microwave Fish** Baked Potato, Tossed Salad	**Baked Sirloin Cubes** Twice Baked Potatoes, Broccoli

Fresh Vegetables \ Fruits		*Herbs \ Spices*	*Basics*
corn - 2 green onions - 6 cucumbers - 2 carrots - bundle radishes - bunch iceberg lettuce - 2 green leaf lettuce - 1 green bell pepper - 2 white onions - 2 pearl onions - 6	garlic pod - 1 parsley bunch lemon- 1 broccoli bunches - 2 red bell pepper - 1 tomatoes - 5 potatoes - 8 mushrooms - 2 celery bundle	tarragon bay leaf cayenne pepper thyme celery salt ground nutmeg basil leaves	Dijon mustard peanut oil cornstarch Converted Rice soy sauce

Entrée Food	*Dairy*	*Miscellaneous*	*Cans \ Jars*
skinless, boneless chicken breasts - 2 ham slices - 2 all-beef frankfurters ½ lb. raw shrimp - ½ lb. halibut steak ½ lb. butterfly pork chops - 2 fish fillets any choice - 2 sirloin steak - 1 ½ lb.	butter - 1 stick margarine - 1 stick sour cream - 2 T eggs - 2 Mozzarella slices - 2 Parmesan cheese ¼ lb. bacon - 9 slices Cheddar cheese ¼ C milk - ¼ C **Frozen** cheese ravioli pkg	instant chicken bouillon - 1 T French rolls - 6 almond extract ½ t French bread - 2 loaves Capellini pasta 1 lb. teriyaki sauce - 2 T **Wine** dry white wine - 1 C red wine - ½ C	pimentos - 4 oz ripe olives - 4 oz. beef gravy - 1 whole tomatoes - 1 Italian stewed tomatoes - 1 chicken broth - 2 jellied cranberry sauce - 6 oz. cream of mushroom soup - 1 beef bouillon - 2

CHICKEN DIJON

with House Salad and Confetti Corn

2 whole skinless, boneless chicken breasts
2 Tbsps. butter
1 cup dry white wine
¼ teaspoon tarragon
Pinch thyme
1 small bay leaf
¼ teaspoon salt
¼ teaspoon pepper
2 ears corn
½ green bell pepper
Pimentos
2 slices ham
2 slices Mozzarella
2 egg yolks
2 Tbsps. sour cream
2 Tbsps. Dijon style mustard
Pinch cayenne pepper

House Salad Ingredients:
iceberg lettuce
carrots stalks, pencil size
radishes, in rounds
cucumber, in rounds
ripe olives

A good first course is a **house salad.** Wash and dry all vegetables. Peel lettuce off in layers. Cut the carrots into pencil-size shapes. Cut the radishes and cucumber into rounds then quarter to make pie-slices. Toss all together then add the ripe olives.

Pound **chicken** to achieve an even thickness. Heat butter in skillet. Add chicken and cook until lightly browned on both sides. Add white wine, tarragon, thyme, bay leaf, salt and pepper. Bring to a boil. Cover and simmer chicken 30 minutes or until tender.

While chicken cooks, prepare the **corn** by placing in boiling water for about 10 minutes. When done strip corn from cob into bowl. Add chopped green pepper and pieces of pimento.

Five minutes before chicken is done, add sliced ham to chicken. Top with slice of Mozzarella cheese. Remove and keep warm.

Blend sauce remaining in skillet pan with egg yolks. Add sour cream, mustard and cayenne pepper. When everything is ready, heat sauce stirring briskly. *DO NOT ALLOW TO BOIL.* Pour over chicken.

FRANKFURTER HASH

with Rice and Celery Salad

½ lb. (all-beef) frankfurters, cut into 1-inch pieces
¼ green bell pepper, chopped
1 Tbsp. butter or margarine
¼ onion, chopped
½ can beef gravy
¼ cup whole tomatoes, chopped

Converted Rice
Sautéed Celery Salad:
1 Tbsp. peanut oil
5 stalks of celery, sliced
1 Tbsp. instant chicken bouillon
½ teaspoon salt
dash celery salt
2 Tbsps. sliced pimentos

Cook **rice** according to package directions.

Meanwhile, in skillet, brown **frankfurters.** Add peppers, butter and onions; cook until vegetables are tender, about 15 minutes.

While the hash cooks, prepare the **sautéed celery**. Cook and stir celery slices in skillet with 1 tablespoon peanut oil. Add the instant bouillon, salt, celery salt and cook over medium heat, turning often until the celery is tender, about 8 minutes.

Toss in the pimentos with the frankfurters to heat before serving. Stir in gravy and tomatoes. Heat; stir now and then.

Serve over **rice.**

SEAFOOD RAVIOLI SOUP

with French Rolls and Green Salad

½ lb. halibut steak
1 (8-10 oz.) pkg. fresh or frozen cheese ravioli
2 (14 oz.) cans Italian stewed tomatoes
2 (14 oz.) cans chicken broth
½ lb. raw shrimp, cleaned

¼ lb. Parmesan cheese

6 - 8 French rolls

Green Salad Ingredients:
iceberg lettuce
green leaf lettuce
cucumber
celery, julienned
parsley

If baking **fresh bread**, pre-heat the oven to temperature stated on package or 350° F, if unstated.

Make the **green salad** first. Wash, dry and tear the lettuces into bite-size pieces. Slice cucumber thinly, julienne the celery stalk into 2-inch lengths. Add parsley as a garnish.

Bake the French rolls before proceeding.

For the **seafood soup**: cut the halibut into ½ inch-wide strips. If using steaks, trim away the skin; cut meat away from bones, then cut into ½ inch wide strips or cubes. Cook **ravioli** in 2 quarts of water until tender and flood with cold water to halt cooking process; set aside.

In a separate soup pot, add stewed tomatoes with their liquid and chicken broth; cover and bring to a boil. Add pasta to stewed tomatoes then place shrimp and halibut fish strips on top. Cover and simmer until fish is opaque in center, 4 to 6 minutes.

Serve the seafood with a sprinkling of Parmesan cheese.

CHRISTMAS PORK CHOPS

with Rice and Broccoli Salad

2 butterfly pork chops
Salt

1 (6 oz.) can jellied cranberry sauce
1 teaspoon lemon juice
½ teaspoon almond extract
¼ teaspoon ground nutmeg

Broccoli Salad Ingredients:
broccoli
red bell pepper, julienned
onion, in thin rings
tomato, in wedges
lettuce, shredded
Packaged fresh bread
Converted Rice

Preheat the oven for the **fresh bread**, following package directions.

While bread cooks, prepare the **broccoli salad** in a salad bowl. Cut broccoli into small florets. Cut red pepper into julienne strips. Slice onion into thin rings. Cut the tomato into narrow wedges. Toss all together. Serve over shredded lettuce.

Prepare the **rice** according to package directions.

Pre-heat the oven broiler for the **pork chops**. Place rack about 6 inches from the heating source. Place chops in a baking dish or pan that has a rim for holding liquids. Pour ½ cup of water into pan and lay in the pork chops. Broil pork chops about 2-3 minutes on each side. Sprinkle with salt after broiling. Remove and set aside.

Make the **cranberry seasoning**. Heat a small skillet to low heat. Add the cranberry sauce, lemon juice, almond extract and nutmeg; stir until blended. Cook until the cranberry is heated then brush the pork chops with this mixture. Place chops back under the broiler, brush on more sauce and cook for another 6-7 minutes before turning, coating with cranberry sauce and broiling for another 6-7 minutes.

Brush on any remaining sauce when serving.

TOMATO PASTA SALAD NIGHT

with French Bread and Green Wedge Salad

9 slices bacon, cut up
3 Tbsps. sliced green onions
1 clove garlic, minced
3 medium tomatoes, peeled and chopped
1 teaspoon basil leaves
½ teaspoon salt
Dash pepper
1 lb. capellini*, cooked

Green Wedge Salad Ingredients:
½ head iceberg lettuce
½ cucumber, in thick slices
2 radishes, in thin slices
2 celery stalks, julienned

Packaged French bread

Parsley, as garnish

** Capellini is angel hair spaghetti.*

If you're having packaged **French bread**, pre-heat the oven for cooking now. Follow package directions. We like to purchase the ready-to-bake versions.

To prepare the **green wedge salad**, cut the iceberg lettuce in half and then into wide wedges. Remove center portion and chop, spreading on salad plate. Cut the cucumber and place in the remaining curved portion of lettuce wedge. Slice the radishes and place on cucumbers. Julienne the celery and place on top of and around the wedge.

While the bread cooks, in large skillet, fry bacon until crisp. Drain, retaining ¼ cup drippings; return drippings to skillet. Add cooked bacon, green onions and garlic; cook 1 minute. Stir in tomatoes, basil, salt and pepper. Simmer 5 minutes.

Prepare **angel hair spaghetti** according to package directions. Add pasta to bacon-tomato mixture; garnish with sprigs of parsley and serve hot.

MICROWAVE FISH

with Baked Potato and Tossed Salad

2 fish fillets - cod, orange roughy sole, snapper
2 Tbsps. teriyaki sauce
1 teaspoon minced green onions

4 potatoes, for baking

Tossed Salad Ingredients:
iceberg lettuce
green leaf lettuce
cucumber
radishes
tomato
ripe olives
croutons

To prepare the **tossed salad,** wash and dry all vegetables. Tear the lettuces into bite-size pieces. Slice the cucumber and radishes. Cut the tomato into wedges. Toss all together, then add the ripe olives. Refrigerate. When serving, add the croutons.

Bake **potatoes** according to your favorite method. We typically use the microwave to completely bake or to at least partially bake the potatoes. Wash the potatoes and pierce with fork. Place potatoes in the microwave and cook on HIGH for 4 minutes per potato per side, turning once. (3 or 4 potatoes will cook in 24 minutes.)

Rinse **fish** and pat dry. Place fish in a baking dish. Brush fish with teriyaki sauce. (Any spicy sauce may substitute: Dijon mustard, sesame, soy, Cajun.) Spread the minced green onion on top of fish. Cover baking dish with plastic wrap. Microwave on HIGH until fish flakes when prodded with a fork, about 2 to 3 minutes.

Remove dish from microwave, open the wrap and let stand 2 minutes before serving. The fish will continue to cook while sitting.

BAKED SIRLOIN CUBES

with Broccoli and Twice-Baked Potatoes

2 fresh mushrooms, sliced
2 Tbsps. butter, divided
1 Tbsp. peanut oil
1 ½ lbs. sirloin, cut into 1 inch cubes
½ cup beef bouillon
½ cup red wine
1 Tbsp. soy sauce
1 clove garlic, minced
6 pearl onions
1 Tbsp. cornstarch
¼ cup beef bouillon
¼ can cream of mushroom soup (optional)
Salt, to taste
Twice-Baked Potatoes **(Facing Page==>)**
1 bunch of broccoli
¼ cup grated cheddar cheese

Prepare the **baked sirloin cubes** first. This requires a skillet and a 2-quart stew pot. In the skillet, sauté mushrooms in 1 tablespoon of butter; remove from skillet and place in the 2 quart pot. To the skillet, add 1 tablespoon peanut oil and remaining 1 tablespoon butter. Add the sirloin meat cubes and brown; remove meat from skillet and pour over mushrooms in the stew pot. To the skillet, add ½ cup bouillon, wine, soy sauce, garlic and onion. Blend together cornstarch and ¼ cup bouillon; add to wine mixture. Cook and stir until smooth. Pour into the stew pot over the meat. Cover and bake at 275° F for ¾ hour.

While the cubes cook, prepare the **twice-baked potatoes** according to the instructions on the Facing Page===>).

After the sirloin cubes have cooked for ¾ hour, add cream of mushroom soup and salt to taste. Bake an extra 10 minutes to heat thoroughly.

Prepare the **broccoli spears**. Remove any large leaves from the broccoli bunch. Cut the stalks lengthwise from end to broccoli head to make spears. Cook by steaming over boiling water for about five minutes. When serving, sprinkle with Cheddar cheese.

TWICE - BAKED POTATOES

4 potatoes, for baking
¼ cup milk
3 Tbsps. butter or margarine
Salt and pepper, to taste
2 green onions, minced
¼ green bell pepper

While the sirloin cubes bake, prepare the **twice-baked potatoes.** Bake potatoes according to your favorite method. We typically use the microwave to completely bake or to at least partially bake the potatoes. Wash the potatoes and pierce with fork. Place potatoes in the microwave and cook on HIGH for 4 minutes per potato per side, turning once. (3 or 4 potatoes will cook in 24 minutes.)

Cut the potatoes lengthwise in order to scoop out the insides, leaving about ¼ inch of potatoes on the sides. In a separate bowl, mash the potatoes, adding the milk, butter, salt and pepper. Taste. Beat until the potatoes become fluffy. Fill the potato shell to the brim. Add a sprinkling of chopped green peppers. Place in microwave or conventional oven to re-heat, about 15 minutes conventional, or 5 minutes microwave.

NEW YEAR'S RESOLUTIONS

It's that time of year

We offer for consideration some dietary resolutions:

- Substitute yogurt for sour cream
- Use low-fat products where possible, except for those special menus you care about.
- Use leaner cuts of beef and pork.
- Eat more fish and seafood
- Lower the individual portions of food that you eat. We eventually arrived at the 4 - 5 oz. serving. It wasn't until 1996 that the American medical Association stated that eating less is healthier. It'll takes some doing, but well worth it.
- Enjoy conversation with your food instead of the TV or newspaper.

We offer the following for good health:

- Develop an exercise ritual, regardless of how light it may be.
- Live life forward. Kierkegaard: "It is true, as philosophers say, that life must be understood backward. But they forget the other proposition, that it must be lived forward."
- Eat well, be happy and prosper.

The ultimate resolution:

- Write Kathy and Leonard Heerensperger and tell them how you've used their book. They would be thrilled to hear from you.

Fourth week DECEMBER

Sunday	*Monday*	*Tuesday*	*Wednesday*	*Thursday*	*Friday*	*Saturday*
Xmas Chicken Wild Rice, Tossed Salad, Dinner Rolls	**Stuffed Tomatoes** Spinach, Corn	**Shrimp Louis Salad** Potato Flats	**Roasted Pork Loin** Stuffed Prunes, Rice or Noodles	**Tortilla Soup** Rice, Avocado Salad	**Broiled Swordfish** Pasta, Red Peppers	Plan Ahead **A Great Flank Steak** Cole Slaw, Baked Beans

Fresh Vegetables / Fruits		*Herbs / Spices*	*Basics*
green onions - 12 fresh mushrooms - 3 fruit of choice - 1 iceberg lettuce - 1 green leaf lettuce - 1 cucumber - 1 radishes - bunch avocados - 2 jalapeño - 2 red bell pepper - 1 green bell peppers 2 cabbage head	garlic pod unripened large tomatoes - 6 ripe tomatoes - 2 spinach - bunch mustard greens or collards or turnip greens 2 C potatoes - 2 white onions - 3 prunes - 6-8 parsley bunch	cayenne pepper ground ginger ground allspice red pepper sauce ground cumin ground coriander basil bay leaf dry mustard celery seeds	sugar cornstarch Dijon mustard extra-virgin olive oil peanut oil mayonnaise Worcestershire sauce flour red wine vinegar vegetable oil white vinegar converted rice tarragon vinegar soy sauce

Entrée Food	*Dairy*	*Miscellaneous*	*Cans / Jars*
chicken breasts - 4 ground chuck ¾ lb. cooked shrimp 12-20 pork loin - 2 lbs. flank steak 1 ½ lb. swordfish - 1 lb. **Frozen** Frozen corn - pkg	butter - 3 sticks eggs - 3 nonfat yogurt - 1 C sour cream - 1 C Monterey Jack cheese 1 C bacon - 2 slices **Wine** white - 1 C	wild rice pkg. dinner rolls - 12 corn tortillas 10-12 navy beans ½ lb. French dressing 4 oz. chili sauce - ¼ C fettuccini pasta - 1 lb brown sugar - 2 T molasses - 2 T liquid smoke - 1 T	ripe olives - 4 oz. chicken broth - 4 Mandarin oranges 1 can - 11 oz. Rotel tomatoes - 3 whole tomatoes - 1 pimentos - 4 oz. stuffed olives- 4 oz. beef broth - 2 tomato paste - 1

Grocery List ______________ Grocery List ______________

CHRISTMAS CHICKEN

with Wild Rice, Tossed Salad and Dinner Rolls

4 chicken breasts
Pepper and salt, to taste
5 Tbsps. butter, divided
9 green onions, diced
3 fresh mushrooms
1 teaspoon minced garlic
½ cup white wine, sauterne
2 Tbsps. fresh parsley or chives

1 fruit of choice, in wedges

Wild Rice
Tossed Salad Ingredients:
- **iceberg lettuce**
- **green leaf lettuce**
- **cucumber**
- **radishes**
- **tomato**
- **ripe olives**

Dinner Rolls

If you're having fresh **dinner rolls** preheat the oven to temperature stated on package.

To prepare the **tossed salad,** wash and dry all vegetables. Tear the lettuces into bite-size pieces. Slice the cucumber and radishes. Cut the tomato into wedges. Toss all together, then add the ripe olives. Refrigerate until ready to serve.

Cook **wild rice** according to package directions.

While the rice cooks, prepare the **chicken breasts.** Pound chicken breasts to achieve an even thickness. Season with salt and pepper. Melt 2 tablespoons of butter in a large skillet and sauté the green onions for a minute or two. Add the mushrooms and continue to sauté another minute or two. Remove mushrooms and onions to a plate. Melt 3 tablespoons of butter in the same skillet. Add minced garlic. Sauté chicken breasts over medium heat 5-6 minutes on each side. Add the white wine to chicken skillet. Stir in onion-mushroom mixture; cook for a minute or two. Garnish with parsley sprig when serving.

Serve with the tossed salad, wild rice and dinner rolls. A fruit cut into wedges makes a nice garnish.

STUFFED TOMATOES

with Spinach and Corn

¾ lb. ground chuck
2 Tbsps. peanut oil
4-6 unripened large tomatoes
1 clove garlic, crushed
¾ cup uncooked Converted Rice
1 teaspoon salt
½ teaspoon pepper
2 (14 ½ oz.) cans chicken broth
1 teaspoon sugar
1 Tbsp. cornstarch

1 package frozen corn

Spinach Salad:
2 hard-cooked eggs
1 teaspoon Dijon mustard
3 Tbsps. tarragon vinegar
pepper to taste
2 Tbsps. extra-virgin olive oil
1 bunch spinach leaves

Cook ground chuck in peanut oil until it loses redness.

Remove the top of each **tomato**, carving it much like you would a pumpkin, so that the top will fit on like a hat. Mix meat, garlic, rice, salt and pepper together. Fill tomatoes to brim with rice mixture. Place hat back on top. (*It should not fit, but rather rest on top of the stuffing.*) Save remaining rice mixture to place in liquid. Place tomatoes in a heavy saucepan, grouping them tightly. Mix together the chicken broth and sugar. Pour around peppers. Pour remainder of rice mixture into pot. Cover and cook slowly for about 30 minutes.

Prepare the **spinach salad**. Prepare the hard-cooked eggs using the ten-ten method: ten minutes in boiling water then remove from heat and let eggs sit in hot water for another ten minutes. When eggs are cool, peel and cut the eggs in half and remove yolks. In a small bowl combine the yolks, the mustard, the tarragon vinegar, and pepper. Beat and gradually add the extra-virgin olive oil. In a large salad bowl, tear the spinach leaves into bite-size pieces. Chop the egg whites and add. When placing the spinach on the individual salad plates, pour the mustard sauce over the spinach.

After the salad is made and before the peppers are done, prepare the **corn**. Cook corn in boiling water for ten minutes.

SHRIMP LOUIS SALAD

with Potato Flats

¼ cup mayonnaise
¼ cup plain yogurt
3 Tbsps. sour cream
3 Tbsps. chili sauce
1 teaspoon Worcestershire sauce
1 clove garlic, minced
Dash cayenne pepper
¼ cup minced green bell pepper
2 green onions, chopped

16-20 cooked shrimp

Potato Flats Ingredients:
2 potatoes
1 egg, beaten
¼ cup minced onions
3 Tbsps. flour
1 teaspoon salt
4 Tbsps. butter
2 cups shredded greens: mustard, collards, spinach, turnip greens
Tomato wedges
Avocado slices

Boil the **potatoes** and cut into quarters. Boil them in salted water until barely done, about 15 minutes. Let them cool. Dry the potatoes then shred or slice very thinly. Beat an egg in a small bowl. Add the potatoes, onions, flour and salt. Shape potato mixture into 6-8 patties. Melt butter in skillet and add the patties. Cook over medium heat until golden brown on both sides.

Make the **dressing**. In a small mixing bowl, combine mayonnaise, yogurt, sour cream, chili sauce and Worcestershire sauce. Stir well to blend. Add the minced garlic, cayenne pepper and the green bell pepper. Finally, add the chopped green onion. Stir well.

Place variety of torn greens in a large salad bowl. Mix well and place on serving dishes. Arrange the **cooked shrimp** on top of lettuce. Place the tomato wedges and the avocado slices on top. Drizzle the dressing over salad.

Serve salad with the potato flats on side.

ROASTED PORK LOIN

with Stuffed Prunes and Rice or Noodles

6-8 prunes
2 lbs. pork loin
1 (11 oz.) can Mandarin oranges, reserved juice
1 teaspoon salt
½ teaspoon ground ginger
¼ teaspoon ground allspice
¼ teaspoon ground pepper

Pan juices
Reserved Mandarin orange juice
1 cup water, divided
½ cup white wine
½ tsp. salt
¼ teaspoon ground ginger
¼ teaspoon ground allspice
2 Tbsps. cornstarch
Converted Rice or noodles

Cook **prunes** for 5 minutes in boiling water; drain and remove pits. Prepare the **pork loins** for stuffing. Make a cut into the edge of the loin, cutting the pork almost in half. Stuff the cooked, pitted prunes into the cuts. If necessary, secure the opening with toothpicks.

Preheat the oven to 325° F.

Place stuffed pork in shallow baking sheet.

Measure 2 tablespoons juice from Mandarin oranges, reserving some juice and fruit for the spiced wine sauce. Combine 2 tablespoons juice with the salt, ginger, allspice and pepper spices and rub into pork. Place any excess orange juice around the pork.

Roast for 2 hours or until done.

If you would like a heavier meal, you can make **rice** or **noodles** before the pork is done, following package directions.

Remove pork and keep warm while you make the wine sauce: skim any fat from pan juices. Combine reserved Mandarin juice with ½ cup water, wine and spices. Stir into pan juices and simmer about 5 minutes. Blend cornstarch with remaining ½ cup water and stir into juices. Cook stirring constantly, until mixture thickens. Add oranges and simmer an additional 3 minutes.

TORTILLA SOUP

with Avocado Salad and Rice

1 stick butter
1 onion, chopped
2 cloves garlic, chopped
1 jalapeño, chopped
3 cans Rotel Tomatoes
2 cans beef broth
2 - 3 Tbsps. chopped fresh parsley
10-12 corn tortillas, cut into strips or squares
Dash Tabasco
Grated Monterey Jack cheese

Converted Rice

Tossed Avocado Salad:
iceberg lettuce
ripe avocado
½ cup French dressing
1 Tbsp. chili sauce

Prepare the **avocado salad**. Tear lettuce into bite-size pieces. Cut 1 avocado lengthwise into halves; cut halves into slices. Make the dressing, mixing ½ cup French dressing with 1 tablespoon chili sauce. Pour sauce over the avocados and mix well. Refrigerate until serving.

Cook **rice** according to package directions.

Meanwhile, prepare the **tortilla soup.** In a large skillet melt butter and sauté onions and garlic until they become clear. Add the chopped **jalapeño.** Add Rotel tomatoes or whole tomatoes, beef broth and parsley. Simmer 15 to 20 minutes.

When things are ready to serve, pour the tortillas into the soup, then top with grated Monterey Jack cheese.

BROILED SWORDFISH

with Pasta and Red Peppers

2 Tbsps. butter
1 teaspoon fresh jalapeño pepper
1 (6 oz.) can tomato paste
¼ teaspoon ground cumin
¼ teaspoon ground coriander
Swordfish *

1 red bell pepper
½ pkg. fettucine
1 (8 oz.) can whole tomatoes
1 teaspoon basil leaves

** You can always substitute with any of the firm full-flavored fish such as tuna or salmon.*

For the **fish sauce** melt butter in small saucepan. Mince the jalapeño pepper and toss into the melted butter. Add a teaspoon of tomato paste, the ground cumin and coriander. Mix well and transfer to a bowl. Set aside .

Pre-heat the oven broiler. Wash the **swordfish** and pat dry. Lay fish on aluminum foil on a baking sheet. Bake for 10 minutes, turning once.

Julienne the **red bell pepper** and while fish cooks prepare the **fettuccini pasta** according to package directions. Place the julienned bell pepper in the boiling water with the pasta.

While pasta cooks, prepare the **pasta sauce.** Mix together the remaining tomato paste, 1 drained can of crushed tomatoes, basil leaves, salt and pepper. Heat until pasta is ready.

Drain pasta and cover with pasta sauce.

When fish is done, place on plate and top with the fish sauce.

A GREAT FLANK STEAK

with Cole Slaw and Baked Beans

1 ½ lb. flank steak
1 cup soy sauce
¼ cup red wine vinegar
2 cloves garlic, minced
1 bay leaf
½ teaspoon sugar
Pepper to taste

Baked beans
(Facing Page===>)

Cole Slaw
(Facing Page===>)

This barbecued meat should be marinated overnight!

Prepare the marinade. In a large bowl, mix the soy sauce, wine vinegar, minced garlic, sugar and bay leaf. Place steak in baking dish and pour the marinade over it making sure that all of the meat is coated. Marinate in refrigerator *overnight*. Turn the steak when the thought hits you.

At the same time as you prepare the marinade, you can also prepare the **baked beans** and the **cole slaw**. See facing page for instructions.

When you are ready to cook, prepare the grill, or preheat the oven broiler. The coals should be the color of white ash when you throw on the steak.

Brush **steak** frequently with sauce and season with pepper. Grill for about 10-15 minutes each side.

BAKED BEANS

2 cups water
½ lb. dried navy beans
1 Tbsp. liquid smoke
½ medium onion, sliced
2 strips of bacon
2 Tbsps. brown sugar
2 Tbsps. molasses
1 teaspoon salt
Dash dry mustard
Dash pepper

Heat **beans** placed in hot water to boiling in Dutch oven. Boil about 2 minutes. Remove from heat. Add 1 tablespoon of liquid smoke to water. Let beans stand for an hour.

Add additional water to barely cover the beans. Add remaining ingredients: onion, bacon, brown sugar, molasses, salt, mustard and pepper. Cover and simmer until tender, about 1-1 ½ hours.

COLE SLAW

1 teaspoon salt
¼ teaspoon pepper
½ teaspoon dry mustard
Scant teaspoon celery seeds
1 Tbsp. sugar
¼ cup chopped green bell pepper
1 Tbsp. chopped pimento
1 teaspoon grated onion
3 Tbsps. vegetable oil
¼ cup white vinegar
3 cups cabbage, finely chopped or julienned
¼ cup chopped stuffed olives

Into a large salad bowl, place all of the ingredients above. The cabbage may be chopped or cut into very thin, julienne strips to suit your taste.

Mix well.

Cover and chill through.

Garnish with sliced, stuffed olives just before serving.

Fifth week DECEMBER

Sunday	*Monday*	*Tuesday*	*Wednesday*	*Thursday*	*Friday*	*Saturday*
Sherry Baked Chicken Mashed Potatoes, Green Peas	**Ground Beef Nachos** Sour Cream, Guacamole Salad	**Pepper Chicken Fettucine Toss** Celery Salad	**Veal Cordon Bleu** Noodles, Broccoli	**Marinated Fish Steak** Baked Potatoes, Roasted Peppers	**Herb Crusted Salmon Fillet** Baked Potato, Corn	**Round Beef Confetti** Mashed Potatoes, Green Peas

Fresh Vegetables \ Fruits		*Herbs \ Spices*	*Basics*
potatoes - 14 white onions - 4 green onions - 4 tomatoes - 2 iceberg lettuce - 1 avocado - 1 green chili pepper - 1 broccoli bunch corn - 2 orange - 1	garlic pod lime - 1 lemon - 1 red bell peppers - 2 yellow bell pepper - 1 green bell peppers - 2 mushrooms - 2 celery bundle cucumber - 1 parsley bunch	ground cumin marjoram ground allspice dried rosemary dries thyme tarragon red pepper sauce	mayonnaise olive oil flour Dijon mustard peanut oil shortening

Entrée Food	*Dairy*	*Miscellaneous*	*Cans \ Jars*
skinless, boneless chicken breasts - 3 ground beef - 1 lb. veal cutlets - 4 Canadian bacon - 6 slices swordfish steak - 1 salmon fillet - 1 lb. top round beef - 4 slices **Frozen** green peas - 2 pkg	eggs - 2 milk - 1 C Romano cheese ⅓ C sour cream - ½ cup Monterey Jack cheese - 2 oz. Parmesan cheese 2 T Swiss cheese slices 4 sharp Cheddar cheese 2 oz. **Wine** sherry wine burgundy wine	brown rice - 1 cup flour tortillas - 6 fettucine pasta ½ lb bread crumbs ½ C extra-wide noodles ½ lb herb salad dressing ½ C cornflakes crumbs 1 oz.	enchilada sauce 1 (16 oz.) black olives - 4 oz dill pickle- 1 oz beef broth - 1

SHERRY BAKED CHICKEN

with Mashed Potatoes and Green Peas

2 whole chicken breasts, skinless, boneless
Salt and ground pepper to taste
1 egg, beaten
¼ cup milk
Dash red pepper sauce
¼ cup grated Romano cheese
½ cup butter or margarine
1 cup sherry wine

3 potatoes
½ stick margarine
¼ cup milk

Frozen green peas

Pound **chicken breasts** to achieve an even thickness. Season chicken breasts with salt and pepper.

In a small bowl mix the egg, milk, and pepper sauce. Place Romano cheese on a sheet of wax paper. Dip chicken pieces in the egg mixture then dredge through the cheese.

Melt butter in a large skillet over medium heat. Add the chicken pieces and cook for 5-6 minutes until brown on both sides. Add sherry wine to chicken. Cover and cook at medium-low heat for 20-30 minutes.

While chicken cooks, prepare **mashed potatoes**. Wash and peel potatoes and cut into halves then quarter into smaller pieces. Heat a pot of water and add in the potato pieces. Salt the water to your taste. Cook for approximately 20 minutes; drain. Into hot potatoes place ½ stick of margarine, ¼ cup of milk and whip to desired smoothness.

Before the potatoes and chicken are done, prepare the **frozen peas**, following package directions.

GROUND BEEF NACHOS

with Sour Cream and Guacamole Salad

Brown rice
1 lb. ground beef
½ onion, chopped
2 teaspoons minced garlic
1 (16 oz.) can enchilada sauce
½ cup sliced ripe olives
½ teaspoon ground cumin
6 large flour tortillas
4 green onions, chopped
1 tomato, chopped
Monterey Jack cheese
½ iceberg lettuce
½ cup sour cream

Guacamole Salad Ingredients:
1 avocado, skinned, cut up
¼ cup chopped white onions
1 small clove garlic, chopped
1 green chili pepper, finely chopped
1 teaspoon lemon juice
½ teaspoon salt
¼ tsp. pepper, ground
¼ teaspoon orange juice
1 Tbsp. mayonnaise
½ tomato, finely chopped

Make the **guacamole salad** first. Beat avocados, onions, garlic, chili pepper, lemon juice, salt, pepper, orange juice and mayonnaise until creamy. Stir in tomato bits. Cover and refrigerate at *least 1 hour* while you proceed with rest of meal.

Make **brown rice** following package directions. You should choose a quick rice.

While rice cooks, pre-heat the oven to 350° F.

In a large skillet, sauté the **ground meat** with the chopped onions and garlic until the meat is well-browned. Drain off and discard any fat. Add the enchilada sauce, the black olives and the ground cumin. Simmer for 10 minutes.

Lightly oil a pan used for making pies. Spoon in a thin layer of cooked rice and beef; add a tortilla as a topping. Repeat this layering for the rest of the rice. Any tortillas left over can be used with the meal. Cut slices of the tomato and lay across top; sprinkle with the Monterrey Jack cheese. Bake in the oven for about 25 minutes.

When ready to serve, prepare a bed of lettuce beside the nachos and spoon on the guacamole salad. Serve the **sour cream** in a separate bowl.

PEPPER-CHICKEN FETTUCCINE TOSS

with Celery Salad

¼ cup olive oil
1 boneless chicken breast, skinned and cut into strips
½ red bell pepper, cut into strips
½ yellow bell pepper, cut into strips
½ green bell pepper, cut into strips
½ small onion, cut into chunks
2 fresh mushrooms, sliced
½ teaspoon marjoram

Celery Salad Ingredients:
iceberg lettuce
celery, julienned
cucumber

½ box fettuccine pasta
2 Tbsps. Parmesan cheese

Make the **celery salad.** Wash the outer layer of the lettuce. If outer layer is damaged, remove it. Shred the lettuce using a grater or by thinly slicing it. Do the shredding over the dinner plate. Next, cut the celery stalk into 2-inch lengths, the size of match sticks. Toss over the lettuce field. Slice cucumber thickly, then quarter. Scatter over the lettuce and celery.

In large skillet, heat olive oil; add chicken strips, pepper, onion, mushrooms and seasoning. Cook and stir over medium heat until chicken is cooked through, about 8 to 10 minutes.

Prepare **fettuccine pasta** according to package directions; drain, rinse in cold water; drain again. Combine hot, cooked fettuccine with the chicken mixture and Parmesan cheese. This makes a dry pasta. Sometimes we add salad dressing to moisten.

VEAL CORDON BLEU

with Noodles and Broccoli

4 veal cutlets
4 slices Swiss cheese
4 thin slices Canadian bacon
2 Tbsps. flour
¼ tsp. ground allspice
½ tsp. each of salt and pepper
1 egg, beaten
½ cup dry bread crumbs
3 Tbsps. peanut oil
2 Tbsps. water

1 bunch broccoli

½ pkg. extra-wide noodles

Noodle Sauce Ingredients:
½ cup pan juices
2 Tbsps. olive oil
2 Tbsps. flour
½ cup milk

Flatten the **veal cutlets** slightly. Place slice of cheese against meat. Top with Canadian bacon. Roll up from narrow end and secure with toothpicks or metal skewers. Mix flour, allspice, salt and pepper. Beat one egg in a small bowl. Dip the veal in the egg then into the flour mixture to coat. Finally, roll veal through the crumbs, coating completely.

Heat peanut oil in frying pan and brown cutlets for about 5-10 minutes. Add water and bring to a boil. Reduce heat to simmer and cook for about 45 minutes.

While the veal cooks, prepare the **broccoli** by the steaming method. In a steamer or in a small pan add a minimum of water. Steam until *al dente,* about 5 minutes.

At the same time, prepare the **extra-wide noodles** following package directions.

To make **gravy** for the meat, drain skillet of the juices, reserving ½ cup. If there is not enough juice, fill to ½ cup level with water. Return liquid to the skillet. Add the olive oil, sprinkle in the flour and stir to mix well. Add milk and season with salt and pepper to taste. Cook until mixture is smooth.

3 hours - Plan ahead

MARINADED FISH STEAK

with Baked Potatoes, Roasted Red and Green Peppers

1 fish steak, swordfish
½ cup herb salad dressing (any Heinz® brand)
Sharp cheese
Crushed cornflake crumbs

4 potatoes, for baking

1 green bell pepper

1 red bell pepper

Place **fish steak** in baking dish. Pour herb salad dressing over fish. *Marinate several hours, turning every 30 minutes or so.*

After 3 hours, preheat oven to 450° F.

While the oven heats, prepare the **baked potatoes** according to your favorite method. We typically use the microwave to completely bake or to at least partially bake the potatoes. Wash the potatoes and pierce with fork. Place potatoes in the microwave and cook on HIGH for 4 minutes per potato per side, turning once. (3 or 4 potatoes will cook in 24 minutes.)

Cut the **bell peppers** in broad strips. Broil the green and red peppers in the still-heating oven in a small baking dish; bake until they begin to brown. Remove and while the fish bakes, cut the peppers into strips.

Before baking fish, grate sharp cheese and combine with equal amount of crushed cornflake crumbs. Roll the **fish steak** in this mixture, coating evenly.

Top with remaining cheese and crumbs.

Bake in a 450° F oven until done, about 15 minutes.

HERB CRUSTED SALMON FILLET

with Baked Potato and Corn

1 lb. salmon fillet
¼ cup parsley, chopped
¼ cup chopped fresh herbs*
(thyme, tarragon, rosemary, chives)
½ Tbsp. grated lime zest (skin)
Salt and pepper

4 potatoes, for baking

4 ears of fresh corn

**Dry herbs may be substituted for the fresh ones listed. Use ¼ teaspoon of dried thyme, tarragon, rosemary and chives.*

Preheat the oven to 375° F.

While oven heats, prepare the **baked potatoes**. We typically use the microwave to completely bake or to at least partially bake the potatoes. Wash the potatoes and pierce with fork. Place potatoes in the microwave and cook on HIGH for 4 minutes per potato per side, turning once. (3 or 4 potatoes will cook in 24 minutes.)

Meanwhile, rinse the **fish** in cold water and pat dry with paper.

In a cereal bowl, combine the chopped parsley, the fresh or died herbs, the skin from the lime, salt and pepper. Sprinkle the fish with this herb mixture, rubbing it into the fish.

Take a piece of aluminum foil, large enough to completely wrap the salmon, and spray it with vegetable oil. Lay the fish on the foil and cover the fish. Seal the ends of foil. Place foiled fish on a shallow baking dish. Cook the fish for twenty minutes maximum. Open the foil carefully and check for doneness.

While the fish bakes, prepare the **corn** by either microwave cooking: 2 minutes per side per piece or by boiling in hot water for ten minutes.

ROUND BEEF CONFETTI

with Mashed Potatoes and Green Peas

4 slices top round beef, cut thinly enough to wrap
½ Tbsp. Dijon mustard
Salt and pepper to taste
½ Tbsp. dried rosemary
½ Tbsp. dried thyme
1 dill pickle, refrigerator style
1 medium onion
2 paper-thin slices Canadian bacon

Flour
2 Tbsps. peanut oil
1 cup burgundy wine
1 can beef broth

3 potatoes
½ stick margarine
¼ cup milk
Green peas, frozen

To make the **round beef confetti**, spread each slice of round beef with mustard. Sprinkle with salt and pepper and add rosemary and thyme spices. Cut the dill pickle in half, lengthwise, then into long quarters. Place in center of beef. Cut the onion into similar quarters and place beside the pickle. Top with a thin slice of Canadian bacon.

Roll the beef round up as much as possible and secure with metal skewers.

Spread some flour on a sheet of wax paper. Press the round beef roll into flour and set aside.

Heat skillet with the peanut oil to medium-high. Place in the beef rolls and allow to brown. Add the burgundy wine, beef broth and cover. Let the beef simmer for about 1 ½ hours.

While the beef cooks prepare **mashed potatoes**. Wash and peel potatoes and cut into halves then quarter into smaller pieces. Heat a pot of water and add in the potato pieces. Salt the water to your taste. Cook for approximately 20 minutes; drain. Into hot potatoes place ½ stick of margarine, ¼ cup of milk and whip to desired smoothness.

While the potatoes cook, prepare the **green peas** following package directions.

The Menu Cookbook ***(More Than Recipes)***
P. O. Box 204015
Austin, TX 78720-4015

ORDER FORM

Number of Sets	Description	Price per Set	Extension
	deluxe set *	**62.95**	
		Shipping & Handling	**6.00**
		Sales Tax (Texas 8.25 %) $ 5.19 per set	
		TOTAL	

Enclosed is __________ payable to **The Menu Cookbook**.

Name:____

Address: ______________________________________

____

City ________________________________

State ___________ Zip __________ Phone (   ) ______________

* The Deluxe Edition Set is two-volume Hard bound with an attractive slip case.
SHIP TO Name & Address:

____

____

____

____

Index

Two indices to serve

A *menu list index* arranged in alphabetical order for each food category so you can easily search for a list of all fish menus, or chicken menus, so on. These indices are arranged alphabetically by category of menu: Chicken, Fish, Monday with Ease, Pasta, Pork, Shrimp, Soup, Red Meat, and Vegetables.

There is also an *ingredient index* arranged in alphabetic order. This index list most side orders used in *More Than Recipes.*

The pages of *More Than Recipes* are numbered sequentially from page 1 to page 645. Volume 2 begins with page 269.

A full index can be found at the end of each volume!

The Format

A note about the format. Each index entry will specify the volume and then the page:

bleu cheese ... 1-101, **2-**265
broccoli ... 1-114, **1-**249

***bleu cheese* is in volume 1 on page 101 and volume 2 page 265.**

Chicken Menus

Chicken Menus - continued

Chicken Menus - continued

Chicken Menus - continued

Fish Menus

Fish Menus - continued

Fish Menus - continued

Fish Menus - continued

Monday with Ease Menus

Monday with Ease Menus - continued

Monday with Ease Menus - continued

Monday with Ease Menus - continued

Pasta Menus

Title **Vol**- page ***Index***

Pasta Menus - continued

Pork Menus

Pork Menus - continued

Pork Menus - continued

Red Meats Menus

Title **Vol**- page ***Index***

Red Meats Menus - continued

Title **Vol**- page ***Index***

Red Meats Menus - continued

Red Meats Menus - continued

Shrimp Menus

Shrimp Menus - continued

Shrimp Menus - continued

Soup Menus

Title **Vol**- page ***Index***

Soup Menus - continued

Title **Vol**-page ***Index***

Vegetable Menus

Two indices to serve

A *menu list index* arranged in alphabetical order for each food category so you can easily search for a list of all fish menus, or chicken menus, so on. These indices are arranged alphabetically by category of menu: Chicken, Fish, Monday with Ease, Pasta, Pork, Shrimp, Soup, Red Meat, and Vegetables.

There is also an *ingredient index* arranged in alphabetic order. This index list most side orders used in *More Than Recipes.*

The pages of *More Than Recipes* are numbered sequentially from page 1 to page 645. Volume 2 begins with page 269.

A full index can be found at the end of each volume!

The Format

A note about the format. Each index entry will specify the volume and then the page:

bleu cheese ... 1-101, **2-**265
broccoli ... 1-114, **1-**249

***bleu cheese* is in volume 1 on page 101 and volume 2 page 265.**

Title **Vol**- page **_Index_**

Title **Vol**- page *Index*